The Complete Crock Pot Cookbook for Beginners 2023

1200 | Super Easy, Delicious & Healthy Crock-pot Recipes for Everyday Meals to Live a Healthy Life

Valerie Albertson

CONTENTS

Lunch & Dinner Recipes 32

Poultry Recipes 43

Vegetable & Vegetarian Recipes 76

Side Dish Recipes 87

Dessert Recipes 121

APPENDIX : Recipes Index 131

What Is a Crock Pot?

Crock Pots are inexpensive to buy and use, making them excellent for making the most of inexpensive ingredients. You can make everything from stews to curries to sweets in a simple Crock Pot. Put your ingredients in the machine and let it handle the rest—ideal for busy weeknights and family dinners.

The majority of Crock Pot recipes recommend cooking on low for eight hours. However, timings can vary. During that period, though, you will not be actively working on the meal. Therefore, the time you spend preparing your dinner for the cook is significantly reduced.

Crock Pot Choosing Tips

When purchasing a Crock Pot, many different models and features are considered. Some of the available options and features are listed below. When you buy a Crock Pot, becoming informed about the alternatives available can help you make the best decision.

Method of Heating

There are two fundamental types of heating systems. One example is a metal pot with electric heating elements enclosed in the walls. This pot contains the crock. The other is a griddle-style heating unit that rests on the container. The characteristics of each are listed below.

INTRODUCTION

The Crock Pot is among the most versatile cooking appliances in your kitchen thanks to its range of settings and the flexibility they bring. And with the warm, homey dishes it can produce than you might believe, it's no wonder why this appliance has stood the test of time. And while they may not be known for being trendy or cutting edge, Crock Pots are back on our radar now more than ever and have a wide variety of uses beyond just cooking meats and vegetables. Are you ready to enjoy some homemade delicious food? Then, the Crock Pot cookbook is the guide for you.

I'm a huge fan of Crock Pots. I love that you can throw ingredients into the pot and leave it alone for several hours. It makes dinner time much easier if you're at home all day. In addition, I enjoy experimenting with new dishes, with methods and techniques I learn.

The Crock Pot is great for making meals, but it's also a fantastic resource for finding delicious sweet treats! This cookbook is brimming with wonderfully wholesome recipes for vegetables, meat, beans and rice, etc. These tasty food are the perfect way to reward yourself after a long day of working hard in your store or looking after those children. Don't you deserve it? This cookbook contains slow-cooking recipes anyone can follow.

Griddle Sort: Rather than "Low-High" controls, this type of heating equipment features a dial temperature control. This device will have more changing degrees of temperature, making it more difficult to control. This unit's crock can be used on the cooktop and in the oven. Other meals can be cooked on the heating device, which can also be used as a griddle.

Electric Heating: These components are located in the sidewalls and bottom of the metal pot-type heating unit. There are numerous heating control options available with this sort of heating equipment. "Off-Low-High" is the most basic heating control choice. Crock Pots with these essential features are suitable for most needs, but there are many different variations available, each with its own set of advantages.

Lid Material

The lids mustn't seal to prevent pressure from building up in the cooker during the lengthy cooking process.

The lids are usually straightforward, allowing you to see the food while cooking without removing the cover. The plastic lids are convenient since they are lighter and easier to handle, but they can become hazy with time, making it difficult to see through them.

Shapes for Crock Pot

The most common shapes for Crock Pots are round or oval. However, rectangle cookers are also available. The form you choose will be determined by the types of foods you intend to use most frequently.

Soups, stews, side dishes, and casseroles: A round Crock Pot is ideal for soups, stews, side dishes, and casseroles. It's also great for steaming desserts in round baking pans and some types of appetizers. Unfortunately, larger cuts of meat, like roasts and rib racks, don't work as well.

Larger portions of meat, such as roasts, chops, and racks of ribs, are best cooked in an oval-shaped cooker. It's ideal for steam-cooking delicacies in rectangular baking pans. Small

whole fish can also be cooked in an oval-shaped cooker.

A rectangle-shaped cooker usually has a deep-sided non-stick metal pot. The pot is placed on a base with a temperature control dial for heating. The pot's shape and dimensions allow it to be used for more significant cuts, but it also works well for soups, stews, and casseroles.

Crock Pot Sizes

Crock Pots are available in sizes, ranging from 1/2 gallon micro cookers to 8-gallon large cookers. The type of food will determine the size you choose, it will be used most frequently and the amount of food you will need to cook. When using a Crock Pot, fill it halfway to three-quarters full. Also, think about the type of food you'll cook in the Crock Pot.

Warming Function

In addition to saving time, low and slow cooking is a great way to ensure that your food is at its best when you eat it (and don't waste any of the ingredients). It also makes it easier to prepare leftovers for the next day to take advantage of your Crock Pot even when you're not home.

Why Slow Cooking Healthy Meals Matters

The recipes in this book fall in line with this healthy-eating philosophy as follows:

Ingredients are natural, whole foods without additives, preservatives, food dyes, or artificial anything.

Refined sugars and hydrogenated oils, which contain trans fats, are not used in any of the recipes. Additionally, few recipes call for oil, keeping added fat to a minimum.

Salt is used sparingly to keep sodium levels to a minimum. You can also choose to eliminate the salt all together, although the small amounts called for in the recipes are beneficial to the overall flavor of the recipe.

Most of the recipes contain a variety of fresh vegetables

BASIC KITCHEN CONVERSIONS & EQUIVALENTS

DRY MEASUREMENTS CONVERSION CHART

3 TEASPOONS = 1 TABLESPOON = 1/16 CUP

6 TEASPOONS = 2 TABLESPOONS = 1/8 CUP

12 TEASPOONS = 4 TABLESPOONS = 1/4 CUP

24 TEASPOONS = 8 TABLESPOONS = 1/2 CUP

36 TEASPOONS = 12 TABLESPOONS = 3/4 CUP

48 TEASPOONS = 16 TABLESPOONS = 1 CUP

METRIC TO US COOKING CONVERSIONS

OVEN TEMPERATURES

120 °C = 250 °F

160 °C = 320 °F

180° C = 350 °F

205 °C = 400 °F

220 °C = 425 °F

LIQUID MEASUREMENTS CONVERSION CHART

8 FLUID OUNCES = 1 CUP = 1/2 PINT = 1/4 QUART

16 FLUID OUNCES = 2 CUPS = 1 PINT = 1/2 QUART

32 FLUID OUNCES = 4 CUPS = 2 PINTS = 1 QUART = 1/4 GALLON

128 FLUID OUNCES = 16 CUPS = 8 PINTS = 4 QUARTS = 1 GALLON

BAKING IN GRAMS

1 CUP FLOUR = 140 GRAMS

1 CUP SUGAR = 150 GRAMS

1 CUP POWDERED SUGAR = 160 GRAMS

1 CUP HEAVY CREAM = 235 GRAMS

VOLUME

1 MILLILITER = 1/5 TEASPOON

5 ML = 1 TEASPOON

15 ML = 1 TABLESPOON

240 ML = 1 CUP OR 8 FLUID OUNCES

1 LITER = 34 FL. OUNCES

WEIGHT

1 GRAM = .035 OUNCES

100 GRAMS = 3.5 OUNCES

500 GRAMS = 1.1 POUNDS

1 KILOGRAM = 35 OUNCES

US TO METRIC COOKING CONVERSIONS

1/5 TSP = 1 ML

1 TSP = 5 ML

1 TBSP = 15 ML

1 FL OUNCE = 30 ML

1 CUP = 237 ML

1 PINT (2 CUPS) = 473 ML

1 QUART (4 CUPS) = .95 LITER

1 GALLON (16 CUPS) = 3.8 LITERS

1 OZ = 28 GRAMS

1 POUND = 454 GRAMS

BUTTER

1 CUP BUTTER = 2 STICKS = 8 OUNCES = 230 GRAMS = 8 TABLESPOONS

WHAT DOES 1 CUP EQUAL

1 CUP = 8 FLUID OUNCES

1 CUP = 16 TABLESPOONS

1 CUP = 48 TEASPOONS

1 CUP = 1/2 PINT

1 CUP = 1/4 QUART

1 CUP = 1/16 GALLON

1 CUP = 240 ML

BAKING PAN CONVERSIONS

1 CUP ALL-PURPOSE FLOUR = 4.5 OZ

1 CUP ROLLED OATS = 3 OZ 1 LARGE EGG = 1.7 OZ

1 CUP BUTTER = 8 OZ 1 CUP MILK = 8 OZ

1 CUP HEAVY CREAM = 8.4 OZ

1 CUP GRANULATED SUGAR = 7.1 OZ

1 CUP PACKED BROWN SUGAR = 7.75 OZ

1 CUP VEGETABLE OIL = 7.7 OZ

1 CUP UNSIFTED POWDERED SUGAR = 4.4 OZ

BAKING PAN CONVERSIONS

9-INCH ROUND CAKE PAN = 12 CUPS

10-INCH TUBE PAN =16 CUPS

11-INCH BUNDT PAN = 12 CUPS

9-INCH SPRINGFORM PAN = 10 CUPS

9 X 5 INCH LOAF PAN = 8 CUPS

9-INCH SQUARE PAN = 8 CUPS

Appetizers Recipes

Appetizers Recipes

Chili Chicken Wings

Servings: 8 | Cooking Time: 7 1/4 Hours

Ingredients:
- 4 pounds chicken wings
- 1/4 cup maple syrup
- 1 teaspoon garlic powder
- 1 teaspoon chili powder
- 2 tablespoons balsamic vinegar
- 1 tablespoon Dijon mustard
- 1 teaspoon Worcestershire sauce
- 1/2 cup tomato sauce
- 1 teaspoon salt

Directions:
1. Combine the chicken wings and the remaining ingredients in a Crock Pot.
2. Toss around until evenly coated and cook on low settings for 7 hours.
3. Serve the chicken wings warm or chilled.

Southwestern Nacho Dip

Servings: 10 | Cooking Time: 6 1/4 Hours

Ingredients:
- 1 pound ground pork
- 1 cup apple juice
- 4 garlic cloves, chopped
- 2 cups BBQ sauce
- 2 tablespoons brown sugar
- Salt and pepper to taste
- 1 1/2 cups sweet corn
- 1 can black beans, drained
- 1 cup diced tomatoes
- 2 jalapeno peppers, chopped
- 2 tablespoons chopped cilantro
- 2 cups grated Cheddar
- 1 lime, juiced
- Nachos for serving

Directions:
1. Heat a skillet over medium flame and add the pork. Cook for a few minutes, stirring often.
2. Transfer the pork in your Crock Pot and add the apple juice, garlic, BBQ sauce, brown sugar, salt and pepper.
3. Cook on high settings for 2 hours.
4. After 2 hours, add the remaining ingredients and continue cooking for 4 hours on low settings.
5. Serve the dip warm with nachos.

Quick Layered Appetizer

Servings: 10 | Cooking Time: 7 1/2 Hours

Ingredients:
- 4 chicken breasts, cooked and diced
- 1 teaspoon dried basil
- 1 teaspoon dried oregano
- 1 cup cream cheese
- 1/4 teaspoon chili powder
- Salt and pepper to taste
- 4 tomatoes, sliced
- 4 large tortillas
- 2 cups shredded mozzarella

Directions:
1. Mix the chicken, basil, oregano, cream cheese, chili powder, salt and pepper in a bowl.
2. Begin layering the chicken mixture, tomatoes, tortillas and mozzarella in your Crock Pot.
3. Cover and cook on low settings for 7 hours.
4. Allow to cool then slice and serve.

Pepperoni Pizza Dip

Servings: 10 | Cooking Time: 3 1/4 Hours

Ingredients:
- 1 1/2 cups pizza sauce
- 4 peperoni, sliced
- 2 shallots, chopped
- 2 red bell peppers, diced
- 1/2 cup black olives, pitted and chopped
- 1 cup cream cheese
- 1 cup shredded mozzarella
- 1/2 teaspoon dried basil

Directions:
1. Combine the pizza sauce and the rest of the ingredients in your Crock Pot.
2. Cover the pot with its lid and cook on low settings for 3 hours.
3. The dip is best served warm with bread sticks or tortilla chips.

Spicy Glazed Pecans

Servings: 10 | Cooking Time: 3 1/4 Hours

Ingredients:
- 2 pounds pecans
- 1/2 cup butter, melted
- 1 teaspoon chili powder
- 1 teaspoon smoked paprika
- 1 teaspoon dried basil
- 1 teaspoon dried thyme
- 1/4 teaspoon cayenne pepper
- 1/2 teaspoon garlic powder
- 2 tablespoons honey

Directions:
1. Combine all the ingredients in your Crock Pot.

2. Mix well until all the ingredients are well distributed and the pecans are evenly glazed.
3. Cook on high settings for 3 hours.
4. Allow them to cool before serving.

Bacon Chicken Sliders

Servings: 8 | Cooking Time: 4 1/2 Hours

Ingredients:
- 2 pounds ground chicken
- 1 egg
- 1/2 cup breadcrumbs
- 1 shallot, chopped
- Salt and pepper to taste
- 8 bacon slices

Directions:
1. Mix the chicken, egg, breadcrumbs and shallot in a bowl. Add salt and pepper to taste and give it a good mix.
2. Form small sliders then wrap each slider in a bacon slice.
3. Place the sliders in a Crock Pot.
4. Cover with its lid and cook on high settings for 4 hours, making sure to flip them over once during cooking.
5. Serve them warm.

Mediterranean Dip

Servings: 20 | Cooking Time: 6 1/4 Hours

Ingredients:
- 2 tablespoons canola oil
- 1 pound ground beef
- 2 shallots, chopped
- 2 garlic cloves, chopped
- 4 ripe tomatoes, peeled and diced
- 1/2 cup Kalamata olives, pitted and chopped
- 1/2 cup black olives, pitted and chopped
- 1/2 teaspoon dried oregano
- 1 teaspoon dried basil
- 1/4 cup white wine
- 1/2 cup tomato sauce
- Salt and pepper to taste

Directions:
1. Heat the oil in a skillet and stir in the beef. Cook for 5 minutes then add the shallots and garlic and cook for 5 additional minutes.
2. Transfer the mixture in your Crock Pot and add the remaining ingredients.
3. Season with salt and pepper and cook on low settings for 6 hours.
4. Serve the dip warm or chilled.

Classic Bread In A Crock Pot

Servings: 8 | Cooking Time: 1 1/2 Hours

Ingredients:
- 2 teaspoons active dry yeast
- 1 teaspoon sugar
- 1 cup warm water
- 1/2 cup yogurt
- 1 egg
- 2 tablespoons olive oil
- 3 cups all-purpose flour
- 1/2 teaspoon salt

Directions:
1. Mix the yeast, sugar, warm water, yogurt, egg and olive oil in a bowl.
2. Stir in the flour and salt and mix well. Knead the dough for 5-10 minutes until even and non-sticky.
3. Place the dough in your Crock Pot and cover with its lid.
4. Cook on high settings for 1 1/4 hours.
5. Serve the bread warm or chilled.

Cranberry Sauce Meatballs

Servings: 12 | Cooking Time: 7 1/2 Hours

Ingredients:
- 3 pounds ground pork
- 1 pound ground turkey
- 1 egg
- 1/2 cup breadcrumbs
- 1 shallot, chopped
- 1/2 teaspoon ground cloves
- Salt and pepper to taste
- 2 cups cranberry sauce
- 1 cup BBQ sauce
- 1 teaspoon hot sauce
- 1 thyme sprig

Directions:
1. Mix the ground pork, turkey, egg, breadcrumbs, shallot, ground cloves, salt and pepper and mix well.
2. In the meantime, combine the cranberry sauce, BBQ sauce, hot sauce and thyme sprig in your Crock Pot.
3. Form small meatballs and drop them in the sauce.
4. Cook on low settings for 7 hours.
5. Serve the meatballs warm or chilled.

Cheesy Chicken Bites

Servings: 10 | Cooking Time: 6 1/4 Hours

Ingredients:
- 4 chicken breasts, cut into bite-size cubes
- 1/4 cup all-purpose flour
- Salt and pepper to taste
- 1 cup cream cheese
- 2 roasted red bell peppers
- 1 cup shredded mozzarella
- 1/4 teaspoon chili powder

Directions:
1. Mix the cream cheese, bell peppers, chili powder, salt and pepper in a blender and pulse until smooth.
2. Pour the mixture in your Crock Pot and add the remaining ingredients.
3. Cook on low settings for 6 hours.
4. Serve the chicken bites warm or chilled.

Balsamico Pulled Pork

Servings: 6 | Cooking Time: 8 1/4 Hours

Ingredients:
- 2 pounds boneless pork shoulder
- 2 tablespoons honey
- 1/4 cup balsamic vinegar
- 1/4 cup hoisin sauce
- 1 tablespoon Dijon mustard
- 1/4 cup chicken stock
- 2 garlic cloves, minced
- 2 shallots, sliced
- 2 tablespoons soy sauce

Directions:
1. Combine the honey, vinegar, hoisin sauce, mustard, stock, garlic, shallots and soy sauce in your Crock Pot.
2. Add the pork shoulder and roll it in the mixture until evenly coated.
3. Cover the Crock Pot and cook on low settings for 8 hours.
4. When done, shred the meat into fine pieces and serve warm or chilled.

Cheeseburger Dip

Servings: 20 | Cooking Time: 6 1/4 Hours

Ingredients:
- 2 pounds ground beef
- 1 tablespoon canola oil
- 2 sweet onions, chopped
- 4 garlic cloves, chopped
- 1/2 cup tomato sauce
- 1 tablespoon Dijon mustard
- 2 tablespoons pickle relish
- 1 cup shredded processed cheese
- 1 cup grated Cheddar

Directions:
1. Heat the canola oil in a skillet and stir in the ground beef. Sauté for 5 minutes then add the meat in your Crock Pot.
2. Stir in the remaining ingredients and cover with the pot's lid.
3. Cook on low settings for 6 hours.
4. The dip is best served warm.

Asian Marinated Mushrooms

Servings: 8 | Cooking Time: 8 1/4 Hours

Ingredients:
- 2 pounds mushrooms
- 1 cup soy sauce
- 1 cup water
- 1/2 cup brown sugar
- 1/4 cup rice vinegar
- 1/2 teaspoon chili powder

Directions:
1. Combine all the ingredients in your Crock Pot.
2. Cover the Crock Pot and cook on low settings for 8 hours.
3. Allow to cool in the pot before serving.

Sausage And Pepper Appetizer

Servings: 8 | Cooking Time: 6 1/4 Hours

Ingredients:
- 6 fresh pork sausages, skins removed
- 2 tablespoons olive oil
- 1 can fire roasted tomatoes
- 4 roasted bell peppers, chopped
- 1 poblano pepper, chopped
- 1 shallot, chopped
- 1 cup grated Provolone cheese
- Salt and pepper to taste

Directions:
1. Heat the oil in a skillet and stir in the sausage meat. Cook for 5 minutes, stirring often.
2. Transfer the meat in your Crock Pot and add the remaining ingredients.
3. Season with salt and pepper and cook on low settings for 6 hours.
4. Serve the dish warm or chilled.

Marinara Turkey Meatballs

Servings: 8 | Cooking Time: 6 1/2 Hours

Ingredients:
- 2 pounds ground turkey
- 1 carrot, grated
- 1 potato, grated
- 1 shallot, chopped
- 1 tablespoon chopped parsley
- 1 tablespoon chopped cilantro
- 4 basil leaves, chopped
- 1/2 teaspoon dried mint
- 1 egg
- 1/4 cup breadcrumbs
- Salt and pepper to taste
- 2 cups marinara sauce

Directions:
1. Mix the turkey, carrot, potato, shallot, parsley, cilantro, basil, mint, egg and breadcrumbs in a bowl.
2. Add salt and pepper to taste and mix well.
3. Pour the marinara sauce in your Crock Pot then form meatballs and drop them in the sauce.
4. Cover the pot with its lid and cook on low settings for 6 hours.
5. Serve the meatballs warm or chilled.

Spanish Chorizo Dip

Servings: 8 | Cooking Time: 6 1/4 Hours

Ingredients:
- 8 chorizo links, diced
- 1 can diced tomatoes
- 1 chili pepper, chopped
- 1 cup cream cheese
- 2 cups grated Cheddar cheese
- 1/4 cup white wine

Directions:
1. Combine all the ingredients in your Crock Pot.
2. Cook the dip on low settings for 6 hours.
3. Serve the dip warm.

Queso Verde Dip

Servings: 12 | Cooking Time: 4 1/4 Hours

Ingredients:
- 1 pound ground chicken
- 2 shallots, chopped
- 2 tablespoons olive oil
- 2 cups salsa verde
- 1 cup cream cheese
- 2 cups grated Cheddar
- 2 poblano peppers, chopped
- 1 tablespoon Worcestershire sauce
- 4 garlic cloves, minced
- 1/4 cup chopped cilantro
- Salt and pepper to taste

Directions:
1. Combine all the ingredients in your Crock Pot.
2. Add salt and pepper to taste and cook on low heat for 4 hours.
3. The dip is best served warm.

Hoisin Chicken Wings

Servings: 8 | Cooking Time: 7 1/4 Hours

Ingredients:
- 4 pounds chicken wings
- 2/3 cup hoisin sauce
- 4 garlic cloves, minced
- 1 teaspoon grated ginger
- 1 teaspoon sesame oil
- 1 tablespoon molasses
- 1 teaspoon hot sauce
- 1/4 teaspoon ground black pepper
- 1/2 teaspoon salt

Directions:
1. Mix the hoisin sauce, garlic, ginger, sesame oil, molasses, hot sauce, black pepper and salt in your Crock Pot.
2. Add the chicken wings and toss them around until evenly coated.
3. Cover with a lid and cook on low settings for 7 hours.
4. Serve the wings warm or chilled.

Spicy Chicken Taquitos

Servings: 8 | Cooking Time: 6 1/2 Hours

Ingredients:
- 4 chicken breasts, cooked and diced
- 1 cup cream cheese
- 2 jalapeno peppers, chopped
- 1/2 cup canned sweet corn, drained
- 1/2 teaspoon cumin powder
- 4 garlic cloves, minced
- 16 taco-sized flour tortillas
- 2 cups grated Cheddar cheese

Directions:
1. In a bowl, mix the chicken, cream cheese, garlic, cumin, poblano peppers and corn. Stir in the cheese as well.
2. Place your tortillas on your working surface and top each tortilla with the cheese mixture.
3. Roll the tortillas tightly to form an even roll.

4. Place the rolls in your Crock Pot.
5. Cook on low settings for 6 hours.
6. Serve warm.

Blue Cheese Chicken Wings

Servings: 8 | Cooking Time: 7 1/4 Hours

Ingredients:
- 4 pounds chicken wings
- 1/2 cup buffalo sauce
- 1/2 cup spicy tomato sauce
- 1 tablespoon tomato paste
- 2 tablespoons apple cider vinegar
- 1 tablespoon Worcestershire sauce
- 1 cup sour cream
- 2 oz. blue cheese, crumbled
- 1 thyme sprig

Directions:
1. Combine the buffalo sauce, tomato sauce, vinegar, Worcestershire sauce, sour cream, blue cheese and thyme in a Crock Pot.
2. Add the chicken wings and toss them until evenly coated.
3. Cook on low settings for 7 hours.
4. Serve the chicken wings preferably warm.

Quick Parmesan Bread

Servings: 8 | Cooking Time: 1 1/4 Hours

Ingredients:
- 4 cups all-purpose flour
- 1/2 teaspoon salt
- 1/2 cup grated Parmesan cheese
- 1 teaspoon baking soda
- 2 cups buttermilk
- 2 tablespoons olive oil

Directions:
1. Mix the flour, salt, parmesan cheese and baking soda in a bowl.
2. Stir in the buttermilk and olive oil and mix well with a fork.
3. Shape the dough into a loaf and place it in your Crock Pot.
4. Cover with its lid and cook on high heat for 1 hour.
5. Serve the bread warm or chilled.

French Onion Dip

Servings: 10 | Cooking Time: 4 1/4 Hours

Ingredients:
- 4 large onions, chopped
- 2 tablespoons olive oil
- 1 tablespoon butter
- 1 1/2 cups sour cream
- 1 pinch nutmeg
- Salt and pepper to taste

Directions:
1. Combine the onions, olive oil, butter, salt, pepper and nutmeg in a Crock Pot.
2. Cover and cook on high settings for 4 hours.
3. When done, allow to cool then stir in the sour cream and adjust the taste with salt and pepper.
4. Serve the dip right away.

Creamy Spinach Dip

Servings: 30 | Cooking Time: 2 1/4 Hours

Ingredients:
- 1 can crab meat, drained
- 1 pound fresh spinach, chopped
- 2 shallots, chopped
- 2 jalapeno peppers, chopped
- 1 cup grated Parmesan
- 1/2 cup whole milk
- 1 cup sour cream
- 1 cup cream cheese
- 1 cup grated Cheddar cheese
- 1 tablespoon sherry vinegar
- 2 garlic cloves, chopped

Directions:
1. Combine all the ingredients in your Crock Pot.
2. Cover with its lid and cook on high settings for 2 hours.
3. Serve the spinach dip warm or chilled with vegetable stick or your favorite salty snacks.

Sausage Dip

Servings: 8 | Cooking Time: 6 1/4 Hours

Ingredients:
- 1 pound fresh pork sausages
- 1 pound spicy pork sausages
- 1 cup cream cheese
- 1 can diced tomatoes
- 2 poblano peppers, chopped

Directions:
1. Combine all the ingredients in a Crock Pot.
2. Cook on low settings for 6 hours.
3. Serve warm or chilled.

Mixed Olive Dip

Servings: 10 | Cooking Time: 1 3/4 Hours

Ingredients:
- 1 pound ground chicken
- 2 tablespoons olive oil
- 1 green bell pepper, cored and diced
- 1/2 cup Kalamata olives, pitted and chopped
- 1/2 cup green olives, chopped
- 1/2 cup black olives, pitted and chopped
- 1 cup green salsa
- 1/2 cup chicken stock
- 1 cup grated Cheddar cheese
- 1/2 cup shredded mozzarella

Directions:
1. Combine all the ingredients in your Crock Pot.
2. Cover with its lid and cook on high settings for 1 1/2 hours.
3. The dip is best served warm.

Caramelized Onion Dip

Servings: 12 | Cooking Time: 4 1/2 Hours

Ingredients:
- 4 red onions, sliced
- 2 tablespoons butter
- 1 tablespoon canola oil
- 1 cup beef stock
- 1 teaspoon dried thyme
- 1/2 cup white wine
- 2 garlic cloves, chopped
- 2 cups grated Swiss cheese
- 1 tablespoon cornstarch
- Salt and pepper to taste

Directions:
1. Heat the butter and oil in a skillet. Add the onions and cook over medium flame until the onions begin to caramelize.
2. Transfer the onions in your Crock Pot and add the remaining ingredients.
3. Season with salt and pepper and cook on low settings for 4 hours.
4. Serve the dip warm with vegetable sticks or your favorite crunchy snacks.

Party Mix

Servings: 20 | Cooking Time: 1 3/4 Hours

Ingredients:
- 4 cups cereals
- 4 cups crunchy cereals
- 2 cups mixed nuts
- 1 cup mixed seeds
- 1/2 cup butter, melted
- 2 tablespoons Worcestershire sauce
- 1 teaspoon hot sauce
- 1 teaspoon salt
- 1/2 teaspoon cumin powder

Directions:
1. Combine all the ingredients in your Crock Pot and toss around until evenly coated.
2. Cook on high settings for 1 1/2 hours.
3. Serve the mix chilled.

Bacon Wrapped Chicken Livers

Servings: 6 | Cooking Time: 3 1/2 Hours

Ingredients:
- 2 pounds chicken livers
- Bacon slices as needed

Directions:
1. Wrap each chicken liver in one slice of bacon and place all the livers in your Crock Pot.
2. Cook on high heat for 3 hours.
3. Serve warm or chilled.

Sweet Corn Crab Dip

Servings: 20 | Cooking Time: 2 1/4 Hours

Ingredients:
- 2 tablespoons butter
- 1 cup canned sweet corn, drained
- 2 red bell peppers, cored and diced
- 2 garlic cloves, chopped
- 2 poblano peppers, chopped
- 1 cup sour cream
- 1 can crab meat, drained
- 1 teaspoon Worcestershire sauce
- 1 teaspoon hot sauce
- 1 cup grated Cheddar cheese

Directions:
1. Mix all the ingredients in your Crock Pot.
2. Cover the pot with its lid and cook on low settings for 2 hours.
3. Serve the dip warm or chilled.

White Bean Hummus

Servings: 8 | Cooking Time: 8 1/4 Hours

Ingredients:
- 1 pound dried white beans, rinsed
- 2 cups water
- 2 cups chicken stock
- 1 bay leaf
- 1 thyme sprig
- 4 garlic cloves, minced
- Salt and pepper to taste
- 2 tablespoons canola oil
- 2 large sweet onions, sliced

Directions:
1. Combine the white beans, water, stock, bay leaf and thyme in your Crock Pot.
2. Add salt and pepper to taste and cook the beans on low settings for 8 hours.
3. When done, drain the beans well (but reserve 1/4 cup of the liquid) and discard the bay leaf and thyme.
4. Transfer the bean in a food processor. Add the reserved liquid and pulse until smooth.
5. Season with salt and pepper and transfer in a bowl.
6. Heat the canola oil in a skillet and add the onions. Cook for 10 minutes over medium flame until the onions begin to caramelize.
7. Top the hummus with caramelized onions and serve.

Glazed Peanuts

Servings: 8 | Cooking Time: 2 1/4 Hours

Ingredients:
- 2 pounds raw, whole peanuts
- 1/4 cup brown sugar
- 1/2 teaspoon garlic powder
- 2 tablespoons salt
- 1 tablespoon Cajun seasoning
- 1/2 teaspoon red pepper flakes
- 1/4 cup coconut oil

Directions:
1. Combine all the ingredients in your Crock Pot.
2. Cover and cook on high settings for 2 hours.
3. Serve chilled.

Tropical Meatballs

Servings: 20 | Cooking Time: 7 1/2 Hours

Ingredients:
- 1 can pineapple chunks (keep the juices)
- 2 poblano peppers, chopped
- 1/4 cup brown sugar
- 2 tablespoons soy sauce
- 2 tablespoons cornstarch
- 1 tablespoon lemon juice
- 2 pounds ground pork
- 1 pound ground beef
- 4 garlic clove, minced
- 1 teaspoon dried basil
- 1 egg
- 1/4 cup breadcrumbs
- Salt and pepper to taste

Directions:
1. Mix the pineapple, poblano peppers, brown sugar, soy sauce, cornstarch and lemon juice in a Crock Pot.
2. Combine the ground meat, garlic, basil, egg and breadcrumbs in a bowl. Add salt and pepper to taste and mix well.
3. Form small meatballs and place them in the sauce.
4. Cover and cook on low settings for 7 hours.
5. Serve the meatballs warm or chilled.

Swiss Cheese Fondue

Servings: 10 | Cooking Time: 4 1/4 Hours

Ingredients:
- 1 garlic cloves
- 2 cups dry white wine
- 2 cups grated Swiss cheese
- 1 cup grated Cheddar
- 2 tablespoons cornstarch
- 1 pinch nutmeg

Directions:
1. Rub the inside of your Crock Pot with a garlic clove. Discard the clove once done.
2. Add the remaining ingredients and cook on low heat for 4 hours.
3. Serve the fondue warm with vegetable sticks, croutons or pretzels.

Mexican Chili Dip

Servings: 20 | Cooking Time: 2 1/4 Hours

Ingredients:
- 1 can black beans, drained
- 1 can red beans, drained
- 1 can diced tomatoes
- 1/2 teaspoon cumin powder
- 1/2 teaspoon chili powder
- 1/2 cup beef stock
- Salt and pepper to taste
- 1 1/2 cups grated Cheddar

Directions:
1. Combine the beans, tomatoes, cumin powder, chili and stock in your Crock Pot.
2. Add salt and pepper to taste and top with grated cheese.
3. Cook on high settings for 2 hours.
4. The dip is best served warm.

Maple Syrup Glazed Carrots

Servings: 8 | Cooking Time: 6 1/4 Hours

Ingredients:
- 3 pounds baby carrots
- 4 tablespoons butter, melted
- 3 tablespoons maple syrup
- 1/8 teaspoon pumpkin pie spices
- 1 teaspoon salt

Directions:
1. Place the baby carrots in your Crock Pot and add the remaining ingredients.
2. Mix until the carrots are evenly coated.
3. Cover and cook on low settings for 6 hours.
4. Serve the carrots warm or chilled.

Beer Bbq Meatballs

Servings: 10 | Cooking Time: 7 1/2 Hours

Ingredients:
- 2 pounds ground pork
- 1 pound ground beef
- 1 carrot, grated
- 2 shallots, chopped
- 1 egg
- 1/2 cup breadcrumbs
- 1/2 teaspoon cumin powder
- Salt and pepper to taste
- 1 cup dark beer
- 1 cup BBQ sauce
- 1 bay leaf
- 1/2 teaspoon chili powder
- 1 teaspoon apple cider vinegar

Directions:
1. Mix the ground pork and beef in a bowl. Add the carrot, shallots, egg, breadcrumbs, cumin, salt and pepper and mix well. Form small meatballs and place them on your chopping board.
2. For the beer sauce, combine the beer, BBQ sauce, bay leaf, chili powder and vinegar in a Crock Pot.
3. Place the meatballs in the pot and cover with its lid.

4. Cook on low settings for 7 hours.
5. Serve the meatballs warm or chilled.

Green Vegetable Dip

Servings: 12 | Cooking Time: 2 1/4 Hours

Ingredients:
- 10 oz. frozen spinach, thawed and drained
- 1 jar artichoke hearts, drained
- 1 cup chopped parsley
- 1 cup cream cheese
- 1 cup sour cream
- 1/2 cup grated Parmesan cheese
- 1/2 cup feta cheese, crumbled
- 1/2 teaspoon onion powder
- 1/4 teaspoon garlic powder

Directions:
1. Combine all the ingredients in your Crock Pot and mix gently.
2. Cover with its lid and cook on high settings for 2 hours.
3. Serve the dip warm or chilled with crusty bread, biscuits or other salty snacks or even vegetable sticks.

Turkey Meatloaf

Servings: 8 | Cooking Time: 6 1/4 Hours

Ingredients:
- 1 1/2 pounds ground turkey
- 1 carrot, grated
- 1 sweet potato, grated
- 1 egg
- 1/4 cup breadcrumbs
- 1/4 teaspoon chili powder
- Salt and pepper to taste
- 1 cup shredded mozzarella

Directions:
1. Mix all the ingredients in a bowl and season with salt and pepper as needed.
2. Give it a good mix then transfer the mixture in your Crock Pot.
3. Level the mixture well and cover with the pot's lid.
4. Cook on low settings for 6 hours.
5. Serve the meatloaf warm or chilled.

Oriental Chicken Bites

Servings: 10 | Cooking Time: 7 1/4 Hours

Ingredients:
- 4 chicken breasts, cubed
- 2 sweet onions, sliced
- 1 teaspoon grated ginger
- 4 garlic cloves, minced
- 1/2 teaspoon cinnamon powder
- 1 teaspoon smoked paprika
- 1 teaspoon cumin powder
- 1 cup chicken stock
- 1/2 lemon, juiced
- 2 tablespoons olive oil
- Salt and pepper to taste

Directions:

1. Combine all the ingredients in your Crock Pot.
2. Add salt and pepper to taste and mix well until the ingredients are evenly distributed.
3. Cover and cook on low settings for 7 hours.
4. Serve the chicken bites warm or chilled.

Taco Dip

Cooking Time: 6 1/2 Hours

Servings: 20 | Ingredients:

- 2 pounds ground beef
- 2 tablespoons canola oil
- 1 can black beans, drained
- 1/2 cup beef stock
- 1 cup tomato sauce
- 1 tablespoon taco seasoning
- 2 cups Velveeta cheese, shredded

Directions:
1. Heat the oil in a skillet and add the beef. Cook for 10 minutes, stirring often.
2. Transfer the beef in your Crock Pot.
3. Add the remaining ingredients and cook on low settings for 6 hours.
4. Serve the dip warm.

Five-spiced Chicken Wings

Servings: 8 | Cooking Time: 7 1/4 Hours

Ingredients:
- 1/2 cup plum sauce
- 1/2 cup BBQ sauce
- 2 tablespoons butter
- 1 tablespoon five-spice powder
- 1 teaspoon salt
- 1/2 teaspoon chili powder
- 4 pounds chicken wings

Directions:
1. Combine the plum sauce and BBQ sauce, as well as butter, five-spice, salt and chili powder in a Crock Pot.
2. Add the chicken wings and mix well until well coated.
3. Cover and cook on low settings fir 7 hours.
4. Serve warm or chilled.

Spicy Monterey Jack Fondue

Servings: 6 | Cooking Time: 4 1/4 Hours

Ingredients:
- 1 garlic clove
- 1 cup white wine
- 2 cups grated Monterey Jack cheese
- 1/2 cup grated Parmesan
- 1 red chili, seeded and chopped
- 1 tablespoon cornstarch
- 1/2 cup milk
- 1 pinch nutmeg
- 1 pinch salt
- 1 pinch ground black pepper

Directions:
1. Rub the inside of your Crock Pot's pot with a garlic clove just to infuse it with aroma.

2. Add the white wine into the pot and stir in the cheeses, red chili, cornstarch and milk.
3. Season with nutmeg, salt and black pepper and cook on low heat for 4 hours.
4. The fondue is best served warm with bread sticks or vegetables.

Beer Cheese Fondue

Servings: 8 | Cooking Time: 2 1/4 Hours

Ingredients:
- 1 shallot, chopped
- 1 garlic clove, minced
- 1 cup grated Gruyere cheese
- 2 cups grated Cheddar
- 1 tablespoon cornstarch
- 1 teaspoon Dijon mustard
- 1/2 teaspoon cumin seeds
- 1 cup beer
- Salt and pepper to taste

Directions:
1. Combine the shallot, garlic, cheeses, cornstarch, mustard, cumin seeds and beer in your Crock Pot.
2. Add salt and pepper to taste and mix well.
3. Cover the pot with its lid and cook on high settings for 2 hours.
4. Serve the fondue warm.

Bacon Black Bean Dip

Servings: 6 | Cooking Time: 6 1/4 Hours

Ingredients:
- 6 bacon slices
- 2 cans black beans, drained
- 2 shallots, sliced
- 1 garlic cloves, chopped
- 1 cup red salsa
- 1/2 cup beef stock
- 1 tablespoon brown sugar
- 1 tablespoon molasses
- 1/2 teaspoon chili powder
- 1 tablespoon apple cider vinegar
- 2 tablespoons Bourbon
- Salt and pepper to taste

Directions:
1. Heat a skillet over medium flame and add the bacon. Cook until crisp then transfer the bacon and its fat in your Crock Pot.
2. Stir in the remaining ingredients and cook on low settings for 6 hours.
3. When done, partially mash the beans and serve the dip right away.

Honey Glazed Chicken Drumsticks

Servings: 8 | Cooking Time: 7 1/4 Hours

Ingredients:
- 3 pounds chicken drumsticks
- 1/4 cup soy sauce
- 1/4 cup honey
- 1 teaspoon rice vinegar
- 1/2 teaspoon sesame oil
- 2 tablespoons tomato paste
- 1/2 teaspoon dried Thai basil

Directions:
1. Combine all the ingredients in your Crock Pot and toss them around until the drumsticks are evenly coated.
2. Cover the pot with its lid and cook on low settings for 7 hours.
3. Serve the chicken drumsticks warm or chilled.

Chipotle Bbq Sausage Bites

Servings: 10 | Cooking Time: 2 1/4 Hours

Ingredients:
- 3 pounds small smoked sausages
- 1 cup BBQ sauce
- 2 chipotle peppers in adobo sauce
- 1 tablespoon tomato paste
- 1/4 cup white wine
- Salt and pepper to taste

Directions:
1. Combine all the ingredients in your Crock Pot.
2. Add salt and pepper if needed and cover with a lid.
3. Cook on high settings for 2 hours.
4. Serve the sausage bites warm or chilled.

Creamy Chicken Dip

Servings: 6 | Cooking Time: 3 1/4 Hours

Ingredients:
- 1 cup cream cheese
- 1 1/2 cups cooked and diced chicken
- 2 cups shredded Monterey Jack cheese
- 1/4 cup white wine
- 1 lime, juiced
- 1/4 teaspoon cumin powder
- 2 garlic cloves, chopped
- Salt and pepper to taste

Directions:
1. Combine all the ingredients in your Crock Pot.
2. Add salt and pepper to taste and cook on low settings for 3 hours.
3. The dip is best served warm with tortilla chips or bread sticks.

Bean Queso

Servings: 10 | Cooking Time: 6 1/4 Hours

Ingredients:
- 1 can black beans, drained
- 1 cup chopped green chiles
- 1/2 cup red salsa
- 1 teaspoon dried oregano
- 1/2 teaspoon cumin powder
- 1 cup light beer
- 1 1/2 cups grated Cheddar
- Salt and pepper to taste

Directions:
1. Combine the beans, chiles, oregano, cumin, salsa, beer and cheese in your Crock Pot.
2. Add salt and pepper as needed and cook on low settings for 6 hours.
3. Serve the bean queso warm.

Caramelized Onion And Cranberry Dip

Servings: 16 | Cooking Time: 6 1/4 Hours

Ingredients:
- 2 tablespoons olive oil
- 4 red onions, sliced
- 1 apple, peeled and diced
- 1 cup frozen cranberries
- 1/4 cup balsamic vinegar
- 1/4 cup fresh orange juice
- 2 tablespoons brown sugar
- 1 teaspoon orange zest
- 1 bay leaf
- 1 thyme sprig
- 1 teaspoon salt

Directions:
1. Heat the oil in a skillet and stir in the onions. Cook for 10 minutes until the onions begin to caramelize.
2. Transfer the onions in a Crock Pot and stir in the remaining ingredients.
3. Cover with a lid and cook on low settings for 6 hours.
4. Serve the dip chilled.

Sweet Corn Jalapeno Dip

Servings: 10 | Cooking Time: 2 1/4 Hours

Ingredients:
- 4 bacon slices, chopped
- 3 cans sweet corn, drained
- 4 jalapenos, seeded and chopped
- 1 cup sour cream
- 1 cup grated Cheddar cheese
- 1/2 cup cream cheese
- 1 pinch nutmeg
- 2 tablespoons chopped cilantro

Directions:
1. Combine the corn, jalapenos, sour cream, Cheddar, cream cheese and nutmeg in a Crock Pot.
2. Cook on high settings for 2 hours.
3. When done, stir in the cilantro and serve the dip warm.
4. Store it in an airtight container in the fridge for up to 2 days. Re-heat it when need it.

Breakfast Recipes

Breakfast Recipes

Cinnamon Quinoa

Servings: 4 | Cooking Time: 4 Hours

Ingredients:
- 1 cup quinoa
- 2 cups milk
- 2 cups water
- ¼ cup stevia
- 1 teaspoon cinnamon powder
- 1 teaspoon vanilla extract

Directions:
1. In your Crock Pot, mix quinoa with milk, water, stevia, cinnamon and vanilla, stir, cover, cook on Low for 3 hours and 30 minutes, stir, cook for 30 minutes more, divide into bowls and serve for breakfast.

Nutrition Info:
- calories 172, fat 4, fiber 3, carbs 8, protein 2

Ginger Apple Bowls

Servings: 2 | Cooking Time: 6 Hours

Ingredients:
- 2 apples, cored, peeled and cut into medium chunks
- 1 tablespoon sugar
- 1 tablespoon ginger, grated
- 1 cup heavy cream
- ¼ teaspoon cinnamon powder
- ½ teaspoon vanilla extract
- ¼ teaspoon cardamom, ground

Directions:
1. In your Crock Pot, combine the apples with the sugar, ginger and the other ingredients, toss, put the lid on and cook on Low for 6 hours.
2. Divide into bowls and serve for breakfast.

Nutrition Info:
- calories 201, fat 3, fiber 7, carbs 19, protein 4

Orange Pudding

Servings: 4 | Cooking Time: 4 Hours

Ingredients:
- 1 cup carrot, grated
- 2 cups of milk
- 1 tablespoon cornstarch
- 1 teaspoon vanilla extract
- ½ teaspoon ground nutmeg

Directions:
1. Put the carrot in the Crock Pot.
2. Add milk, vanilla extract, and ground nutmeg.
3. Then add cornstarch and stir the ingredients until cornstarch is dissolved.
4. Cook the pudding on low for 4 hours.

Nutrition Info:
- Per Serving: 84 calories, 4.3g protein, 10.8g carbohydrates, 2.6g fat, 0.8g fiber, 10mg cholesterol, 77mg sodium, 161mg potassium.

Sweet Quinoa

Servings:4 | Cooking Time: 3 Hours

Ingredients:
- 1 cup quinoa
- ¼ cup dates, chopped
- 3 cups of water
- 1 apricot, chopped
- ½ teaspoon ground nutmeg

Directions:
1. Put quinoa, dates, and apricot in the Crock Pot.
2. Add ground nutmeg and mix the mixture.
3. Cook it on high for 3 hours.

Nutrition Info:
- Per Serving: 194 calories, 6.4g protein, 36.7g carbohydrates, 2.8g fat, 4.1g fiber, 0mg cholesterol, 8g sodium, 338mg potassium.

Egg Scramble

Servings:4 | Cooking Time: 2.5 Hours

Ingredients:
- 4 eggs, beaten
- 1 tablespoon butter, melted
- 2 oz Cheddar cheese, shredded
- ¼ teaspoon cayenne pepper
- 1 teaspoon ground paprika

Directions:
1. Mix eggs with butter, cheese, cayenne pepper, and ground paprika.
2. Then pour the mixture in the Crock Pot and close the lid.
3. Cook it on high for 2 hours.
4. Then open the lid and scramble the eggs.
5. Close the lid and cook the meal on high for 30 minutes.

Nutrition Info:
- Per Serving: 147 calories, 9.2g protein, 0.9g carbohydrates, 12g fat, 0.2g fiber, 186mg cholesterol, 170mg sodium, 88mg potassium.

Seafood Eggs

Servings:4 | Cooking Time: 2.5 Hours

Ingredients:
- 4 eggs, beaten
- 2 tablespoons cream cheese
- 1 teaspoon Italian seasonings
- 6 oz shrimps, peeled
- 1 teaspoon olive oil

Directions:
1. Mix cream cheese with eggs.
2. Add Italian seasonings and shrimps.
3. Then brush the ramekins with olive oil and pour the egg mixture inside.
4. Transfer the ramekins in the Crock Pot.
5. Cook the eggs on High for 2.5 hours.

Nutrition Info:
• Per Serving: 144 calories, 15.6g protein, 1.3g carbohydrates, 8.4g fat, 0g fiber, 260mg cholesterol, 181mg sodium, 138mg potassium

Boiled Bacon Eggs

Servings: 6 | Cooking Time: 2 Hrs

Ingredients:
• 7 oz. bacon, sliced
• 1 tsp salt
• 6 eggs, hard-boiled, peeled
• ½ cup cream
• 3 tbsp mayonnaise
• 1 tbsp minced garlic
• 1 tsp ground black pepper
• 4 oz. Parmesan cheese, shredded
• 1 tsp dried dill

Directions:
1. Place a non-skillet over medium heat and add bacon slices.
2. Drizzle salt and black pepper on top, then cook for 1 minute per side.
3. Transfer the bacon slices to a plate and keep them aside.
4. Whisk mayonnaise with minced garlic, dried dill, and cream in a bowl.
5. Spread this creamy mixture into the base of your Crock Pot.
6. Take the peeled eggs and wrap then with cooked bacon slices.
7. Place the wrapped eggs in the creamy mixture.
8. Drizzle shredded cheese over the wrapped eggs.
9. Put the cooker's lid on and set the cooking time to 2 hours on High settings.
10. Serve and devour.

Nutrition Info:
• Per Serving: Calories 381, Total Fat 31g, Fiber 1g, Total Carbs 8.07g, Protein 19g

Apple And Chia Mix

Servings: 2 | Cooking Time: 8 Hours

Ingredients:
• ¼ cup chia seeds
• 2 apples, cored and roughly cubed
• 1 cup almond milk
• 2 tablespoons maple syrup
• 1 teaspoon vanilla extract
• ½ tablespoon cinnamon powder
• Cooking spray

Directions:
1. Grease your Crock Pot with the cooking spray, add the chia seeds, milk and the other ingredients, toss, put the lid on and cook on Low for 8 hours.
2. Divide the mix into bowls and serve for breakfast.

Nutrition Info:
• calories 453, fat 29.3, fiber 8, carbs 51.1, protein 3.4

Bacon, Cheese & Spinach Breakfast

Servings: 6 (5.9 Ounces Per Serving)
Cooking Time: 2 Hours And 5 Minutes
Ingredients:
• 1 cup baby spinach, packed
• 6 organic eggs
• 1 cup Parmesan cheese, shredded
• ½ cup cheddar cheese, shredded
• 1/3 cup mushrooms, fresh, diced
• ½ teaspoon garlic powder
• ½ teaspoon onion powder
• ½ teaspoon thyme
• 1 cup plain yogurt
• 1 cup bacon, cooked, crumbled
• Salt and pepper to taste
• Olive oil

Directions:
1. In a bowl, whisk together dry herbs, salt, pepper, and eggs. Stir in crumbled bacon, shredded cheese, and spinach. Grease the bottom of Crock-Pot with olive oil. Pour the eggs mixture into Crock-Pot, cover and cook on HIGH for about 2 hours. Serve hot.

Nutrition Info:
• Calories: 225.6 , Total Fat: 13.9 g, Saturated Fat: 7.15 g, Cholesterol: 215.12 mg, Sodium: 434.51 mg, Potassium: 294.32 mg, Total Carbohydrates: 6.91 g, Fiber: 0.87 g, Sugar: 4.32 g, Protein: 18.44 g

Chicken Burrito Bowl

Servings: 6 | Cooking Time: 7 Hrs

Ingredients:
• 10 oz. chicken breast, sliced
• 1 tbsp chili flakes
• 1 tsp salt
• 1 tsp onion powder
• 1 tsp minced garlic
• ½ cup white beans, canned
• ¼ cup green peas
• 1 cup chicken stock
• ½ avocado, pitted and chopped
• 1 tsp ground black pepper

Directions:
1. Place the chicken breast in the Crock Pot.
2. Drizzle salt, onion powder, chili flakes, black pepper, and minced garlic on top.
3. Pour the chicken stock on top of the chicken.
4. Put the cooker's lid on and set the cooking time to 2 hours on High settings.
5. Now add white beans and green peas to the chicken.
6. Close the lid again and cook for 5 hours on Low setting.
7. Shred the slow-cooked chicken and return to the bean's mixture.
8. Mix well and add chopped avocado.
9. Serve the burrito with avocado on top.

Nutrition Info:
• Per Serving: Calories 192, Total Fat 7.7g, Fiber 5g, Total Carbs 15.66g, Protein 16g

Apricot Butter

Servings:4 | Cooking Time: 7 Hours

Ingredients:
- 1 cup apricots, pitted, chopped
- 3 tablespoons butter
- 1 teaspoon ground cinnamon
- 1 teaspoon brown sugar

Directions:
1. Put all ingredients in the Crock Pot and stir well
2. Close the lid and cook them on Low for 7 hours.
3. Then blend the mixture with the help of the immersion blender and cool until cold.

Nutrition Info:
- Per Serving: 99 calories, 0.6g protein, 5.5g carbohydrates, 8.9g fat, 1.1g fiber, 23mg cholesterol, 62mg sodium, 106mg potassium.

Broccoli Omelet

Servings:4 | Cooking Time: 2 Hours

Ingredients:
- 5 eggs, beaten
- 1 tablespoon cream cheese
- 3 oz broccoli, chopped
- 1 tomato, chopped
- 1 teaspoon avocado oil

Directions:
1. Mix eggs with cream cheese and transfer in the Crock Pot.
2. Add avocado oil, broccoli, and tomato.
3. Close the lid and cook the omelet on High for 2 hours.

Nutrition Info:
- Per Serving: 99 calories, 7.9g protein, 2.6g carbohydrates, 6.6g fat, 0.8g fiber, 207mg cholesterol, 92mg sodium, 184mg potassium.

Ham Stuffed Pockets

Servings: 6 | Cooking Time: 1.5 Minutes

Ingredients:
- 6 pita bread, sliced
- 7 oz. mozzarella, sliced
- 1 tsp minced garlic
- 7 oz. ham, sliced
- 1 big tomato, sliced
- 1 tbsp mayo
- 1 tbsp heavy cream

Directions:
1. First, heat your Crock Pot for 30 minutes on High setting.
2. Meanwhile, whisk the mayonnaise with garlic and cream.
3. Layer inside each half of the pita bread with mayo-garlic mixture.
4. Now add a slice of tomato, ham, and mozzarella to the bread.
5. Wrap the bread pieces with a foil sheet.
6. Place the packed pita bread in the Crock Pot.
7. Put the cooker's lid on and set the cooking time to 1 hour 30 minutes on Low settings.
8. Remove the bread from the foil.

9. Serve.

Nutrition Info:
- Per Serving: Calories 273, Total Fat 3.3g, Fiber 2g, Total Carbs 38.01g, Protein 22g

Breakfast Muffins

Servings:4 | Cooking Time: 3 Hours

Ingredients:
- 7 eggs, beaten
- 1 bell pepper, diced
- ½ teaspoon salt
- ½ teaspoon cayenne pepper
- 2 tablespoons almond meal
- 1 teaspoon avocado oil

Directions:
1. Brush the muffin molds with avocado oil.
2. In the mixing bowl, mix eggs, bell pepper, salt, cayenne pepper, and almond meal.
3. Pour the muffin mixture in the muffin molds and transfer in the Crock Pot.
4. Cook the muffins on high for 3 hours.

Nutrition Info:
- Per Serving: 139 calories, 10.7g protein, 3.7g carbohydrates, 9.4g fat, 0.9g fiber, 286mg cholesterol, 399mg sodium, 189mg potassium

Sausage Pie

Servings:4 | Cooking Time: 3 Hours

Ingredients:
- ½ cup flour
- ¼ cup skim milk
- 1 teaspoon baking powder
- 1 teaspoon salt
- ½ teaspoon chili flakes
- 4 sausages, chopped
- 1 egg, beaten
- Cooking spray

Directions:
1. Mix flour with skin milk and baking powder.
2. Then add salt, chili flakes, and egg. Stir the mixture until smooth. You will get the batter.
3. Spray the Crock Pot with cooking spray from inside.
4. Then pour the batter in the Crock Pot.
5. Add chopped sausages and close the lid.
6. Cook the pie on High for 3 hours.

Nutrition Info:
- Per Serving: 171 calories, 8.7g protein, 13.4g carbohydrates, 8.9g fat, 0.5g fiber, 64mg cholesterol, 809mg sodium, 262mg potassium

Eggs And Sausage Casserole

Servings: 4 | Cooking Time: 8 Hours

Ingredients:
- 8 eggs, whisked
- 1 yellow onion, chopped
- 1 pound pork sausage, chopped
- 2 teaspoons basil, dried
- 1 tablespoon garlic powder
- Salt and black pepper to the taste
- 1 yellow bell pepper, chopped
- 1 teaspoon olive oil

Directions:
1. Grease your Crock Pot with the olive oil, add eggs, onion, pork sausage, basil, garlic powder, salt, pepper and yellow bell pepper, toss, cover and cook on Low for 8 hours.
2. Slice, divide between plates and serve for breakfast.

Nutrition Info:
- calories 301, fat 4, fiber 4, carbs 14, protein 7

Vegetable Omelet

Servings: 4 | Cooking Time: 2 Hours 10 Minutes

Ingredients:
- 6 eggs
- ½ cup milk
- ¼ teaspoon salt
- Black pepper, to taste
- 1/8 teaspoon garlic powder
- 1/8 teaspoon chili powder
- 1 cup broccoli florets
- 1 red bell pepper, thinly sliced
- 1 small yellow onion, finely chopped
- 1 garlic clove, minced
- For Garnishing
- Chopped tomatoes
- Fresh parsley
- Shredded cheddar cheese
- Chopped onions

Directions:
1. Mix together eggs, milk, garlic powder, chili powder, salt and black pepper in a large mixing bowl.
2. Grease a crockpot and add garlic, onions, broccoli florets and sliced peppers.
3. Stir in the egg mixture and cover the lid.
4. Cook on HIGH for about 2 hours.
5. Top with cheese and allow it to stand for about 3 minutes.
6. Dish out the omelet into a serving plate and garnish with chopped onions, chopped tomatoes and fresh parsley.

Nutrition Info:
- Calories: 136 Fat: 7.4g Carbohydrates: 7.8g

Vanilla Maple Oats

Servings: 4 | Cooking Time: 8 Hrs

Ingredients:
- 1 cup steel-cut oats
- 2 tsp vanilla extract
- 2 cups vanilla almond milk
- 2 tbsp maple syrup
- 2 tsp cinnamon powder
- 2 cups of water
- 2 tsp flaxseed
- Cooking spray
- 2 tbsp blackberries

Directions:
1. Coat the base of your Crock Pot with cooking spray.
2. Stir in oats, almond milk, vanilla extract, cinnamon, maple syrup, flaxseeds, and water.
3. Put the cooker's lid on and set the cooking time to 8 hours on Low settings.
4. Stir well and serve with blackberries on top.
5. Devour.

Nutrition Info:
- Per Serving: Calories 200, Total Fat 3g, Fiber 6g, Total Carbs 9g, Protein 3g

Parmesan Quinoa

Servings: 2 | Cooking Time: 6 Hours

Ingredients:
- 1 cup quinoa
- 2 cups veggie stock
- 1 tablespoon chives, chopped
- 1 carrot, peeled and grated
- ½ cup parmesan, grated
- ¼ cup heavy cream
- Salt and black pepper to the taste
- Cooking spray

Directions:
1. Grease your Crock Pot with the cooking spray, add the quinoa mixed with the stock and the other ingredients except the parmesan and the cream, toss, put the lid on and cook on High for 3 hours.
2. Add the remaining ingredients, toss the mix again, cook on High for 3 more hours, divide into bowls and serve for breakfast.

Nutrition Info:
- calories 261, fat 6, fiber 8, carbs 26, protein 11

Quinoa Breakfast Bake

Servings: 4 | Cooking Time: 7 Hours

Ingredients:
- 1 cup quinoa
- 4 tablespoons olive oil
- 2 cups water
- ½ cup dates, chopped
- 3 bananas, chopped
- ¼ cup coconut, shredded
- 2 teaspoons cinnamon powder
- 2 tablespoons brown sugar

- 1 cup walnuts, toasted and chopped

Directions:

1. Put the oil in your Crock Pot, add quinoa, water, dates, bananas, coconut, cinnamon, brown sugar and walnuts, stir, cover and cook on Low for 7 hours.
2. Divide into bowls and serve for breakfast.

Nutrition Info:

- calories 241, fat 4, fiber 8, carbs 16, protein 6

Romano Cheese Frittata

Servings:4 | Cooking Time: 3 Hours

Ingredients:

- 4 oz Romano cheese, grated
- 5 eggs, beaten
- ¼ cup of coconut milk
- ½ cup bell pepper, chopped
- ½ teaspoon ground white pepper
- 1 teaspoon olive oil
- ½ teaspoon ground coriander

Directions:

1. Mix eggs with coconut milk, ground white pepper, bell pepper, and ground coriander.
2. Then brush the Crock Pot bowl with olive oil.
3. Pour the egg mixture in the Crock Pot.
4. Cook the frittata on High for 2.5 hours.
5. Then top the frittata with Romano cheese and cook for 30 minutes on High.

Nutrition Info:

- Per Serving: 238 calories, 16.5g protein, 3.6g carbohydrates, 17.9g fat, 0.6g fiber, 234mg cholesterol, 420mg sodium, 169mg potassium.

Radish Bowl

Servings:4 | Cooking Time: 1.5 Hours

Ingredients:

- 2 cups radish, halved
- 1 tablespoon dried dill
- 1 tablespoon olive oil
- 4 eggs, beaten
- ¼ teaspoon salt
- ¼ cup milk

Directions:

1. Mix radish with dried dill, olive oil, salt, and milk and transfer in the Crock Pot.
2. Cook the radish on High for 30 minutes.
3. Then shake the vegetables well and add eggs. Mix the mixture gently and close the lid.
4. Cook the meal on High for 1 hour.

Nutrition Info:

- Per Serving: 112 calories, 6.6g protein, 3.5g carbohydrates, 8.3g fat, 1g fiber, 165mg cholesterol, 240mg sodium, 229mg potassium

Raspberry Chia Pudding

Servings:2 | Cooking Time: 2 Hours

Ingredients:

- 4 tablespoons chia seeds
- 1 cup of coconut milk
- 2 teaspoons raspberries

Directions:

1. Put chia seeds and coconut milk in the Crock Pot and cook it for 2 hours on Low.
2. Then transfer the cooked chia pudding in the glasses and top with raspberries.

Nutrition Info:

- Per Serving: 423 calories, 7.7g protein, 19.6g carbohydrates, 37.9g fat, 13.1g fiber, 0mg cholesterol, 23mg sodium, 442mg potassium.

Quinoa And Oats Mix

Servings: 6 | Cooking Time: 7 Hours

Ingredients:

- ½ cup quinoa
- 1 and ½ cups steel cut oats
- 4 and ½ cups almond milk
- 2 tablespoons maple syrup
- 4 tablespoons brown sugar
- 1 and ½ teaspoons vanilla extract
- Cooking spray

Directions:

1. Grease your Crock Pot with cooking spray, add quinoa, oats, almond milk, maple syrup, sugar and vanilla extract, cover and cook on Low for 7 hours.
2. Stir, divide into bowls and serve for breakfast.

Nutrition Info:

- calories 251, fat 8, fiber 8, carbs 20, protein 5

Butternut Squash Quinoa

Servings: 6 | Cooking Time: 6 Hours

Ingredients:

- 1 yellow onion, chopped
- 1 tablespoon olive oil
- 3 garlic cloves, minced
- 2 teaspoons oregano, dried
- 1 and ½ pound chicken breasts, skinless, boneless and chopped
- 2 teaspoons parsley, dried
- 2 teaspoons curry powder
- ½ teaspoon chili flakes
- Salt and black pepper to the taste
- 1 butternut squash, peeled and cubed
- 2/3 cup quinoa
- 12 ounces canned tomatoes, chopped
- 4 cups veggie stock

Directions:

1. In your Crock Pot, mix onion with oil, garlic, oregano, chicken, parsley, curry powder, chili, squash, quinoa, salt, pepper, tomatoes and stock, stir, cover and cook on Low for 6 hours.

2. Divide into bowls and serve for breakfast.

Nutrition Info:
- calories 231, fat 4, fiber 6, carbs 20, protein 5

Tropical Granola

Servings: 6 | Cooking Time: 1 Hour And 30 Minutes

Ingredients:
- 1 cup almonds, sliced
- 4 cups old-fashioned oats
- ½ cup pecans, chopped
- ½ teaspoon ginger, ground
- ½ cup coconut oil
- ½ cup dried coconut
- ½ cup raisins
- ½ cup dried cherries
- ½ cup pineapple, dried

Directions:
1. In your Crock Pot, mix oil with almonds, oats, pecans, ginger, coconut, raisins, cherries and pineapple, toss, cover, cook on High for 1 hour and 30 minutes, stir again, divide into bowls and serve for breakfast.

Nutrition Info:
- calories 172, fat 5, fiber 8, carbs 10, protein 4

Tomato Hot Eggs

Servings:3 | Cooking Time: 2.5 Hours

Ingredients:
- 3 eggs, beaten
- 2 tomatoes, chopped
- 1 teaspoon coconut oil
- 1 bell pepper, diced
- 1 tablespoon hot sauce

Directions:
1. Grease the Crock Pot with coconut oil from inside.
2. Then mix hot sauce with beaten eggs.
3. Add chopped tomatoes and bell pepper.
4. Pour the mixture in the Crock Pot and close the lid.
5. Cook the meal on high for 2.5 hours.

Nutrition Info:
- Per Serving: 104 calories, 6.7g protein, 6.6g carbohydrates, 6.2g fat, 1.5g fiber, 164mg cholesterol, 193mg sodium, 335mg potassium.

Chocolate Vanilla Toast

Servings: 4 | Cooking Time: 4 Hrs

Ingredients:
- Cooking spray
- 1 loaf of bread, cubed
- ¾ cup brown sugar
- 3 eggs
- 1 and ½ cups of milk
- 1 tsp vanilla extract
- ¾ cup of chocolate chips
- 1 tsp cinnamon powder

Directions:
1. Cover the base of your Crock Pot with cooking spray.

2. Spread the bread pieces in the cooker.
3. Beat eggs with vanilla, milk, sugar, chocolate chips, and cinnamon in a bowl.
4. Pour this egg-chocolate mixture over the bread pieces.
5. Put the cooker's lid on and set the cooking time to 4 hours on Low settings.
6. Serve.

Nutrition Info:
- Per Serving: Calories 261, Total Fat 6g, Fiber 5g, Total Carbs 19g, Protein 6g

Ham Pockets

Servings:4 | Cooking Time: 1 Hour

Ingredients:
- 4 pita bread
- ½ cup Cheddar cheese, shredded
- 4 ham slices
- 1 tablespoon mayonnaise
- 1 teaspoon dried dill

Directions:
1. Mix cheese with mayonnaise and dill.
2. Then fill the pita bread with sliced ham and cheese mixture.
3. Wrap the stuffed pitas in the foil and place it in the Crock Pot.
4. Cook them on High for 1 hour.

Nutrition Info:
- Per Serving: 283 calories, 13.7g protein, 35.7g carbohydrates, 9.1g fat, 1.7g fiber, 32mg cholesterol, 801mg sodium, 175mg potassium.

Breakfast Pork Ground

Servings:4 | Cooking Time: 7 Hours

Ingredients:
- 1 cup ground pork
- 1 teaspoon tomato paste
- 1 red onion, diced
- ½ cup Mozzarella, shredded
- ½ cup corn kernels
- 1 tablespoon butter

Directions:
1. Mix ground pork with tomato paste, mozzarella, butter, and corn kernels.
2. Transfer the mixture in the Crock Pot and cook on low for 7 hours.
3. Then transfer the cooked meal in the serving plates and top with diced onion.

Nutrition Info:
- Per Serving: 122 calories, 7g protein, 6.6g carbohydrates, 7.8g fat, 1.2g fiber, 28mg cholesterol, 67mg sodium, 106mg potassium

Butter Oatmeal

Servings:4 | Cooking Time: 10 Minutes

Ingredients:
- 1 tablespoon liquid honey
- 1 tablespoon coconut shred
- 1 teaspoon vanilla extract
- 1 cup of water
- ½ cup heavy cream
- 1 cup oatmeal
- 2 tablespoons butter

Directions:
1. Put butter, oatmeal, heavy cream, water, vanilla extract, and coconut shred in the Crock Pot.
2. Carefully stir the ingredients and close the lid.
3. Cook the meal on Low for 5 hours.
4. Then add liquid honey, stir it, and transfer in the serving bowls.

Nutrition Info:
- Per Serving: 212 calories, 3.1g protein, 19.2g carbohydrates, 13.9g fat, 2.3g fiber, 36mg cholesterol, 51mg sodium, 92mg potassium.

Hash Brown And Bacon Casserole

Servings: 2 | Cooking Time: 3 Hours

Ingredients:
- 5 ounces hash browns, shredded
- 2 bacon slices, cooked and chopped
- ¼ cup mozzarella cheese, shredded
- 2 eggs, whisked
- ¼ cup sour cream
- 1 tablespoon cilantro, chopped
- 1 tablespoon olive oil
- A pinch of salt and black pepper

Directions:
1. Grease your Crock Pot with the oil, add the hash browns mixed with the eggs, sour cream and the other ingredients, toss, put the lid on and cook on High for 4 hours.
2. Divide the casserole into bowls and serve.

Nutrition Info:
- calories 383, fat 26.9, fiber 2.3, carbs 26.6, protein 9.6

Tropical Cherry Granola

Servings: 6 | Cooking Time: 1 Hr And 30 Minutes

Ingredients:
- 1 cup almonds, sliced
- 4 cups old-fashioned oats
- ½ cup pecans, chopped
- ½ tsp ginger, ground
- ½ cup of coconut oil
- ½ cup dried coconut
- ½ cup raisins
- ½ cup dried cherries
- ½ cup pineapple, dried

Directions:
1. Toss oil with pecans, ginger, almonds, and all other ingredients in the Crock Pot.

2. Put the cooker's lid on and set the cooking time to 1 hour 30 minutes on High settings.
3. Mix well and serve.

Nutrition Info:
- Per Serving: Calories 172, Total Fat 5g, Fiber 8g, Total Carbs 10g, Protein 4g

Breakfast Zucchini Oatmeal

Servings: 4 | Cooking Time: 8 Hours

Ingredients:
- ½ cup steel cut oats
- 1 carrot, grated
- 1 and ½ cups coconut milk
- ¼ zucchini, grated
- A pinch of cloves, ground
- A pinch of nutmeg, ground
- ½ teaspoon cinnamon powder
- 2 tablespoons brown sugar
- ¼ cup pecans, chopped

Directions:
1. In your Crock Pot, mix oats with carrot, milk, zucchini, cloves, nutmeg, cinnamon and sugar, stir, cover and cook on Low for 8 hours.
2. Add pecans, toss, divide into bowls and serve.

Nutrition Info:
- calories 251, fat 6, fiber 8, carbs 19, protein 6

Eggs With Spinach And Yogurt

Servings:4 | Cooking Time: 3 Hours

Ingredients:
- 1 clove of garlic, minced
- 2/3 cup plain Greek yogurt
- 2 tablespoons grass-fed butter, unsalted
- 4 large eggs, beaten
- 1 teaspoon fresh oregano, chopped
- Salt and pepper to taste
- 2 tablespoons olive oil
- 10 cups fresh spinach, chopped
- ¼ teaspoon red pepper flakes, crushed
- 2 tablespoon scallions, chopped

Directions:
1. In a mixing bowl, combine garlic, yogurt, butter, and eggs. Stir in oregano and season with salt and pepper to taste.
2. Grease the bottom of the CrockPot with olive oil.
3. Arrange the spinach and pour over the egg mixture.
4. Sprinkle with pepper flakes and scallions on top.
5. Close the lid and cook on high for 2 hours or on low for 3 hours.

Nutrition Info:
- Calories per serving: 247; Carbohydrates: 6.8g; Protein: 17.8g; Fat: 21.4g; Sugar: 0g; Sodium: 410mg; Fiber: 3.5g

Kale & Feta Breakfast Frittata

Servings: 6 (4.8 Ounces Per Serving) | Cooking Time: 3 Hours And 5 Minutes

Ingredients:
- 2 cups kale, chopped
- ½ cup feta, crumbled
- 2 teaspoons olive oil
- Salt and pepper to taste
- 3 green onions, chopped
- 1 large green pepper, diced
- 8 eggs

Directions:
1. Heat the olive oil in Crock-Pot and sauté the kale, diced pepper, and chopped green onion for about 2-3 minutes. Beat the eggs in a mixing bowl, pour over other ingredients, and stir. Add salt and pepper and sprinkle crumbled feta cheese on top. Cover and cook on LOW for 2-3 hours, or until the cheese has melted. Serve hot.

Nutrition Info:
- Calories: 160.1, Total Fat: 10.71 g, Saturated Fat: 4.2 g, Cholesterol: 259.13 mg, Sodium: 245.78 mg, Potassium: 263.49 mg, Total Carbohydrates: 4.92 g, Fiber: 1.06 g, Sugar: 1.52 g, Protein: 11.24 g

Light Egg Scramble

Servings:2 | Cooking Time: 4 Hours

Ingredients:
- 1 tablespoon butter, melted
- 6 eggs, beaten
- 1 teaspoon salt
- 1 teaspoon ground paprika

Directions:
1. Pour the melted butter in the Crock Pot.
2. Add eggs and salt and stir.
3. Cook the eggs on Low for 4 hours. Stir the eggs every 15 minutes.
4. When the egg scramble is cooked, top it with ground paprika.

Nutrition Info:
- Per Serving: 243 calories, 16.8g protein, 1.6g carbohydrates, 19g fat, 0.4g fiber, 506mg cholesterol, 1389mg sodium, 203mg potassium

Ham Stuffed Peppers

Servings: 3 | Cooking Time: 4 Hrs

Ingredients:
- 3 bell peppers, halved and deseeded
- Salt and black pepper to the taste
- 4 eggs
- ½ cup milk
- 2 tbsp green onions, chopped
- ½ cup ham, chopped
- ¼ cup spinach, chopped
- ¾ cup cheddar cheese, shredded

Directions:
1. Beat eggs with green onion, salt, black pepper, spinach, milk, half of the cheese and ham in a medium bowl.
2. Cover the base of your Crock Pot with aluminum foil.
3. Divide the egg-spinach mixture into the bell pepper halves.
4. Place these stuffed pepper halves in the Crock Pot.
5. Drizzle the cheese over the bell peppers.
6. Put the cooker's lid on and set the cooking time to 4 hours on Low settings.
7. Serve warm.
8. Devour.

Nutrition Info:
- Per Serving: Calories 162, Total Fat 4g, Fiber 1g, Total Carbs 6g, Protein 11g

Nutty Sweet Potatoes

Servings: 8 | Cooking Time: 6 Hrs

Ingredients:
- 2 tbsp peanut butter
- ¼ cup peanuts
- 1 lb. sweet potato, peeled and cut in strips.
- 1 garlic clove, peeled and sliced
- 2 tbsp lemon juice
- 1 cup onion, chopped
- ½ cup chicken stock
- 1 tsp salt
- 1 tsp paprika
- 1 tsp ground black pepper

Directions:
1. Toss the sweet potato with lemon juice, paprika, salt, black pepper, and peanut butter in a large bowl.
2. Place the sweet potatoes in the Crock Pot.
3. Add onions and garlic clove on top of the potatoes.
4. Put the cooker's lid on and set the cooking time to 6 hours on Low settings.
5. Serve with crushed peanuts on top.
6. Devour.

Nutrition Info:
- Per Serving: Calories 376, Total Fat 22.4g, Fiber 6g, Total Carbs 39.36g, Protein 5g

Chocolate Quinoa

Servings: 4 | Cooking Time: 6 Hours

Ingredients:
- 1 cup quinoa
- 1 cup coconut milk
- 1 cup milk
- 2 tablespoons cocoa powder
- 3 tablespoons maple syrup
- 4 dark chocolate squares, chopped

Directions:
1. In your Crock Pot, mix quinoa with coconut milk, milk, cocoa powder, maple syrup and chocolate, stir, cover and cook on Low for 6 hours.
2. Stir quinoa mix again, divide into bowls and serve.

Nutrition Info:
- calories 215, fat 5, fiber 8, carbs 17, protein 4

Tomato Ground Chicken

Servings:4 | Cooking Time: 6 Hours

Ingredients:
- 10 oz ground chicken
- 1 cup tomatoes, chopped
- ¼ cup cream
- 1 teaspoon chili powder

Directions:
1. Mix ground chicken with cream and chili powder and transfer in the Crock Pot.
2. Add tomatoes and close the lid.
3. Cook the meal on Low for 6 hours.
4. Then carefully mix the chicken.

Nutrition Info:
- Per Serving: 154 calories, 21.1g protein, 2.6g carbohydrates, 6.3g fat, 0.8g fiber, 66mg cholesterol, 75mg sodium, 297mg potassium

Bacon Eggs

Servings:2 | Cooking Time: 2 Hours

Ingredients:
- 2 bacon slices
- 2 eggs, hard-boiled, peeled
- ¼ teaspoon ground black pepper
- 1 teaspoon olive oil
- ½ teaspoon dried thyme

Directions:
1. Sprinkle the bacon with ground black pepper and dried thyme.
2. Then wrap the eggs in the bacon and sprinkle with olive oil.
3. Put the eggs in the Crock Pot and cook on High for 2 hours.

Nutrition Info:
- Per Serving: 187 calories, 12.6g protein, 0.9g carbohydrates, 14.7g fat, 0.2g fiber, 185mg cholesterol, 501mg sodium, 172mg potassium.

Squash Butter

Servings:4 | Cooking Time: 2 Hours

Ingredients:
- 1 cup butternut squash puree
- 1 teaspoon allspices
- 4 tablespoons applesauce
- 2 tablespoons butter
- 1 teaspoon cornflour

Directions:
1. Put all ingredients in the Crock Pot and mix until homogenous.
2. Then close the lid and cook the butter on High for 2 hours.
3. Transfer the cooked squash butter in the plastic vessel and cool it well.

Nutrition Info:
- Per Serving: 78 calories, 0.2g protein, 6.3g carbohydrates, 5.8g fat, 0.8g fiber, 15mg cholesterol, 44mg sodium, 20mg potassium

Carrot Pudding

Servings:4 | Cooking Time: 5 Hours

Ingredients:
- 3 cups carrot, shredded
- 1 tablespoon potato starch
- 3 tablespoons maple syrup
- 1 teaspoon ground cinnamon
- 4 cups of milk

Directions:
1. Mix potato starch with milk and pour the liquid in the Crock Pot.
2. Add ground cinnamon, maple syrup, and carrot.
3. Close the lid and cook the pudding on Low for 5 hours.

Nutrition Info:
- Per Serving: 206 calories, 8.7g protein, 33.1g carbohydrates, 5g fat, 2.3g fiber, 20mg cholesterol, 173mg sodium, 437mg potassium

Cheesy Sausage Casserole

Servings: 6-8 | Cooking Time: 4-5 Hours

Ingredients:
- 1 ½ cups cheddar cheese, shredded
- ½ cup mayonnaise
- 2 cups green cabbage, shredded
- 2 cups zucchini, diced
- ½ cup onion, diced
- 8 large eggs
- 1 lb. pork sausage
- 1 teaspoon sage, ground, dried
- 2 teaspoons prepared yellow mustard
- Cayenne pepper to taste
- ¼ teaspoon sea salt
- ¼ teaspoon black pepper

Directions:
1. Using cooking spray, grease the inside of the Crock-Pot. In a mixing bowl, whisk together eggs, mayonnaise, cheese, mustard, dried ground sage, cayenne pepper, salt, and black pepper. Layer half of the sausage, cabbage, zucchini, and onions into the Crock-Pot. Repeat with the remaining ingredients of zucchini, onion, sausage and cabbage. Pour the egg mixture onto the layered ingredients. Cook for 4-5 hours on LOW, until it is golden brown on the edges and set. Serve warm.

Nutrition Info:
- Calories: 484, Total Fat: 38.85 g, Saturated Fat: 21.6 g, Net Carbs: 6.39 g, Dietary Fiber: 1.8 g, Protein: 26.4 g

Peppers, Kale And Cheese Omelet

Servings: 4 | Cooking Time: 3 Hours

Ingredients:
- 1 teaspoon olive oil
- 7 ounces roasted red peppers, chopped
- 6 ounces baby kale
- Salt and black pepper to the taste
- 6 ounces feta cheese, crumbled
- ¼ cup green onions, sliced
- 7 eggs, whisked

Directions:
1. In a bowl, mix the eggs with cheese, kale, red peppers, green onions, salt and pepper, whisk well, pour into the Crock Pot after you've greased it with the oil, cover, cook on Low for 3 hours, divide between plates and serve right away.

Nutrition Info:
- calories 231, fat 7, fiber 4, carbs 7, protein 14

Blueberry Quinoa Oatmeal

Servings: 4 | Cooking Time: 8 Hours

Ingredients:
- ½ cup quinoa
- 1 cup steel cut oats
- 1 teaspoon vanilla extract
- 5 cups water
- Zest of 1 lemon, grated
- 1 teaspoon vanilla extract
- 2 tablespoons flaxseed
- 1 tablespoon butter, melted
- 3 tablespoons maple syrup
- 1 cup blueberries

Directions:
1. In your Crock Pot, mix butter with quinoa, water, oats, vanilla, lemon zest, flaxseed, maple syrup and blueberries, stir, cover and cook on Low for 8 hours.
2. Divide into bowls and serve for breakfast.

Nutrition Info:
- calories 189, fat 5, fiber 5, carbs 20, protein 5

Chia Seeds And Chicken Breakfast

Servings: 4 | Cooking Time: 3 Hours

Ingredients:
- 1 pound chicken breasts, skinless, boneless and cubed
- ½ teaspoon basil, dried
- ¾ cup flaxseed, ground
- ¼ cup chia seeds
- ¼ cup parmesan, grated
- ½ teaspoon oregano, chopped
- Salt and black pepper to the taste
- 2 eggs
- 2 garlic cloves, minced

Directions:
1. In a bowl, mix flaxseed with chia seeds, parmesan, salt, pepper, oregano, garlic and basil and stir.
2. Put the eggs in a second bowl and whisk them well.
3. Dip chicken in eggs mix, then in chia seeds mix, put them

in your Crock Pot after you've greased it with cooking spray, cover and cook on High for 3 hours.
4. Serve them right away for a Sunday breakfast.

Nutrition Info:
- calories 212, fat 3, fiber 4, carbs 17, protein 4

Shrimp Omelet

Servings:4 | Cooking Time: 3.5 Hours

Ingredients:
- 4 eggs, beaten
- 4 oz shrimps, peeled
- ½ teaspoon ground turmeric
- ½ teaspoon ground paprika
- ¼ teaspoon salt
- Cooking spray

Directions:
1. Mix eggs with shrimps, turmeric, salt, and paprika.
2. Then spray the Crock Pot bowl with cooking spray.
3. After this, pour the egg mixture inside. Flatten the shrimps and close the lid.
4. Cook the omelet for 3.5 hours on High.

Nutrition Info:
- Per Serving: 98 calories, 12.1g protein, 1.1g carbohydrates, 4.9g fat, 0.2g fiber, 223mg cholesterol, 278mg sodium, 120mg potassium.

Granola Bowls

Servings: 2 | Cooking Time: 4 Hours

Ingredients:
- ½ cup granola
- ¼ cup coconut cream
- 2 tablespoons brown sugar
- 2 tablespoons cashew butter
- 1 teaspoon cinnamon powder
- ½ teaspoon nutmeg, ground

Directions:
1. In your Crock Pot, mix the granola with the cream, sugar and the other ingredients, toss, put the lid on and cook on Low for 4 hours.
2. Divide into bowls and serve for breakfast.

Nutrition Info:
- calories 218, fat 6, fiber 9, carbs 17, protein 6

Lunch & Dinner Recipes

Lunch & Dinner Recipes

Lime Bean Stew

Servings: 8 | Cooking Time: 6 1/4 Hours

Ingredients:
- 2 cups dried lime beans
- 2 carrots, sliced
- 2 celery stalks, sliced
- 1 head cauliflower, cut into florets
- 1 teaspoon grated ginger
- 1 cup diced tomatoes
- 1 cup tomato sauce
- 2 cups vegetable stock
- 1 bay leaf
- 1 thyme sprig
- Salt and pepper to taste

Directions:
1. Combine the beans, carrots, celery, cauliflower, ginger, tomatoes, tomato sauce, stock, salt and pepper, as well as bay leaf and thyme in your Crock Pot.
2. Season with salt and pepper as needed and cook on low settings for 6 hours.
3. The stew is best served warm.

Spring Pilaf

Servings:5 | Cooking Time: 4 Hours

Ingredients:
- ½ cup carrot, diced
- ½ cup green peas, frozen
- 1 cup long-grain rice
- 2 oz chives, chopped
- 1 tablespoon olive oil
- 2.5 cups chicken stock
- ½ cup fresh parsley, chopped

Directions:
1. Mix rice with olive oil and put it in the Crock Pot.
2. Add chicken stock and all remaining ingredients.
3. Close the lid and cook the pilaf on High for 4 hours.

Nutrition Info:
- Per Serving: 186 calories, 4.4g protein, 34g carbohydrates, 3.5g fat, 2g fiber, 0mg cholesterol, 396mg sodium, 187mg potassium.

Cheesy Potato Casserole

Servings: 6 | Cooking Time: 6 1/2 Hours

Ingredients:
- 2 1/2 pounds potatoes, peeled and sliced
- 2 large onions, sliced
- 2 tomatoes, sliced
- 4 garlic cloves, minced
- 1 1/2 cups tomato sauce
- 1/2 teaspoon dried oregano
- 1/2 teaspoon dried thyme
- 1/2 cup vegetable stock
- Salt and pepper to taste
- 1 1/2 cups grated Cheddar

Directions:
1. Layer the potatoes and onions in your Crock Pot.
2. Finish the layering with tomatoes.
3. Mix the garlic, tomato sauce, oregano, thyme and stock in a bowl. Add salt and pepper to taste then pour this mixture over the potatoes.
4. Top with cheese and cook on low settings for 6 hours.
5. Serve the casserole warm and fresh.

Garlic Bean Dip

Servings:8 | Cooking Time: 5 Hours

Ingredients:
- 1 cup red kidney beans, canned
- 1 tablespoon tomato paste
- 1 teaspoon minced garlic
- 1 teaspoon dried cilantro
- 1 teaspoon ground paprika
- ½ cup of water

Directions:
1. Mix water with tomato paste and pour the liquid in the Crock Pot.
2. Add red kidney beans, ground paprika, minced garlic, and cilantro.
3. Close the lid and cook the mixture on low for 5 hours.
4. Then blend the mixture gently with the help of the blender.

Nutrition Info:
- Per Serving: 80 calories, 5.3g protein, 14.7g carbohydrates, 0.3g fat, 3.7g fiber, 0mg cholesterol, 5mg sodium, 341mg potassium.

Beef Strips

Servings: 4 | Cooking Time: 6 Hours

Ingredients:
- ½ pound baby mushrooms, sliced
- 1 yellow onion, chopped
- 1 pound beef sirloin steak, cubed
- Salt and black pepper to the taste
- 1/3 cup red wine
- 2 teaspoons olive oil
- 2 cups beef stock
- 1 tablespoon Worcestershire sauce

Directions:
1. In your Crock Pot, mix beef strips with onion, mushrooms, salt, pepper, wine, olive oil, beef stock and Worcestershire sauce, toss, cover and cook on Low for 6 hours.
2. Divide between plates and serve for lunch.

Nutrition Info:
- calories 212, fat 7, fiber 1, carbs 8, protein 26

Curried Tofu Lentils

Servings: 6 | Cooking Time: 6 1/4 Hours

Ingredients:
- 8 oz. firm tofu, cubed
- 2 tablespoons canola oil
- 2 tablespoons red curry paste
- 1 cup red lentils
- 2 cups vegetable stock
- 2 cups cauliflower florets
- 2 tablespoons tomato paste
- 1 bay leaf
- 1/2 lemongrass stalk, crushed
- 1/2 teaspoon grated ginger
- Salt and pepper to taste

Directions:
1. Heat the oil in a skillet and add the tofu. Cook on all sides until golden brown and crusty then transfer in your Crock Pot.
2. Add the remaining ingredients and season with salt and pepper.
3. Cook on low settings for 6 hours.
4. Serve the dish warm and fresh.

Veggie Soup

Servings: 2 | Cooking Time: 4 Hours

Ingredients:
- ½ pound gold potatoes, peeled and roughly cubed
- 1 carrot, sliced
- 1 zucchini, cubed
- 1 eggplant, cubed
- 1 cup tomatoes, cubed
- 4 cups veggie stock
- A pinch of salt and black pepper
- 3 tablespoons tomato paste
- 1 sweet onion, chopped
- 1 tablespoon lemon juice
- 1 tablespoon chives, chopped

Directions:
1. In your Crock Pot, mix the potatoes with the carrot, zucchini and the other ingredients, toss, put the lid on and cook on Low for 4 hours.
2. Divide the soup into bowls and serve.

Nutrition Info:
- calories 392, fat 7, fiber 8, carbs 12, protein 28

Sweet Potato Stew

Servings: 8 | Cooking Time: 8 Hours

Ingredients:
- 1 yellow onion, chopped
- ½ cup red beans, dried
- 2 red bell peppers, chopped
- 2 tablespoons ginger, grated
- 4 garlic cloves, minced
- 2 pounds sweet, peeled and cubed
- 3 cups chicken stock
- 14 ounces canned tomatoes, chopped
- 2 jalapeno peppers, chopped
- Salt and black pepper to the taste

- ½ teaspoon cumin, ground
- ½ teaspoon coriander, ground
- ¼ teaspoon cinnamon powder
- ¼ cup peanuts, roasted and chopped
- Juice of ½ lime

Directions:
1. In your Crock Pot, mix onion with red beans, red bell peppers, ginger, garlic, potatoes, stock, tomatoes, jalapenos, salt, pepper, cumin, coriander and cinnamon, stir, cover and cook on Low for 8 hours.
2. Divide into bowls, divide peanuts on top, drizzle lime juice and serve for lunch.

Nutrition Info:
- calories 259, fat 8, fiber 7, carbs 42, protein 8

Barley Black Bean Stew

Servings: 6 | Cooking Time: 3 1/4 Hours

Ingredients:
- 1 shallot, chopped
- 1 garlic clove, chopped
- 1 can (15 oz.) black beans, drained
- 1 cup canned corn, drained
- 1/2 cup pearl barley
- 1 1/2 cups vegetable stock
- 1/2 cup diced tomatoes
- 1/4 teaspoon chili powder
- 1/4 teaspoon cumin powder
- Salt and pepper to taste
- 2 tablespoons chopped cilantro
- 1 green onion, chopped

Directions:
1. Combine the shallot, garlic, black beans, corn, pearl barley and stock in your Crock Pot.
2. Add the stock, tomatoes, chili powder and cumin powder and season with salt and pepper.
3. Cook on high settings for 3 hours.
4. When done, stir in the cilantro and green onion.
5. Serve the soup warm.

Asian Style Beef Short Ribs

Servings: 6 | Cooking Time: 7 1/4 Hours

Ingredients:
- 4 pounds beef short ribs
- 1 large onion, sliced
- 1 carrot, sliced
- 1/2 cup light soy sauce
- 2 tablespoons brown sugar
- 4 garlic cloves, chopped
- 1 star anise
- 2 tablespoons rice vinegar
- 1 cup beef stock
- 2 green onions, chopped for serving

Directions:
1. Mix the onion, carrot, soy sauce, sugar, garlic, star anise, vinegar and stock in your Crock Pot.
2. Add the beef ribs and coat them well in the mixture.
3. Cover with a lid and cook on low settings for 7 hours.
4. When done, top with chopped green onions and serve right away.

Coconut Bean Curry

Servings: 6 | Cooking Time: 6 1/2 Hours

Ingredients:
- 2 cans pinto beans, drained
- 1 tablespoon olive oil
- 1 shallot, chopped
- 2 garlic cloves, chopped
- 1 teaspoon grated ginger
- 1/2 teaspoon chili powder
- 1/2 teaspoon cumin powder
- 1 teaspoon curry powder
- 1 cup coconut milk
- 1 cup vegetable stock
- 2 tablespoons tomato paste
- 1 bay leaf
- 1 teaspoon brown sugar
- Salt and pepper to taste

Directions:
1. Combine the beans and the remaining ingredients in your Crock Pot.
2. Season with salt and pepper.
3. Cook on low settings for 6 hours.
4. Serve the bean curry warm.

Honey Orange Glazed Tofu

Servings: 4 | Cooking Time: 4 1/4 Hours

Ingredients:
- 12 oz. firm tofu, cubed
- 1 tablespoon grated ginger
- 1 garlic clove, minced
- 1 orange, zested and juiced
- 2 tablespoons soy sauce
- 1 teaspoon Worcestershire sauce
- 1/4 cup vegetable stock

Directions:
1. Combine all the ingredients in your Crock Pot.
2. Cover and cook on low settings for 4 hours.
3. The tofu is best served warm with your favorite side dish.

Peppercorn Artichoke Casserole

Servings: 6 | Cooking Time: 6 1/4 Hours

Ingredients:
- 1 jar artichoke hearts, drained and chopped
- 4 peppercorns, chopped
- 1 tablespoon lemon juice
- 2 celery stalks, sliced
- 1 cup vegetable stock
- 1 cup Alfredo sauce
- Salt and pepper to taste

Directions:
1. Combine all the ingredients in your Crock Pot.
2. Add salt and pepper to taste and cook on low settings for 6 hours.
3. The dish is best served warm, but it can also be re-heated.

Beef Barley Stew

Servings: 6 | Cooking Time: 6 1/2 Hours

Ingredients:
- 1 pound beef chuck roast, cut into thin strips
- 2 tablespoons canola oil
- 1 shallot, chopped
- 2 garlic cloves, chopped
- 1 carrot, diced
- 1 celery stalk, diced
- 1 cup pearl barley
- 1/4 cup dried currants
- 1/4 cup pine nuts
- 2 cups beef stock
- Salt and pepper to taste

Directions:
1. Heat the oil in a frying pan and add the beef. Cook for a few minutes on all sides then transfer in your Crock Pot.
2. Add the shallot, garlic, carrot, celery, pearl barley, currants, pine nuts and stock.
3. Add salt and pepper to taste and cook on low settings for 6 hours.
4. The stew is great served both warm and chilled.

Squash And Chicken Soup

Servings: 2 | Cooking Time: 6 Hours

Ingredients:
- ½ pound chicken thighs, skinless, boneless and cubed
- ½ small yellow onion, chopped
- ½ red bell pepper, chopped
- ½ green bell pepper, chopped
- 3 cups chicken stock
- ½ cup butternut squash, peeled and cubed
- 2 ounces canned green chilies, chopped
- ½ teaspoon oregano, dried
- A pinch of salt and black pepper
- ½ tablespoon lime juice
- 1 tablespoon cilantro, chopped

Directions:
1. In your Crock Pot, mix the chicken with the onion, bell pepper and the other ingredients, toss, put the lid on and cook on High for 6 hours.
2. Ladle the soup into bowls and serve.

Nutrition Info:
- calories 365, fat 11.2, fiber 10.2, carbs 31.4, protein 38

Puttanesca Pizza

Servings: 6 | Cooking Time: 2 1/2 Hours

Ingredients:
- Dough:
- 2 cups all-purpose flour
- 1 teaspoon active dry yeast
- 1 cup warm water
- 1/4 teaspoon salt
- 2 tablespoons olive oil
- Topping:
- 1/2 cup crushed fire roasted tomatoes
- 1/4 cup Kalamata olives, pitted and sliced

- 1/4 cup green olives, sliced
- 1 tablespoon capers, chopped
- 1/2 teaspoon dried basil
- 1/2 teaspoon dried oregano

Directions:
1. To make the dough, combine all the ingredients in a bowl and knead for a few minutes in a bowl.
2. Roll the dough into a round that fits in your Crock Pot.
3. Top with tomatoes, olives, capers and dried herbs.
4. Cook on high settings for 1 1/2 hours.
5. Serve the pizza warm.

Indian Style Tofu Stew

Servings: 6 | Cooking Time: 2 1/4 Hours

Ingredients:
- 2 tablespoons olive oil
- 8 oz. firm tofu, cubed
- 1 teaspoon cumin powder
- 1/2 teaspoon chili powder
- 1/4 teaspoon ground coriander
- 1/2 teaspoon turmeric powder
- 1 1/2 cups coconut milk
- 1 head cauliflower, cut into florets
- 1 bay leaf
- 1/2 lemongrass stalk, crushed
- Salt and pepper to taste

Directions:
1. Season the tofu with cumin, chili, coriander and turmeric powder.
2. Heat the oil in a skillet and add the tofu. Cook on all sides until golden and fragrant.
3. Transfer in your Crock Pot and add the remaining ingredients.
4. Cook on high settings for 2 hours.
5. Serve the stew warm or chilled.

Sauerkraut Cumin Pork

Servings: 6 | Cooking Time: 6 1/4 Hours

Ingredients:
- 1 1/2 pounds pork shoulder, cubed
- 1 1/2 pounds sauerkraut, shredded
- 1 large onion, chopped
- 2 carrots, grated
- 1 1/2 teaspoons cumin seeds
- 1/4 teaspoon red pepper flakes
- 1 cup chicken stock
- 1 bay leaf
- Salt and pepper to taste

Directions:
1. Combine all the ingredients in your Crock Pot.
2. Add enough salt and pepper and cook on low settings for 6 hours.
3. Serve the pork and sauerkraut warm and fresh.

Green Pea Tomato Stew

Servings: 6 | Cooking Time: 2 1/4 Hours

Ingredients:
- 2 shallots, chopped
- 2 garlic cloves, chopped
- 2 tablespoons olive oil
- 1 celery stalk, sliced
- 1 red bell pepper, cored and diced
- 1 carrot, diced
- 1 pound frozen green peas
- 1 cup diced tomatoes
- 1 bay leaf
- Salt and pepper to taste

Directions:
1. Heat the oil in a skillet and stir in the shallots and garlic. Cook for 2 minutes until softened then transfer in your Crock Pot.
2. Add the remaining ingredients and season with salt and pepper.
3. Cook on high for 2 hours.
4. Serve the stew warm or chilled.

Caramelized Onions Chicken Stew

Servings: 6 | Cooking Time: 6 1/2 Hours

Ingredients:
- 2 chicken breasts, cubed
- 2 tablespoons canola oil
- 4 bacon slices, chopped
- 3 large onions, sliced
- 1 celery stalk, sliced
- 2 red bell peppers, cored and sliced
- 1/4 cup dry white wine
- 1 can fire roasted tomatoes
- 1/2 teaspoon dried thyme
- Salt and pepper to taste

Directions:
1. Heat the oil in a skillet and add the bacon. Cook until crisp then stir in the onions.
2. Cook for 10 minutes until the onions are soft and begin to caramelize.
3. Transfer in your Crock Pot. Add the remaining ingredients and season with salt and pepper.
4. Cook on low settings for 6 hours.
5. Serve the stew warm and fresh.

Vegetable Shepherd's Pie

Servings: 6 | Cooking Time: 7 1/2 Hours

Ingredients:
- 1 cup frozen green peas
- 1 cup frozen corn
- 2 large carrots, diced
- 2 cups sliced mushrooms
- 1 tablespoon cornstarch
- Salt and pepper to taste
- 1 1/2 cups vegetable stock
- 1/2 teaspoon dried oregano
- 1 1/2 pounds potatoes, peeled and cubed

Directions:

1. Begin by cooking the potatoes. Once cooked, mash them with a potato masher, adding part of the cooking liquid to obtain a smooth puree.
2. Combine the vegetables with cornstarch, salt and pepper in a bowl.
3. Transfer in your Crock Pot and add the stock.
4. Top with the mashed potatoes and cook on low settings for 7 hours.
5. Serve the pie warm or chilled. It can also be re-heated.

Saffron Beef Tagine

Servings: 6 | Cooking Time: 7 1/4 Hours

Ingredients:

- 2 pounds beef sirloin, cubed
- 2 tablespoons olive oil
- 1 large onion, chopped
- 4 garlic clove, chopped
- 1 celery stalk, sliced
- 2 ripe tomatoes, peeled and diced
- 1 cup dried plums, chopped
- 1/2 teaspoon saffron threads
- 1/2 cup couscous
- 1 1/2 cups vegetable stock
- Salt and pepper to taste
- 1 orange, sliced
- 2 tablespoons sliced almonds
- Chopped parsley for serving
- Lime juice for serving

Directions:

1. Heat the oil in a skillet and add the beef. Cook for a few minutes and transfer in your Crock Pot.
2. Stir in the remaining ingredients and season with salt and pepper.
3. Cook the tagine on low settings for 7 hours and serve it warm and fresh, topped with chopped parsley and a drizzle of lime juice.

Honey Apple Pork Chops

Servings: 4 | Cooking Time: 5 1/4 Hours

Ingredients:

- 4 pork chops
- 2 red, tart apples, peeled, cored and cubed
- 1 shallot, chopped
- 2 garlic cloves, chopped
- 1 tablespoon olive oil
- 1 red chili, chopped
- 1 heirloom tomato, peeled and diced
- 1 cup apple cider
- 2 tablespoons honey
- Salt and pepper to taste

Directions:

1. Mix all the ingredients in your Crock Pot.
2. Add salt and pepper to taste and cook on low settings for 5 hours.
3. Serve the chops warm and fresh.

Beef Broccoli Sauté

Servings: 4 | Cooking Time: 2 1/4 Hours

Ingredients:

- 2 flank steaks, cut into thin strips
- 1 tablespoon peanut oil
- 1 pound broccoli florets
- 1/4 cup peanuts, chopped
- 1 tablespoon tomato paste
- 2 tablespoons soy sauce
- 1/4 cup beef stock
- 1 teaspoon hot sauce
- 1/2 teaspoon sesame oil
- 1 tablespoon sesame seeds
- Salt and pepper to taste

Directions:

1. Combine all the ingredients in your Crock Pot.
2. Add salt and pepper to taste and cook on high settings for 2 hours.
3. Serve the sauté warm.

Mexican Lunch Mix

Servings: 12 | Cooking Time: 7 Hours

Ingredients:

- 12 ounces beer
- ¼ cup flour
- 2 tablespoons tomato paste
- 1 jalapeno pepper, chopped
- 1 bay leaf
- 4 teaspoons Worcestershire sauce
- 2 teaspoons red pepper flakes, crushed
- 1 and ½ teaspoons cumin, ground
- 2 teaspoons chili powder
- Salt and black pepper to the taste
- 2 garlic cloves, minced
- ½ teaspoon sweet paprika
- ½ teaspoon red vinegar
- 3 pounds pork shoulder butter, cubed
- 2 potatoes, chopped
- 1 yellow onion, chopped

Directions:

1. In your Crock Pot, mix pork with potatoes, onion, beef, flour, tomato paste, jalapeno, bay leaf, Worcestershire sauce, pepper flakes, cumin, chili powder, garlic, paprika and vinegar, toss, cover and cook on Low for 7 hours.
2. Divide between plates and serve for lunch.

Nutrition Info:

- calories 261, fat 12, fiber 2, carbs 16, protein 21

Pork And Chorizo Lunch Mix

Servings: 8 | Cooking Time: 4 Hours

Ingredients:
- 1 pound chorizo, ground
- 1 pound pork, ground
- 3 tablespoons olive oil
- 1 tomato, chopped
- 1 avocado, pitted, peeled and chopped
- Salt and black pepper to the taste
- 1 small red onion, chopped
- 2 tablespoons enchilada sauce

Directions:
1. Heat up a pan with the oil over medium-high heat, add pork, stir, brown for a couple of minutes, transfer to your Crock Pot, add salt, pepper, chorizo, onion and enchilada sauce, stir, cover and cook on Low for 4 hours.
2. Divide between plates and serve with chopped tomato and avocado on top.

Nutrition Info:
- calories 300, fat 12, fiber 3, carbs 15, protein 17

Coq Au Vin

Servings: 8 | Cooking Time: 8 1/2 Hours

Ingredients:
- 1 whole chicken, cut into smaller pieces
- 2 tablespoons canola oil
- 1 cup miniature onions
- 4 carrots, sliced
- 1 pound button mushrooms
- 1/2 cup red wine
- 1 cup tomato sauce
- 2 ripe tomatoes, peeled and diced
- 2 bay leaves
- Salt and pepper to taste
- 1 thyme sprig
- 1 rosemary sprig

Directions:
1. Heat the canola oil in a skillet and add the chicken. Fry on all sides for a few minutes until golden then transfer the chicken in your Crock Pot.
2. Add the remaining ingredients and season with salt and pepper.
3. Cook the coq au vin on low settings for 8 hours.
4. Serve the dish warm, simple as it is.

White Beans In Sauce

Servings:4 | Cooking Time: 5 Hours

Ingredients:
- 1 cup white beans, soaked
- 1 cup BBQ sauce
- 1 cup chicken stock
- 3 cups of water
- 1 onion, diced
- 1 teaspoon dried sage

Directions:
1. Mix BBQ sauce, chicken stock, and water in the Crock Pot.
2. Add onion, dried sage, and white beans.

3. Close the lid and cook the beans on High for 5 hours.
4. Serve the cooked beans with BBQ sauce gravy.

Nutrition Info:
- Per Serving: 278 calories, 13.1g protein, 56g carbohydrates, 0.7g fat, 8.7g fiber, 0mg cholesterol, 841mg sodium, 1080mg potassium.

Spiced Lentil Stew

Servings: 6 | Cooking Time: 3 1/4 Hours

Ingredients:
- 2 tablespoons olive oil
- 1 large onion, chopped
- 2 garlic cloves, chopped
- 1/2 teaspoon cumin powder
- 1/4 teaspoon chili powder
- 1/2 teaspoon grated ginger
- 1/2 teaspoon coriander seeds
- 1/2 teaspoon turmeric powder
- 1 cup red lentils
- 2 cups vegetable stock
- 1/2 cup tomato sauce
- Salt and pepper to taste
- Chopped cilantro for serving

Directions:
1. Heat the oil in a skillet and stir in the onion and garlic. Cook for 2 minutes until softened then add the spices and sauté for 30 seconds just until the flavors are released.
2. Transfer the mixture in your Crock Pot and add the remaining ingredients.
3. Season with salt and pepper and cook on high settings for 3 hours.
4. Serve the stew warm and fresh, topped with chopped cilantro.

Red Beans Saute

Servings:4 | Cooking Time: 7 Hours

Ingredients:
- 1 cup red beans, soaked
- 1 cup carrot, chopped
- 1 yellow onion, chopped
- 5 cups chicken stock
- 1 teaspoon Italian seasonings
- 1 teaspoon tomato paste

Directions:
1. Mix chicken stock with tomato paste and pour the liquid in the Crock Pot.
2. Add Italian seasonings, onion, carrot, and soaked red beans.
3. Close the lid and cook the saute on Low for 7 hours.

Nutrition Info:
- Per Serving: 194 calories, 11.8g protein, 34.8g carbohydrates, 1.6g fat, 8.3g fiber, 1mg cholesterol, 982mg sodium, 786mg potassium.

Apple Cherry Pork Chops

Servings: 6 | Cooking Time: 3 1/4 Hours

Ingredients:
- 6 pork chops
- 4 red, tart apples, cored and sliced
- 1 cup frozen sour cherries
- 1/2 cup apple cider vinegar
- 1/2 cup tomato sauce
- 1 onion, chopped
- 1 garlic clove, minced
- 1 bay leaf
- Salt and pepper to taste

Directions:
1. Combine the pork chops, apples, sour cherries, tomato sauce, onion, garlic and bay leaf in your Crock Pot.
2. Add salt and pepper to taste and cook on high settings for 3 hours.
3. Serve the pork chops warm and fresh.

Arroz Con Pollo

Servings: 8 | Cooking Time: 6 1/4 Hours

Ingredients:
- 1 cup wild rice
- 1 cup green peas
- 2 celery stalks, sliced
- 1 onion, chopped
- 1 red chili, chopped
- 2 ripe tomatoes, peeled and diced
- 1 cup sliced mushrooms
- 2 cups vegetable stock
- 4 chicken breasts, halved
- Salt and pepper to taste
- 1 thyme sprig
- 1 rosemary sprig

Directions:
1. Combine the rice, green peas, celery, onion, red chili, tomatoes, mushrooms, stock and chicken in your Crock Pot.
2. Add the thyme sprig, rosemary, salt and pepper and cook the dish on low settings for 6 hours.
3. Serve the dish warm and fresh.

Chunky Pasta Sauce

Servings: 8 | Cooking Time: 8 1/4 Hours

Ingredients:
- 1 can (15 oz.) black beans, drained
- 1 can (15 oz.) kidney beans
- 2 cups tomato sauce
- 1 cup fire roasted tomatoes
- 1 cup frozen corn
- 1 cup green peas
- 1 celery stalk, sliced
- 1 teaspoon cumin powder
- 1 teaspoon dried oregano
- 1 cup vegetable stock
- Salt and pepper to taste

Directions:
1. Combine all the ingredients in your Crock Pot.

2. Add salt and pepper to taste and cook on low settings for 8 hours.
3. Serve the sauce right away or freeze it into individual portions for later serving.

Creamy Lentil Stew

Servings: 8 | Cooking Time: 7 1/4 Hours

Ingredients:
- 1 cup red lentils
- 1 large sweet potato, peeled and diced
- 1 carrot, diced
- 2 ripe tomatoes, peeled and diced
- 2 cups vegetable stock
- 1/2 teaspoon cumin seeds
- 1/2 red chili, chopped
- Salt and pepper to taste
- 1 bay leaf

Directions:
1. Combine all the ingredients in your Crock Pot.
2. Add salt and pepper to taste and cook on low settings for 7 hours.
3. Serve the stew warm and fresh.

Kale White Bean Stew

Servings: 8 | Cooking Time: 5 1/4 Hours

Ingredients:
- 2 pounds beef roast, cut into small cubes
- 2 tablespoons canola oil
- 2 cans (15 oz. each) white beans, drained
- 2 shallots, chopped
- 4 garlic cloves, chopped
- 1 teaspoon dried oregano
- 1/2 teaspoon dried sage
- 1 bunch kale, shredded
- Salt and pepper to taste

Directions:
1. Heat the oil in a frying pan and add the beef. Cook for a few minutes on all sides then transfer in your Crock Pot.
2. Add the remaining ingredients and season with salt and pepper.
3. Cover the pot and cook for 5 hours on low settings.
4. Serve the stew warm and fresh.

Turmeric Lentils Stew

Servings: 2 | Cooking Time: 5 Hours

Ingredients:
- 2 cups veggie stock
- ½ cup canned red lentils, drained
- 1 carrot, sliced
- 1 eggplant, cubed
- ½ cup tomatoes, chopped
- 1 red onion, chopped
- 1 garlic clove, minced
- 1 teaspoon turmeric powder
- ¼ tablespoons ginger, grated
- ½ teaspoons mustard seeds
- ¼ teaspoon sweet paprika

- ½ cup tomato paste
- 1 tablespoon dill, chopped
- Salt and black pepper to the taste

Directions:
1. In your Crock Pot, combine the lentils with the stock, tomatoes, eggplant and the other ingredients, toss, put the lid on, cook on High for 5 hours, divide into bowls and serve.

Nutrition Info:
- calories 303, fat 4, fiber 8, carbs 12, protein 4

Buffalo Cauliflower

Servings: 6 | Cooking Time: 6 1/4 Hours

Ingredients:
- 1 head cauliflower, cut into florets
- 1 onion, chopped
- 1 can diced tomatoes
- 1 can fire roasted green chilies, chopped
- 1 teaspoon hot sauce
- 1/2 cup tomato sauce
- 1 teaspoon cumin powder
- 1 can (15 oz.) cannellini beans, drained
- Salt and pepper to taste
- Grated Cheddar for serving

Directions:
1. Combine the cauliflower and the rest of the ingredients in your Crock Pot.
2. Add salt and pepper to taste and cook on low settings for 6 hours.
3. Serve the dish warm.

Mustard Pork Chops And Carrots

Servings: 2 | Cooking Time: 4 Hours

Ingredients:
- 1 tablespoon butter
- 1 pound pork chops, bone in
- 2 carrots, sliced
- 1 cup beef stock
- ½ tablespoon honey
- ½ tablespoon lime juice
- 1 tablespoon lime zest, grated

Directions:
1. In your Crock Pot, mix the pork chops with the butter and the other ingredients, toss, put the lid on and cook on High for 4 hours.
2. Divide between plate sand serve.

Nutrition Info:
- calories 300, fat 8, fiber 10, carbs 16, protein 16

Chili Bbq Ribs

Servings: 8 | Cooking Time: 8 1/2 Hours

Ingredients:
- 6 pounds pork short ribs
- 2 cups BBQ sauce
- 1 1/2 teaspoons chili powder
- 1 teaspoon cumin powder
- 2 tablespoons brown sugar
- 2 tablespoons red wine vinegar
- 1 teaspoon Worcestershire sauce
- Salt and pepper to taste

Directions:
1. Mix the BBQ sauce, chili powder, sugar, vinegar, Worcestershire sauce, salt and pepper in a Crock Pot.
2. Add the short ribs and mix until well coated.
3. Cover with a lid and cook on low settings for 8 1/4 hours.
4. Serve the ribs warm and fresh.

Mediterranean Chickpea Feta Stew

Servings: 8 | Cooking Time: 8 1/4 Hours

Ingredients:
- 2 cups dried chickpeas, rinsed
- 1 large onion, chopped
- 2 carrots, diced
- 1 celery stalk, diced
- 1 teaspoon dried oregano
- 1 teaspoon dried basil
- 1 pinch chili powder
- 2 heirloom tomatoes, peeled and diced
- 2 cups vegetable stock
- Salt and pepper to taste
- 8 oz. feta cheese for servings

Directions:
1. Combine the chickpeas, onion, carrots, celery, oregano, basil, chili powder, tomatoes, salt and pepper, as well as stock in your Crock Pot.
2. Cover and cook on low settings for 8 hours.
3. Serve the stew warm, topped with crumbled feta cheese.

Zucchini Rolls In Tomato Sauce

Servings: 8 | Cooking Time: 7 Hours

Ingredients:
- 2 large zucchinis
- 2 carrots, cut into match sticks
- 2 parsnips, cut into matchsticks
- 1 large eggplant, cut into sticks
- 1 cup tomato sauce
- 1 cup vegetable stock
- 1 bay leaf
- 1 teaspoon dried thyme
- 1/2 teaspoon dried oregano
- Salt and pepper to taste

Directions:
1. Using a vegetable peeler, cut thin ribbons of zucchini and lay them flat on your chopping board.
2. Place a few sticks of parsnip, carrot and eggplant at one end of each zucchini ribbon then tightly roll.

3. Arrange the rolls in your Crock Pot and add the remaining ingredients.
4. Season with salt and pepper and cook on low settings for 6 hours.
5. Serve warm.

Rosemary Garlic Beef Stew

Servings: 6 | Cooking Time: 5 1/4 Hours

Ingredients:
- 2 pounds beef roast, cubed
- 1 celery stalk, sliced
- 1 sweet onion, sliced
- 1 leek, sliced
- 4 garlic cloves, minced
- 2 pounds red potatoes, peeled and cubed
- 1 tablespoon Dijon mustard
- 1 teaspoon Worcestershire sauce
- 1 tablespoon soy sauce
- 1 tablespoon brown sugar
- 1 tablespoon dried rosemary
- 1 cup diced tomatoes
- 1 cup beef stock
- 1 bay leaf
- Salt and pepper to taste

Directions:
1. Mix all the ingredients in your Crock Pot.
2. Add enough salt and pepper and cook on low settings for 5 hours.
3. The stew is best served warm.

Beef Bolognese Sauce

Servings: 6 | Cooking Time: 6 1/4 Hours

Ingredients:
- 2 tablespoons canola oil
- 2 pounds ground beef
- 1 carrot, grated
- 1 celery stalk, finely chopped
- 4 garlic cloves, minced
- 1 can (15 oz.) diced tomatoes
- 2 tablespoons tomato paste
- 1/2 teaspoon dried oregano
- 1/2 teaspoon dried basil
- 1/4 cup red wine
- 1/2 cup beef stock
- Salt and pepper to taste
- Grated Parmesan cheese for serving
- Cooked pasta of your choice for serving

Directions:
1. Heat the oil in a frying pan and add the ground beef. Cook for a few minutes then transfer in your Crock Pot.
2. Add the rest of the ingredients and adjust the taste with salt and pepper.
3. Cook on low settings for 6 hours.
4. Serve the sauce warm, over cooked past, topped with grated cheese or freeze the sauce into individual portions for later serving.

Bulgur Chili

Servings: 8 | Cooking Time: 8 1/4 Hours

Ingredients:
- 1 cup bulgur wheat
- 1 large onion, chopped
- 2 cups sliced mushrooms
- 1 red bell pepper, cored and diced
- 2 garlic cloves, chopped
- 2 cups vegetable stock
- 1 cup diced tomatoes
- 1 can (15 oz.) black beans, drained
- 1 can (15 oz.) kidney beans, drained
- 1 tablespoon brown sugar
- 1 teaspoon apple cider vinegar
- 1 teaspoon chili powder
- Salt and pepper to taste
- 1 bay leaf
- 1 thyme sprig

Directions:
1. Combine the bulgur and the remaining ingredients in your Crock Pot.
2. Add salt and pepper to taste and cook on low settings for 8 hours, mixing a few times during the cooking time to make sure it's cooked evenly.
3. Serve the chili warm.

Balsamic Roasted Root Vegetables

Servings: 4 | Cooking Time: 3 1/4 Hours

Ingredients:
- 1/2 pound baby carrots
- 2 sweet potatoes, peeled and cubed
- 2 parsnips, sliced
- 1 turnip, peeled and sliced
- 1 large red onion, sliced
- 2 tablespoons olive oil
- 1 tablespoon brown sugar
- 2 tablespoons balsamic vinegar
- 1/4 cup vegetable stock
- Salt and pepper to taste

Directions:
1. Combine all the ingredients in your Crock Pot.
2. Add salt and pepper to taste and cook on high settings for 3 hours.
3. Serve the vegetables warm and fresh.

Alfredo Green Bean Casserole

Servings: 6 | Cooking Time: 3 1/4 Hours

Ingredients:
- 1 pound green beans, trimmed and chopped
- 1 cup Alfredo sauce
- 1 cup water chestnuts, chopped
- 2 cups sliced mushrooms
- 1/2 cup grated Parmesan cheese
- 1 shallot, sliced
- 1/2 cup vegetable stock
- Salt and pepper to taste

Directions:

1. Combine all the ingredients in a Crock Pot. Add salt and pepper to taste.
2. Cook on high settings for 3 hours.
3. Serve the casserole warm and fresh.

Fall Crock Pot Roast

Servings: 6 | Cooking Time: 6 Hours

Ingredients:
- 2 sweet potatoes, cubed
- 2 carrots, chopped
- 2 pounds beef chuck roast, cubed
- ¼ cup celery, chopped
- 1 tablespoon canola oil
- 2 garlic cloves, minced
- 1 yellow onion, chopped
- 1 tablespoon flour
- 1 tablespoon brown sugar
- 1 tablespoon sugar
- 1 teaspoon cumin, ground
- Salt and black pepper to the taste
- ¾ teaspoon coriander, ground
- ½ teaspoon oregano, dried
- 1 teaspoon chili powder
- 1/8 teaspoon cinnamon powder
- ¾ teaspoon orange peel grated
- 15 ounces tomato sauce

Directions:
1. In your Crock Pot, mix potatoes with carrots, beef cubes, celery, oil, garlic, onion, flour, brown sugar, sugar, cumin, salt pepper, coriander, oregano, chili powder, cinnamon, orange peel and tomato sauce, stir, cover and cook on Low for 6 hours.
2. Divide into bowls and serve for lunch.

Nutrition Info:
- calories 278, fat 12, fiber 2, carbs 16, protein 25

Apple Corned Beef With Red Cabbage

Servings: 6 | Cooking Time: 6 1/2 Hours

Ingredients:
- 1 1/2 pounds beef chuck roast, cubed
- 1 red cabbage, shredded
- 1/2 teaspoon cumin seeds
- 1 cinnamon stick
- 1 star anise
- 1/2 cup red wine
- 1 tablespoon red wine vinegar
- 1/2 cup beef stock
- 2 red apples, cored and diced
- 1 bay leaf
- Salt and pepper to taste

Directions:
1. Mix the chuck roast, cabbage, cumin seeds, cinnamon, star anise, red wine, vinegar, stock and apples in your Crock Pot.
2. Add the bay leaf, salt and pepper and cook on low settings for 6 hours.
3. The dish is best served warm.

Cuban Flank Steaks

Servings: 6 | Cooking Time: 8 1/4 Hours

Ingredients:
- 6 beef flank steaks
- 2 red onions, sliced
- 1 teaspoon cumin seeds
- 1 teaspoon chili powder
- 1 teaspoon dried oregano
- 1 cup beef stock
- 1 chipotle pepper, chopped
- 2 limes, juiced
- Salt and pepper to taste

Directions:
1. Combine the steaks in your Crock Pot and add salt and pepper.
2. Cover and cook for 8 hours on low settings.
3. Serve the steaks warm.

Leek Potato Stew

Servings: 6 | Cooking Time: 4 1/2 Hours

Ingredients:
- 2 tablespoons olive oil
- 2 leeks, sliced
- 2 celery stalks, sliced
- 2 carrots, diced
- 1 1/2 pounds potatoes, peeled and cubed
- 2 tablespoons tomato paste
- 1/2 cup diced tomatoes
- 1 bay leaf
- 1 thyme sprig
- Salt and pepper to taste

Directions:
1. Heat the oil in your Crock Pot and add the leeks. Cook for 5 minutes until softened then transfer the mix in your Crock Pot.
2. Add the remaining ingredients and season with salt and pepper.
3. Cook on low settings for 4 hours.
4. The stew is best served warm.

Poultry Recipes

Poultry Recipes

Salsa Chicken Wings

Servings:5 | Cooking Time: 6 Hours

Ingredients:
- 2-pounds chicken wings
- 2 cups salsa
- ½ cup of water

Directions:
1. Put all ingredients in the Crock Pot.
2. Carefully mix the mixture and close the lid.
3. Cook the chicken wings on low for 6 hours.

Nutrition Info:
- Per Serving: 373 calories, 54.1g protein, 6.5g carbohydrates, 13.6g fat, 1.7g fiber, 161mg cholesterol, 781mg sodium, 750mg potassium.

Lime Dipped Chicken Drumsticks

Servings: 7 | Cooking Time: 3.5 Hours

Ingredients:
- 3 oz. garlic, peeled and minced
- 17 oz. chicken drumsticks
- 1 lime, finely chopped
- 1 tsp lemon zest
- 1 tsp kosher salt
- 1 tsp coriander
- 1 tsp butter

Directions:
1. Add butter, chicken and all other ingredients to the Crock Pot.
2. Put the cooker's lid on and set the cooking time to 3.5 hours on High settings.
3. Serve warm.

Nutrition Info:
- Per Serving: Calories: 136, Total Fat: 7g, Fiber: 0g, Total Carbs: 4.68g, Protein: 13g

Turmeric Meatballs

Servings:4 | Cooking Time: 2.5 Hours

Ingredients:
- 1-pound ground chicken
- 1 tablespoon ground turmeric
- ½ teaspoon ground ginger
- 1 teaspoon salt
- 1 tablespoon corn starch
- ½ cup cream

Directions:
1. Mix ground chicken with ground turmeric, ginger, salt, and corn starch.
2. Then make the medium-size meatballs.
3. Preheat the skillet well.
4. Put the meatballs in the hot skillet and cook them for 30 seconds per side.
5. Then transfer the meatballs in the Crock Pot, add cream, and close the lid.
6. Cook the meatballs on High for 2.5 hours.

Nutrition Info:
- Per Serving: 250 calories, 33.2g protein, 4.5g carbohydrates, 10.3g fat, 0.4g fiber, 107mg cholesterol, 689mg sodium, 333mg potassium.

Alfredo Chicken

Servings: 4 | Cooking Time: 2 Hours And 30 Minutes

Ingredients:
- 1 pound chicken breasts, skinless and boneless
- 4 tablespoons soft butter
- 1 cup chicken stock
- 2 cups heavy cream
- Salt and black pepper to the taste
- ½ teaspoon Italian seasoning
- ½ teaspoon garlic powder
- 1/3 cup parmesan, grated
- ½ pound rigatoni

Directions:
1. In your Crock Pot, mix chicken with butter, stock, cream, salt, pepper, garlic powder and Italian seasoning, stir, cover and cook on High for 2 hours.
2. Shred meat, return to Crock Pot, also add rigatoni and parmesan, cover and cook on High for 30 minutes more.
3. Divide between plates and serve.

Nutrition Info:
- calories 300, fat 7,fiber 7, carbs 17, protein 12

Halved Chicken

Servings:4 | Cooking Time: 5 Hours

Ingredients:
- 2-pounds whole chicken, halved
- 1 tablespoon salt
- 1 teaspoon ground black pepper
- 2 tablespoons mayonnaise
- ½ cup of water

Directions:
1. Mix the ground black pepper with salt and mayonnaise.
2. Then rub the chicken halves with mayonnaise mixture and transfer in the Crock Pot.
3. Add water and close the lid.
4. Cook the chicken on High for 5 hours.

Nutrition Info:
- Per Serving: 461 calories, 65.7g protein, 2.1g carbohydrates, 19.3g fat, 1.2g fiber, 0.1mg cholesterol, 1993mg sodium, 559mg potassium.

Goose And Sauce

Servings: 4 | Cooking Time: 5 Hours

Ingredients:
- 1 goose breast half, skinless, boneless and cut into thin slices
- ¼ cup olive oil
- 1 sweet onion, chopped
- 2 teaspoons garlic, chopped
- Salt and black pepper to the taste
- ¼ cup sweet chili sauce

Directions:
1. In your Crock Pot, mix goose with oil, onion, garlic, salt, pepper and chili sauce, stir, cover and cook on Low for 5 hours.
2. Divide between plates and serve.

Nutrition Info:
- calories 192, fat 4, fiber 8, carbs 12, protein 22

Crockpot Chicken, Egg And Tomato Stew

Servings: 4 | Cooking Time: 8 Hours

Ingredients:
- 2 tablespoons butter, melted
- 4 chicken breasts, skin and bones removed
- Salt and pepper to taste
- 4 large eggs, unbeaten
- ½ cup organic tomato sauce

Directions:
1. Pour the melted butter in the crockpot.
2. Arrange the chicken pieces and season with salt and pepper to taste.
3. Pour the tomato sauce.
4. Carefully, crack the eggs into the chicken and tomato sauce.
5. Close the lid and cook on high for 8 hours or on low for 6 hours.

Nutrition Info:
- Calories per serving: 616; Carbohydrates: 3.3g; Protein: 63.8g; Fat: 37.2g; Sugar: 0g; Sodium: 637mg; Fiber: 2.4g

Turkey And Corn

Servings: 2 | Cooking Time: 7 Hours

Ingredients:
- 1 red onion
- 1 cup corn
- 1 pound turkey breasts, skinless, boneless and cubed
- 1 cup heavy cream
- 2 tablespoons olive oil
- 1 tablespoon cumin, ground
- ½ cup chicken stock
- ½ teaspoon rosemary, dried
- A pinch of salt and black pepper
- 1 tablespoon cilantro, chopped

Directions:
1. In your Crock Pot, mix the turkey with the corn, onion and the other ingredients, toss, put the lid on and cook on Low for 7 hours.
2. Divide everything into bowls and serve.

Nutrition Info:
- calories 214, fat 14, fiber 2, carbs 6, protein 15

Coca Cola Chicken

Servings: 4 | Cooking Time: 4 Hours

Ingredients:
- 1 yellow onion, minced
- 4 chicken drumsticks
- 1 tablespoon balsamic vinegar
- 1 chili pepper, chopped
- 15 ounces coca cola
- Salt and black pepper to the taste
- 2 tablespoons olive oil

Directions:
1. Heat up a pan with the oil over medium-high heat, add chicken pieces, stir and brown them on all sides and then transfer them to your Crock Pot.
2. Add vinegar, chili, coca cola, salt and pepper, cover and cook on High for 4 hours.
3. Divide chicken mix between plates and serve.

Nutrition Info:
- calories 372, fat 14, fiber 3, carbs 20, protein 15

Chicken Pocket

Servings:4 | Cooking Time: 4 Hours

Ingredients:
- 1-pound chicken fillet, skinless, boneless
- 3 oz prunes, chopped
- 1 teaspoon dried cilantro
- 1 tablespoon olive oil
- 1 teaspoon salt
- ½ cup of water

Directions:
1. Make the horizontal cut in the chicken fillet and fill it with prunes.
2. Then secure the cut and rub the chicken fillet with dried cilantro and salt.
3. Sprinkle the chicken with olive oil and transfer in the Crock Pot.
4. Add water and close the lid.
5. Cook the chicken on High for 4 hours.
6. Drain water and remove the toothpicks.
7. Cut the cooked meal into 4 servings.

Nutrition Info:
- Per Serving: 297 calories, 33.3g protein, 13.6g carbohydrates, 12g fat, 1.5g fiber, 101mg cholesterol, 680mg sodium, 432mg potassium.

Chinese Duck

Servings: 6 | Cooking Time: 8 Hours

Ingredients:
- 1 duck, chopped in medium pieces
- 1 celery stalk, chopped
- 2 carrots, chopped
- 2 cups chicken stock
- Salt and black pepper to the taste
- 1 tablespoon ginger, grated

Directions:
1. In your Crock Pot, mix duck with celery, carrots, stock, salt, pepper and ginger, stir, cover and cook on Low for 8 hours.
2. Divide duck, ginger sauce between plates, and serve.

Nutrition Info:
- calories 200, fat 3, fiber 6, carbs 19, protein 17

Chili Sausages

Servings:4 | Cooking Time: 3 Hours

Ingredients:
- 1-pound chicken sausages, roughly chopped
- ½ cup of water
- 1 tablespoon chili powder
- 1 teaspoon tomato paste

Directions:
1. Sprinkle the chicken sausages with chili powder and transfer in the Crock Pot.
2. Then mix water and tomato paste and pour the liquid over the chicken sausages.
3. Close the lid and cook the meal on High for 3 hours.

Nutrition Info:
- Per Serving: 221 calories, 15g protein, 8.9g carbohydrates, 12.8g fat, 1.4g fiber, 0mg cholesterol, 475mg sodium, 50mg potassium.

Chicken And Green Onion Sauce

Servings: 4 | Cooking Time: 4 Hours

Ingredients:
- 2 tablespoons butter, melted
- 4 green onions, chopped
- 4 chicken breast halves, skinless and boneless
- Salt and black pepper to the taste
- 8 ounces sour cream

Directions:
1. In your Crock Pot, mix chicken with melted butter, green onion, salt, pepper and sour cream, cover and cook on High for 4 hours.
2. Divide chicken between plates, drizzle green onions sauce all over and serve.

Nutrition Info:
- calories 200, fat 7, fiber 2, carbs 11, protein 20

Creamy Spinach And Artichoke Chicken

Servings: 4 | Cooking Time: 4 Hours

Ingredients:
- 4 ounces cream cheese
- 4 chicken breasts, boneless and skinless
- 10 ounces canned artichoke hearts, chopped
- 10 ounces spinach
- ½ cup parmesan, grated
- 1 tablespoon dried onion
- 1 tablespoon garlic, dried
- Salt and black pepper to the taste
- 4 ounces mozzarella, shredded

Directions:
1. Place chicken breasts in your Crock Pot season with salt and pepper, add artichokes, cream cheese, spinach, onion, garlic, spinach and top with mozzarella.
2. Cover Crock Pot, cook on High for 4 hours, toss, divide everything between plates and serve.

Nutrition Info:
- calories 450, fat 23, fiber 1, carbs 14, protein 39

Chicken With Basil And Tomatoes

Servings:4 | Cooking Time: 8 Hours

Ingredients:
- ¾ cup balsamic vinegar
- ¼ cup fresh basil leaves
- 2 tablespoons olive oil
- 8 plum tomatoes, sliced
- 4 boneless chicken breasts, bone and skin removed

Directions:
1. Place balsamic vinegar, basil leaves, olive oil and tomatoes in a blender. Season with salt and pepper to taste. Pulse until fine.
2. Arrange the chicken pieces in the crockpot.
3. Pour over the sauce.
4. Close the lid and cook on low for 8 hours or on high for 6 hours.

Nutrition Info:
- Calories per serving: 177; Carbohydrates:4 g; Protein:24 g; Fat: 115g; Sugar: 0g; Sodium: 171mg; Fiber: 3.5g

Red Sauce Chicken Soup

Servings: 4 | Cooking Time: 3 Hours

Ingredients:
- 3 tbsp butter, melted
- 4 oz. cream cheese
- 2 cups chicken meat, cooked and shredded
- 1/3 cup red sauce
- 4 cups chicken stock
- Salt and black pepper to the taste
- ½ cup sour cream
- ¼ cup celery, chopped

Directions:
1. Blend stock with red sauce, sour cream, black pepper, butter, cream cheese, and salt in a blender.
2. Transfer this red sauce mixture to the Crock Pot along with

chicken and celery.

3. Put the cooker's lid on and set the cooking time to 3 hours on High settings.

4. Serve warm.

Nutrition Info:

• Per Serving: Calories: 400, Total Fat: 23g, Fiber: 5g, Total Carbs: 15g, Protein: 30g

Oregano Chicken Breast

Servings:4 | Cooking Time: 4 Hours

Ingredients:

• 1-pound chicken breast, skinless, boneless, roughly chopped
• 1 tablespoon dried oregano
• 1 bay leaf
• 1 teaspoon peppercorns
• 1 teaspoon salt
• 2 cups of water

Directions:

1. Pour water in the Crock Pot and add peppercorns and bay leaf.

2. Then sprinkle the chicken with the dried oregano and transfer in the Crock Pot.

3. Close the lid and cook the meal on High for 4 hours.

Nutrition Info:

• Per Serving: 135 calories, 24.2g protein, 1.3g carbohydrates, 3g fat, 0.3g fiber, 73mg cholesterol, 643mg sodium, 448mg potassium.

Crock Pot Chicken Breasts

Servings: 4 | Cooking Time: 4 Hours

Ingredients:

• 6 chicken breasts, skinless and boneless
• Salt and black pepper to the taste
• ¼ cup jalapenos, chopped
• 5 bacon slices, chopped
• 8 ounces cream cheese
• ¼ cup yellow onion, chopped
• ½ cup mayonnaise
• ½ cup parmesan, grated
• 1 cup cheddar cheese, grated

Directions:

1. Arrange chicken breasts in your Crock Pot, add salt, pepper, jalapenos, bacon, cream cheese, onion, mayo, parmesan and cheddar, cover and cook on High for 4 hours.

2. Divide between plates and serve.

Nutrition Info:

• calories 340, fat 12, fiber 2, carbs 15, protein 20

Jalapeno Chicken Wings

Servings:6 | Cooking Time: 3 Hours

Ingredients:

• 5 jalapenos, minced
• ½ cup tomato juice
• 2-pounds chicken wings, skinless
• 1 teaspoon salt
• ¼ cup of water

Directions:

1. Mix minced jalapenos with tomato juice, salt, and water.

2. Pour the liquid in the Crock Pot.

3. Add chicken wings and close the lid.

4. Cook the meal on High for 3 hours.

Nutrition Info:

• Per Serving: 294 calories, 44.1g protein, 1.6g carbohydrates, 11.3g fat, 0.4g fiber, 135mg cholesterol, 573mg sodium, 439mg potassium.

Turkey Curry

Servings: 4 | Cooking Time: 4 Hours

Ingredients:

• 18 ounces turkey meat, minced
• 3 ounces spinach
• 20 ounces canned tomatoes, chopped
• 2 tablespoons coconut oil
• 2 tablespoons coconut cream
• 2 garlic cloves, minced
• 2 yellow onions, sliced
• 1 tablespoon coriander, ground
• 2 tablespoons ginger, grated
• 1 tablespoons turmeric powder
• 1 tablespoon cumin, ground
• Salt and black pepper to the taste
• 2 tablespoons chili powder

Directions:

1. In your Crock Pot, mix turkey with spinach, tomatoes, oil, cream, garlic, onion, coriander, ginger, turmeric, cumin, chili, salt and pepper, stir, cover and cook on High for 4 hours.

2. Divide into bowls and serve.

Nutrition Info:

• calories 240, fat 4, fiber 3, carbs 13, protein 12

Continental Beef Chicken

Servings:5 | Cooking Time: 9 Hours

Ingredients:

• 6 oz. dried beef
• 12 oz. chicken breast, diced
• 7 oz. sour cream
• 1 can onion soup
• 3 tbsp flour

Directions:

1. Spread half of the dried beef in the Crock Pot.

2. Top it with chicken breast, sour cream, onion soup, and flour.

3. Spread the remaining dried beef on top.

4. Put the cooker's lid on and set the cooking time to 9 hours on Low settings.

5. Serve warm.

Nutrition Info:

• Per Serving: Calories: 285, Total Fat: 15.1g, Fiber: 1g, Total Carbs: 12.56g, Protein: 24g

Chicken And Broccoli

Servings: 2 | Cooking Time: 5 Hours

Ingredients:
- 1 pound chicken breast, skinless, boneless and sliced
- 1 cup broccoli florets
- ½ cup tomato sauce
- ½ cup chicken stock
- 1 tablespoon avocado oil
- 1 yellow onion, sliced
- 3 garlic cloves, minced
- A pinch of salt and black pepper
- 1 tablespoon cilantro, chopped

Directions:
1. In your Crock Pot, mix the chicken with the broccoli, tomato sauce and the other ingredients, toss, put the lid on and cook on High for 5 hours.
2. Divide the mix between plates and serve hot.

Nutrition Info:
- calories 253, fat 14, fiber 2, carbs 7, protein 16

Sauce Goose

Servings: 4 | Cooking Time: 5 Hours

Ingredients:
- 1 goose breast half, skinless, boneless and cut into thin slices
- ¼ cup olive oil
- 1 sweet onion, chopped
- 2 tsp garlic, chopped
- Salt and black pepper to the taste
- ¼ cup sweet chili sauce

Directions:
1. Add goose, oil and all other ingredients to the Crock Pot.
2. Put the cooker's lid on and set the cooking time to 5 hours on Low settings.
3. Serve warm.

Nutrition Info:
- Per Serving: Calories: 192, Total Fat: 4g, Fiber: 8g, Total Carbs: 12g, Protein: 22g

Orange Duck Fillets

Servings: 4 | Cooking Time: 8 Hours

Ingredients:
- 2 oranges, peeled and sliced
- 1 tbsp honey
- 1 lb. duck fillet, sliced
- 1 tsp salt
- ½ tsp ground black pepper
- ½ tsp cilantro, chopped
- 1 tsp coriander, chopped
- 7 oz. celery stalk, chopped
- 1 tbsp chives, chopped
- ¼ cup of water
- 2 tbsp butter
- 1 tsp cinnamon

Directions:
1. Add butter, duck, and all other ingredients to the Crock Pot.

2. Put the cooker's lid on and set the cooking time to 8 hours on Low settings.
3. Serve warm.

Nutrition Info:
- Per Serving: Calories: 353, Total Fat: 23.2g, Fiber: 3g, Total Carbs: 15.68g, Protein: 21g

Mediterranean Stuffed Chicken

Servings:4 | Cooking Time: 8 Hours

Ingredients:
- 4 chicken breasts, bones and skin removed
- Salt and pepper to taste
- 1 cup feta cheese, crumbled
- 1/3 cup sun-dried tomatoes, chopped
- 2 tablespoons olive oil

Directions:
1. Create a slit in the chicken breasts to thin out the meat. Season with salt and pepper to taste
2. In a mixing bowl, combine the feta cheese and sun-dried tomatoes.
3. Spoon the feta cheese mixture into the slit created into the chicken.
4. Close the slit using toothpicks.
5. Brush the chicken with olive oil.
6. Place in the crockpot and cook on high for 6 hours or on low for 8 hours.

Nutrition Info:
- Calories per serving: 332; Carbohydrates: 3g; Protein:40 g; Fat: 17g; Sugar: 0g; Sodium: 621mg; Fiber:2.4 g

Tomato Chicken Sausages

Servings:4 | Cooking Time: 2 Hours

Ingredients:
- 1-pound chicken sausages
- 1 cup tomato juice
- 1 tablespoon dried sage
- 1 teaspoon salt
- 1 teaspoon olive oil

Directions:
1. Heat the olive oil in the skillet well.
2. Add chicken sausages and roast them for 1 minute per side on high heat.
3. Then transfer the chicken sausages in the Crock Pot.
4. Add all remaining ingredients and close the lid.
5. Cook the chicken sausages on High for 2 hours.

Nutrition Info:
- Per Serving: 236 calories, 15.3g protein, 10.5g carbohydrates, 13.7g fat, 1.1g fiber, 0mg cholesterol, 1198mg sodium, 145mg potassium.

Garlic Duck

Servings:4 | Cooking Time: 5 Hours

Ingredients:
- 1-pound duck fillet
- 1 tablespoon minced garlic
- 1 tablespoon butter, softened
- 1 teaspoon dried thyme
- 1/3 cup coconut cream

Directions:
1. Mix minced garlic with butter, and dried thyme.
2. Then rub the suck fillet with garlic mixture and place it in the Crock Pot.
3. Add coconut cream and cook the duck on High for 5 hours.
4. Then slice the cooked duck fillet and sprinkle it with hot garlic coconut milk.

Nutrition Info:
- Per Serving: 216 calories, 34.1g protein, 2g carbohydrates, 8.4g fat, 0.6g fiber, 8mg cholesterol, 194mg sodium, 135mg potassium.

Crockpot Fajita Chicken

Servings:8 | Cooking Time: 8 Hours

Ingredients:
- 2 ½ pounds chicken thighs and breasts, skin and bones removed
- 1 onion, sliced
- 4 cloves of garlic, minced
- 2 cups bell peppers, sliced
- 1 teaspoon ground coriander
- ½ teaspoon cumin
- ½ teaspoon chipotle pepper, chopped
- 1 cup roma tomatoes, diced
- Salt and pepper to taste

Directions:
1. Place all ingredients in the CrockPot.
2. Close the lid and cook on high for 6 hours or on low for 8 hours.
3. Shred the chicken meat using two forks.
4. Return to the CrockPot and cook on high for another 30 minutes.
5. Garnish with chopped cilantro.

Nutrition Info:
- Calories per serving: 328; Carbohydrates: 3.3g; Protein: 39.5g; Fat: 17.7g; Sugar: 0g; Sodium: 697mg; Fiber: 1.7g

Turkey Wings And Veggies

Servings: 4 | Cooking Time: 8 Hours

Ingredients:
- 4 turkey wings
- 1 yellow onion, chopped
- 1 carrot, chopped
- 3 garlic cloves, minced
- 1 celery stalk, chopped
- 1 cup chicken stock
- Salt and black pepper to the taste
- 2 tablespoons olive oil
- A pinch of rosemary, dried
- 2 bay leaves
- A pinch of sage, dried
- A pinch of thyme, dried

Directions:
1. In your Crock Pot, mix turkey with onion, carrot, garlic, celery, stock, salt, pepper, oil, rosemary, sage, thyme and bay leaves, toss, cover and cook on Low for 8 hours.
2. Divide between plates and serve hot.

Nutrition Info:
- calories 223, fat 5, fiber 7, carbs 18, protein 14

Chicken Pepper Chili

Servings: 4 | Cooking Time: 7 Hrs

Ingredients:
- 16 oz. salsa
- 8 chicken thighs
- 1 yellow onion, chopped
- 16 oz. canned tomatoes, chopped
- 1 red bell pepper, chopped
- 2 tbsp chili powder

Directions:
1. Add salsa and all other ingredients to the Crock Pot.
2. Put the cooker's lid on and set the cooking time to 7 hours on Low settings.
3. Serve warm.

Nutrition Info:
- Per Serving: Calories 250, Total Fat 3g, Fiber 3g, Total Carbs 14g, Protein 8g

Chicken Sausages In Jam

Servings:4 | Cooking Time: 6 Hours

Ingredients:
- ½ cup of strawberry jam
- ½ cup of water
- 1-pound chicken breast, skinless, boneless, chopped
- 1 teaspoon white pepper

Directions:
1. Sprinkle the chicken meat with white pepper and put it in the Crock Pot.
2. Then mix jam with water and pour the liquid over the chicken.
3. Close the lid and cook it on Low for 6 hours.

Nutrition Info:
- Per Serving: 282 calories, 24.1g protein, 37.5g carbohydrates, 2.9g fat, 0.1g fiber, 73mg cholesterol, 59mg sodium, 427mg potassium.

Chicken And Olives

Servings: 2 | Cooking Time: 5 Hours

Ingredients:
- 1 pound chicken breasts, skinless, boneless and sliced
- 1 cup black olives, pitted and halved
- ½ cup chicken stock
- ½ cup tomato sauce
- 1 tablespoon lime juice
- 1 tablespoon lime zest, grated
- 1 teaspoon chili powder
- 2 spring onions, chopped
- 1 tablespoon chives, chopped

Directions:
1. In your Crock Pot, mix the chicken with the olives, stock and the other ingredients except the chives, toss, put the lid on and cook on High for 5 hours.
2. Divide the mix into bowls, sprinkle the chives on top and serve.

Nutrition Info:
- calories 200, fat 7, fiber 1, carbs 5, protein 12

Turkey Cranberry Stew

Servings: 4 | Cooking Time: 8 Hrs

Ingredients:
- 3 lbs. turkey breast, skinless and boneless
- 1 cup cranberries, chopped
- 2 sweet potatoes, chopped
- ½ cup raisins
- ½ cup walnuts, chopped
- 1 sweet onion, chopped
- 2 tbsp lemon juice
- 1 cup of sugar
- 1 tsp ginger, grated
- ½ tsp nutmeg, ground
- 1 tsp cinnamon powder
- ½ cup veggie stock
- 1 tsp poultry seasoning
- Salt and black pepper to the taste
- 3 tbsp olive oil

Directions:
1. Take oil in a nonstick pan and place it over medium-high heat.
2. Stir in walnuts, onion, raisins, cranberries, sugar, lemon juice, cinnamon, nutmeg, ginger, black pepper, and stock.
3. Cook this mixture to a simmer on medium heat.
4. Now place the turkey and sweet potatoes in the Crock Pot.
5. Top them with poultry seasoning and cranberries mixture.
6. Put the cooker's lid on and set the cooking time to 8 hours on Low settings.
7. Slice the slow-cooked turkey and serve with sweet pota-to-cranberry sauce.
8. Enjoy.

Nutrition Info:
- Per Serving: Calories 264, Total Fat 4g, Fiber 6g, Total Carbs 8g, Protein 15g

Stuffed Pasta

Servings:6 | Cooking Time: 4 Hours

Ingredients:
- 12 oz cannelloni
- 9 oz ground chicken
- 1 teaspoon Italian seasonings
- 2 oz Parmesan, grated
- ½ cup tomato juice
- ½ cup of water

Directions:
1. Mix the ground chicken with Italian seasonings and fill the cannelloni.
2. Put the stuffed cannelloni in the Crock Pot.
3. Add all remaining ingredients and close the lid.
4. Cook the meal on High for 4 hours.

Nutrition Info:
- Per Serving: 250 calories, 21.5g protein, 14g carbohydrates, 12.1g fat, 0.8g fiber, 62mg cholesterol, 373mg sodium, 150mg potassium.

Parsley Chicken Mix

Servings: 2 | Cooking Time: 5 Hours

Ingredients:
- 1 pound chicken breast, skinless, boneless and sliced
- ½ cup parsley, chopped
- 2 tablespoons olive oil
- 1 tablespoon pine nuts
- 1 tablespoon lemon juice
- ½ cup chicken stock
- ¼ cup black olives, pitted and halved
- 1 teaspoon hot paprika
- A pinch of salt and black pepper

Directions:
1. In a blender, mix the parsley with the oil, pine nuts and lemon juice and pulse well.
2. In your Crock Pot, mix the chicken with the parsley mix and the remaining ingredients, toss, put the lid on and cook on High for 5 hours.
3. Divide everything between plates and serve.

Nutrition Info:
- calories 263, fat 14, fiber 3, carbs 7, protein 16

Chicken Tomato Salad

Servings: 2 | Cooking Time: 3 Hours

Ingredients:
- 1 chicken breast, skinless and boneless
- 1 cup chicken stock
- 2 cups of water
- Salt and black pepper to the taste
- 1 tbsp mustard
- 3 garlic cloves, minced
- 1 tbsp balsamic vinegar
- 1 tbsp honey
- 3 tbsp olive oil
- Mixed salad greens
- Handful cherry tomatoes halved

Directions:
1. Mix water with a pinch of salt in a bowl and chicken.
2. Soak the chicken and refrigerate for 45 minutes.
3. Drain the chicken and transfer to a Crock Pot.
4. Along with stock, black pepper, and salt.
5. Put the cooker's lid on and set the cooking time to 3 hours on High settings.
6. Transfer the slow-cooked chicken to a cutting board then cut into strips.
7. Mix garlic, salt, black pepper, honey, mustard, olive oil, and vinegar in a bowl.
8. Toss in salad greens, tomatoes, and chicken strips.
9. Mix well and serve.

Nutrition Info:
- Per Serving: Calories: 200, Total Fat: 4g, Fiber: 6g, Total Carbs: 15g, Protein: 12g

Mediterranean Chicken

Servings: 4 | Cooking Time: 4 Hours

Ingredients:
- 1 and ½ pounds chicken breast, skinless and boneless
- Juice of 2 lemons
- 1 rosemary spring, chopped
- ¼ cup olive oil
- 3 garlic cloves, minced
- A pinch of salt and black pepper
- 1 cucumber, chopped
- 1 cup kalamata olives, pitted and sliced
- ¼ cup red onions, chopped
- 2 tablespoons red vinegar

Directions:
1. In your Crock Pot, mix chicken with lemon juice, rosemary, oil, garlic, salt and pepper, stir, cover and cook on High for 4 hours.
2. Transfer chicken to a cutting board, shred with 2 forks, transfer to a bowl, add cucumber, olives, onion and vinegar, toss, divide between plates and serve.

Nutrition Info:
- calories 240, fat 3, fiber 3, carbs 12, protein 3

Horseradish Chicken Wings

Servings:4 | Cooking Time: 6 Hours

Ingredients:
- 3 tablespoons horseradish, grated
- 1 teaspoon ketchup
- 1 tablespoon mayonnaise
- ½ cup of water
- 1-pound chicken wings

Directions:
1. Mix chicken wings with ketchup, horseradish, and mayonnaise,
2. Put them in the Crock Pot and add water.
3. Cook the meal on Low for 6 hours.

Nutrition Info:
- Per Serving: 236 calories, 33g protein, 2.5g carbohydrates, 9.7g fat, 0.4g fiber, 102mg cholesterol, 174mg sodium, 309mg potassium.

Turkey And Plums Mix

Servings: 2 | Cooking Time: 7 Hours

Ingredients:
- 1 pound turkey breast, skinless, boneless and sliced
- 1 cup plums, pitted and halved
- ½ cup chicken stock
- ½ teaspoon chili powder
- ½ teaspoon turmeric powder
- ½ teaspoon cumin, ground
- 1 tablespoon rosemary, chopped
- A pinch of salt and black pepper

Directions:
1. In your Crock Pot, mix the turkey with the plums, stock and the other ingredients, toss, put the lid on and cook on Low for 7 hours.
2. Divide the mix between plates and serve right away.

Nutrition Info:
- calories 253, fat 13, fiber 2, carbs 7, protein 16

Bourbon Honey Chicken

Servings: 6 | Cooking Time: 5 Hours

Ingredients:
- 4 oz. cup bourbon
- 3 tbsp soy sauce
- 1 tbsp honey
- 1 tsp ketchup
- 3 oz. yellow onion, chopped
- 1 tsp minced garlic
- 3 lb. chicken breast, skinless, boneless
- 7 oz. water
- 1 tsp salt

Directions:
1. Add water, garlic, salt, ketchup, honey, and soy sauce in a bowl then mix well.
2. Arrange the chicken breast in the Crock Pot and top it with honey mixture, bourbon, and onion.
3. Put the cooker's lid on and set the cooking time to 5 hours on High settings.
4. Mix well and serve.

Nutrition Info:
- Per Serving: Calories: 461, Total Fat: 24g, Fiber: 0g, Total Carbs: 6.37g, Protein: 48g

Sweet And Hot Chicken Wings

Servings: 6 | Cooking Time: 4 Hours

Ingredients:
- 12 chicken wings, cut into 24 pieces
- 1 pound celery, cut into thin matchsticks
- ¼ cup honey
- 4 tablespoons hot sauce
- Salt to the taste
- ¼ cup tomato puree
- 1 cup yogurt
- 1 tablespoon parsley, chopped

Directions:
1. In your Crock Pot, mix chicken with celery, honey, hot

sauce, salt, tomato puree and parsley, stir, cover and cook on High for 3 hours and 30 minutes.
2. Add yogurt, toss, cover, cook on High for 30 minutes more, divide between plates and serve

Nutrition Info:
- calories 300, fat 4, fiber 4, carbs 14, protein 22

Sichuan Chicken

Servings:4 | Cooking Time: 4 Hours

Ingredients:
- 1 chili pepper, chopped
- 1 oz fresh ginger, chopped
- 1 onion, chopped
- 1-pound chicken fillet, chopped
- 3 oz scallions, chopped
- 1 garlic clove, chopped
- 2 tablespoons mustard
- 1 cup of water

Directions:
1. Mix mustard with chicken and leave for 10 minutes to marinate.
2. Meanwhile, put all remaining ingredients in the Crock Pot.
3. Add marinated chicken and close the lid.
4. Cook the chicken on High for 4 hours.

Nutrition Info:
- Per Serving: 286 calories, 36.5g protein, 11.5g carbohydrates, 10.5g fat, 2.9g fiber, 101mg cholesterol, 107mg sodium, 514mg potassium.

Turkey And Scallions Mix

Servings: 2 | Cooking Time: 7 Hours

Ingredients:
- 1 pound turkey breasts, skinless, boneless and cubed
- 1 tablespoon avocado oil
- ½ cup tomato sauce
- ½ cup chicken stock
- ½ teaspoon sweet paprika
- 4 scallions, chopped
- 1 tablespoons lemon zest, grated
- 1 tablespoon lemon juice
- A pinch of salt and black pepper
- 1 tablespoon chives, chopped

Directions:
1. In your Crock Pot, mix the turkey with the oil, tomato sauce and the other ingredients, toss, put the lid on and cook on Low for 7 hours.
2. Divide everything between plates and serve.

Nutrition Info:
- calories 234, fat 12, fiber 3, carbs 5, protein 7

Chicken And Asparagus

Servings: 2 | Cooking Time: 5 Hours

Ingredients:
- 1 pound chicken breast, skinless, boneless and cubed
- 1 cup asparagus, sliced
- 1 tablespoon olive oil
- 2 scallions, chopped
- A pinch of salt and black pepper
- 1 teaspoon garam masala
- 1 cup chicken stock
- 1 cup tomatoes, cubed
- 1 tablespoon parsley, chopped

Directions:
1. In your Crock Pot, mix the chicken with the asparagus, oil and the other ingredients except the asparagus, toss, put the lid on and cook on High for 4 hours.
2. Add the asparagus, toss, cook on High for 1 more hour, divide everything between plates and serve.

Nutrition Info:
- calories 229, fat 9, fiber 4, carbs 7, protein 16

Okra Chicken Saute

Servings:6 | Cooking Time: 8 Hours

Ingredients:
- 1 cup bell pepper, chopped
- 1 cup tomatoes, chopped
- 2 cups okra, chopped
- 1-pound chicken fillet, chopped
- 1 teaspoon salt
- 1 teaspoon ground black pepper
- 2 cups of water

Directions:
1. Put all ingredients in the Crock Pot.
2. Close the lid and cook the saute on Low for 8 hours.

Nutrition Info:
- Per Serving: 170 calories, 23g protein, 5.4g carbohydrates, 5.8g fat, 1.8g fiber, 67mg cholesterol, 459mg sodium, 397mg potassium.

French-style Chicken

Servings:4 | Cooking Time: 7 Hours

Ingredients:
- 1 can onion soup
- 4 chicken drumsticks
- ½ cup celery stalk, chopped
- 1 teaspoon dried tarragon
- ¼ cup white wine

Directions:
1. Put ingredients in the Crock Pot and carefully mix them.
2. Then close the lid and cook the chicken on low for 7 hours.

Nutrition Info:
- Per Serving: 127 calories, 15.1g protein, 5.8g carbohydrates, 3.7g fat, 0.7g fiber, 40mg cholesterol, 688mg sodium, 185mg potassium.

Pineapple Chicken

Servings:4 | Cooking Time: 8 Hours

Ingredients:
- 12 oz chicken fillet
- 1 cup pineapple, canned, chopped
- ½ cup Cheddar cheese, shredded
- 1 tablespoon butter, softened
- 1 teaspoon ground black pepper
- ¼ cup of water

Directions:
1. Grease the Crock Pot bowl bottom with softened butter.
2. Then cut the chicken fillet into servings and put in the Crock Pot in one layer.
3. After this, top the chicken with ground black pepper, water, pineapple, and Cheddar cheese.
4. Close the lid and cook the meal on Low for 8 hours.

Nutrition Info:
- Per Serving: 266 calories, 28.4g protein, 5.9g carbohydrates, 13.9g fat, 0.7g fiber, 98mg cholesterol, 183mg sodium, 273mg potassium.

Lemon Parsley Chicken

Servings:4 | Cooking Time: 8 Hours

Ingredients:
- 2 tablespoons butter, melted
- 1-pound chicken breasts, bones removed
- Salt and pepper to taste
- 1 lemon, sliced thinly
- ½ cup parsley, chopped

Directions:
1. Line the bottom of the crockpot with foil.
2. Grease the foil with melted butter.
3. Season the chicken breasts with salt and pepper to taste.
4. Arrange on the foil and place lemon slices on top.
5. Sprinkle with chopped parsley.
6. Cook on low for 8 hours or on high for 6 hours

Nutrition Info:
- Calories per serving: 303; Carbohydrates: 3.1g; Protein: 34.5g; Fat: 14g; Sugar: 0.7g; Sodium: 430mg; Fiber: 1g

Rosemary Chicken Thighs

Servings: 2 | Cooking Time: 7 Hours

Ingredients:
- 1 pound chicken thighs, boneless
- 1 teaspoon rosemary, dried
- ½ teaspoon sweet paprika
- ½ teaspoon garam masala
- 1 tablespoon olive oil
- ½ cup chicken stock
- A pinch of salt and black pepper
- 1 tablespoon cilantro, chopped

Directions:
1. In your Crock Pot, mix the chicken with the rosemary, paprika and the other ingredients, toss, put the lid on and cook on Low for 7 hours/
2. Divide the chicken between plates and serve with a side salad.

Nutrition Info:
- calories 220, fat 8, fiber 2, carbs 5, protein 11

Chicken And Cabbage Bowl

Servings:4 | Cooking Time: 7 Hours

Ingredients:
- 1-pound chicken fillet, sliced
- 1 cup white cabbage, shredded
- 1 tablespoon tomato paste
- 1 teaspoon dried rosemary
- 1 teaspoon salt
- 1 teaspoon dried dill
- 2 cups of water

Directions:
1. Mix water with tomato paste and whisk until smooth.
2. Pour the liquid in the Crock Pot.
3. Add cabbage, chicken fillet, and all remaining ingredients.
4. Close the lid and cook the meal on Low for 7 hours.
5. When the meal is cooked, transfer it in the serving bowls.

Nutrition Info:
- Per Serving: 225 calories, 33.3g protein, 2.1g carbohydrates, 8.5g fat, 0.8g fiber, 101mg cholesterol, 690mg sodium, 358mg potassium.

Beef, Pork & Lamb Recipes

Beef, Pork & Lamb Recipes

Sausage Soup

Servings: 6 | Cooking Time: 6 Hours

Ingredients:
- 1 tablespoon avocado oil
- 32 ounces pork sausage meat, ground
- 10 ounces canned tomatoes and jalapenos, chopped
- 10 ounces spinach
- 1 green bell pepper, chopped
- 4 cups beef stock
- 1 teaspoon onion powder
- Salt and black pepper to the taste
- 1 tablespoon cumin
- 1 tablespoon chili powder
- 1 teaspoon garlic powder
- 1 teaspoon Italian seasoning

Directions:
1. Heat up a pan with the oil over medium heat, add sausage, stir, brown for a couple of minutes on all sides and transfer to your Crock Pot.
2. Add green bell pepper, canned tomatoes and jalapenos, stock, onion powder, salt, pepper, cumin, chili powder, garlic powder, Italian seasoning and stock, stir, cover and cook on Low for 5 hours and 30 minutes.
3. Add spinach, cover, cook on Low for 30 minutes more, stir soup, ladle it into bowls and serve.

Nutrition Info:
- calories 524, fat 43, fiber 2, carbs 15, protein 26

Beef Brisket In Orange Juice

Servings:4 | Cooking Time: 5 Hours

Ingredients:
- 1 cup of orange juice
- 2 cups of water
- 2 tablespoons butter
- 12 oz beef brisket
- ½ teaspoon salt

Directions:
1. Toss butter in the skillet and melt.
2. Put the beef brisket in the melted butter and roast on high heat for 3 minutes per side.
3. Then sprinkle the meat with salt and transfer in the Crock Pot.
4. Add orange juice and water.
5. Close the lid and cook the meat on High for 5 hours.

Nutrition Info:
- Per Serving: 237 calories, 26.3g protein, 6.5g carbohydrates, 11.2g fat, 0.1g fiber, 91mg cholesterol, 392mg sodium, 470mg potassium.

Poached Pork Roast

Servings:4 | Cooking Time: 7 Hours

Ingredients:
- 2 cups onion, diced
- 1-pound pork loin
- 1 tablespoon sunflower oil
- 1 teaspoon salt
- 1 teaspoon ground black pepper
- 2 cups of water
- 1 tablespoon flour

Directions:
1. Sprinkle the pork loin with flour.
2. Then heat the sunflower oil in the skillet well.
3. Add pork loin and roast it for 3 minutes per side on high heat.
4. Transfer the meat in the Crock Pot.
5. Add all remaining ingredients and close the lid.
6. Cook the pork roast on low for 7 hours.

Nutrition Info:
- Per Serving: 337 calories, 31.9g protein, 7.2g carbohydrates, 19.4g fat, 1.4g fiber, 91mg cholesterol, 658mg sodium, 574mg potassium

Veal And Tomatoes

Servings: 4 | Cooking Time: 7 Hours

Ingredients:
- 4 medium veal leg steaks
- 1 teaspoon avocado oil
- 2 garlic cloves, minced
- 1 red onion, chopped
- Salt and black pepper to the taste
- 2 teaspoons sage, chopped
- 15 ounces canned tomatoes, chopped
- 2 tablespoons parsley, chopped
- 1 ounce bocconcini, sliced

Directions:
1. Heat up a pan with the oil over medium-high heat, add veal, brown for 2 minutes on each side and transfer to your Crock Pot.
2. Add onion, sage, garlic, tomatoes, parsley, bocconcini, salt and pepper, cover and cook on Low for 7 hours.
3. Divide between plates and serve.

Nutrition Info:
- calories 276, fat 6, fiber 4, carbs 15, protein 36

Lamb And Cabbage

Servings: 2 | Cooking Time: 5 Hours

Ingredients:
- 2 pounds lamb stew meat, cubed
- 1 cup red cabbage, shredded
- 1 cup beef stock
- 1 teaspoon avocado oil
- 1 teaspoon sweet paprika
- 2 tablespoons tomato paste
- A pinch of salt and black pepper
- 1 tablespoon cilantro, chopped

Directions:
1. In your Crock Pot, mix the lamb with the cabbage, stock and the other ingredients, toss, put the lid on and cook on High for 5 hours.
2. Divide everything between plates and serve.

Nutrition Info:
- calories 254, fat 12, fiber 3, carbs 6, protein 16

Ginger And Rosemary Pork Ribs

Servings:4 | Cooking Time: 12 Hours

Ingredients:
- 1/3 cup chicken broth
- 4 racks pork spare ribs
- 3 tablespoons ginger paste or powder
- 1 teaspoon rosemary, dried
- Salt and pepper to taste

Directions:
1. Pour the broth into the crockpot.
2. Season the spare ribs with ginger paste, rosemary, salt and pepper.
3. Place in the crockpot.
4. Close the lid and cook on low for 12 hours or on high for 8 hours.

Nutrition Info:
- Calories per serving: 396; Carbohydrates: 03g; Protein: 27.1g; Fat: 21g; Sugar: 0g; Sodium: 582mg; Fiber: 0g

Wine-braised Beef Heart

Servings:4 | Cooking Time: 5 Hours

Ingredients:
- 10 oz beef heart
- 1/3 cup red wine
- ½ cup beef broth
- ½ cup potatoes, chopped
- 3 oz fennel bulb, chopped
- 1 teaspoon salt
- 1 teaspoon peppercorns
- 1 teaspoon brown sugar
- Cooking spray

Directions:
1. Spray the skillet with cooking spray.
2. Then chop the beef heart roughly and put it in the skillet.
3. Roast the beef heart on high heat for 6 minutes (for 3 minutes per side).
4. Transfer the beef heart in the Crock Pot.

5. Add all remaining ingredients and close the lid.
6. Cook the meal on High for 5 hours.

Nutrition Info:
- Per Serving: 162 calories, 21.4g protein, 6.3g carbohydrates, 3.6g fat, 1.3g fiber, 150mg cholesterol, 732mg sodium, 373mg potassium.

Onion And Bison Soup

Servings:8 | Cooking Time: 10 Hours

Ingredients:
- 6 onions, julienned
- 2 pounds bison meat, cubed
- 3 cups beef stock
- ½ cup sherry
- 3 sprigs of thyme
- 1 bay leaf
- 2 tablespoons olive oil
- Salt and pepper to taste

Directions:
1. Place all ingredients in the CrockPot.
2. Give a good stir.
3. Close the lid and cook on high for 8 hours or on low for 10 hours.

Nutrition Info:
- Calories per serving: 341; Carbohydrates: 9.5g; Protein: 24.5g; Fat: 21.8g; Sugar: 1.7g; Sodium: 809mg; Fiber: 4.8g

Beef And Zucchinis Mix

Servings: 2 | Cooking Time: 8 Hours

Ingredients:
- 1 pound beef stew meat, cut into strips
- 1 tablespoon olive oil
- ¼ cup beef stock
- ½ teaspoon sweet paprika
- ½ teaspoon chili powder
- 2 small zucchinis, cubed
- 1 tablespoon balsamic vinegar
- 1 tablespoon chives, chopped

Directions:
1. In your Crock Pot, mix the beef with the oil, stock and the other ingredients, toss, put the lid on and cook on Low for 8 hours.
2. Divide the mix between plates and serve.

Nutrition Info:
- calories 400, fat 12, fiber 8, carbs 18, protein 20

Fennel Seeds Pork Chops

Servings:4 | Cooking Time: 6 Hours

Ingredients:
- 4 pork chops
- 1 tablespoon fennel seeds
- 3 tablespoons avocado oil
- 1 teaspoon garlic, diced
- ½ cup of water

Directions:
1. Mix fennel seeds with avocado oil and garlic. Mash the

mixture.

2. Then rub the pork chops with fennel seeds mixture and transfer in the Crock Pot.
3. Add water and close the lid.
4. Cook the meat on low for 6 hours.

Nutrition Info:
- Per Serving: 276 calories, 18.4g protein, 1.6g carbohydrates, 21.4g fat, 1.1g fiber, 69mg cholesterol, 59mg sodium, 336mg potassium

Beef Meatballs Casserole

Servings: 8 | Cooking Time: 7 Hours

Ingredients:
- 1/3 cup flour
- 2 eggs
- 1 pound beef sausage, chopped
- 1 pound beef, ground
- Salt and black pepper to taste
- 1 tablespoons parsley, dried
- ¼ teaspoon red pepper flakes
- ¼ cup parmesan, grated
- ¼ teaspoon onion powder
- ½ teaspoon garlic powder
- ¼ teaspoon oregano, dried
- 1 cup ricotta cheese
- 2 cups marinara sauce
- 1 and ½ cups mozzarella cheese, shredded

Directions:
1. In a bowl, mix sausage with beef, salt, pepper, almond flour, parsley, pepper flakes, onion powder, garlic powder, oregano, parmesan and eggs, stir well and shape meatballs out of this mix.
2. Arrange meatballs in your Crock Pot, add half of the marinara sauce, ricotta cheese and top with the rest of the marinara.
3. Add mozzarella at the end, cover and cook on Low for 7 hours.
4. Divide between plates and serve.

Nutrition Info:
- calories 456, fat 35, fiber 3, carbs 12, protein 32

Seasoned Poached Pork Belly

Servings:4 | Cooking Time: 4 Hours

Ingredients:
- 10 oz pork belly
- 1 teaspoon minced garlic
- 1 teaspoon ginger paste
- ¼ cup apple cider vinegar
- 1 cup of water

Directions:
1. Rub the pork belly with minced garlic and garlic paste.
2. Then sprinkle it with apple cider vinegar and transfer in the Crock Pot.
3. Add water and close the lid.
4. Cook the pork belly on High for 4 hours.
5. Then slice the cooked pork belly and sprinkle with hot gravy from the Crock Pot.

Nutrition Info:

- Per Serving: 333 calories, 32.8g protein, 0.7g carbohydrates, 19.1g fat, 0.1g fiber, 82mg cholesterol, 1148mg sodium, 20mg potassium

Pork Loin And Cauliflower Rice

Servings: 6 | Cooking Time: 8 Hours

Ingredients:
- 3 bacon slices, cooked and chopped
- 3 carrots, chopped
- 2 pounds pork loin roast
- 1 rhubarb stalk, chopped
- 2 bay leaves
- ¼ cup red wine vinegar
- 4 garlic cloves, minced
- Salt and black pepper to the taste
- ¼ cup olive oil
- 1 tablespoon garlic powder
- 1 tablespoon Italian seasoning
- 24 ounces cauliflower rice
- 1 teaspoon turmeric powder
- 1 cup beef stock

Directions:
1. In your Crock Pot, mix bacon with carrots, pork, rhubarb, bay leaves, vinegar, salt, pepper, oil, garlic powder, Italian seasoning, stock and turmeric, toss, cover and cook on Low for 7 hours.
2. Add cauliflower rice, cover, cook on Low for 1 more hour, divide between plates and serve.

Nutrition Info:
- calories 310, fat 6, fiber 3, carbs 14, protein 10

Beef With Green Peas Sauce

Servings:4 | Cooking Time: 5 Hours

Ingredients:
- 1-pound beef loin, chopped
- 1 cup green peas, frozen
- 1 bay leaf
- 1 tablespoon butter
- 1 teaspoon flour
- 1 teaspoon chili powder
- ½ cup tomato juice
- 2 cup of water

Directions:
1. Put all ingredients in the Crock Pot and close the lid.
2. Cook the beef on High for 5 hours.
3. Then transfer it in the serving bowls and top with the remaining sauce from the Crock Pot.

Nutrition Info:
- Per Serving: 234 calories, 23.3g protein, 8.9g carbohydrates, 11.3g fat, 2.3g fiber, 68mg cholesterol, 614mg sodium, 175mg potassium

Schweinshaxe

Servings:4 | Cooking Time: 10 Hours

Ingredients:
- 1 tablespoon juniper berries
- ½ cup beer
- 1-pound pork knuckle
- ½ teaspoon sugar
- 1 lemon, halved
- 2 cups of water
- 1 tablespoon sunflower oil

Directions:
1. Put all ingredients in the Crock Pot and close the lid.
2. Cook the meal on Low for 10 hours.

Nutrition Info:
- Per Serving: 311 calories, 29.1g protein, 2.9g carbohydrates, 18.9g fat, 0.4g fiber, 102mg cholesterol, 90mg sodium, 422mg potassium

Lamb With Mint

Servings:4 | Cooking Time: 10 Hours

Ingredients:
- 2 tablespoons ghee
- 1 lamb leg, bone in
- 4 cloves of garlic, minced
- ¼ cup fresh mint, chopped
- ½ teaspoon salt
- A dash of ground black pepper

Directions:
1. Heat oil in skillet over medium flame.
2. Sear the lamb leg for at least 3 minutes on each side.
3. Place in the CrockPot and add the rest of the ingredients.
4. Close the lid and cook on high for 8 hours or on low for 8 hours.

Nutrition Info:
- Calories per serving: 525; Carbohydrates: 6.5g; Protein: 37.4g; Fat: 18.3g; Sugar:0g; Sodium: 748mg; Fiber: 2.4g

Meatballs With Melted Core

Servings:4 | Cooking Time: 4 Hours

Ingredients:
- 4 oz Cheddar cheese, shredded
- 1 tablespoon cream cheese
- 1 cup ground pork
- 1 tablespoon cornflour
- ½ teaspoon smoked paprika
- ½ teaspoon onion powder
- 1 tablespoon olive oil
- ½ cup chicken stock

Directions:
1. Mix ground pork with cornflour, smoked paprika, and onion powder.
2. Then make the ground pork meatballs.
3. After this, make the small balls from the shredded cheese.
4. Fill the pork meatballs with cheese balls and put in the Crock Pot.
5. Sprinkle them with olive oil.
6. Add chicken stock and cream cheese.
7. Close the lid and cook the meatballs on High for 4 hours.

Nutrition Info:
- Per Serving: 395 calories, 27.6g protein, 2.3g carbohydrates, 30.2g fat, 0.3g fiber, 106mg cholesterol, 336mg sodium, 331mg potassium

Burgers

Servings:4 | Cooking Time: 4 Hours

Ingredients:
- 10 oz ground beef
- 1 tablespoon minced onion
- 1 teaspoon dried dill
- 2 tablespoons water
- 1 teaspoon ground black pepper
- 1/3 cup chicken stock

Directions:
1. Mix the minced beef with onion, dill, water, and ground black pepper.
2. Make 4 burgers and arrange them in the Crock Pot bowl.
3. Add chicken stock and close the lid.
4. Cook the burgers on high for 4 hours.

Nutrition Info:
- Per Serving: 135 calories, 21.7g protein, 0.8g carbohydrates, 4.5g fat, 0.2g fiber, 63mg cholesterol, 111mg sodium, 305mg potassium.

Beef Barbecue Cubes

Servings:2 | Cooking Time: 5 Hours

Ingredients:
- 9 oz beef sirloin, chopped
- ½ cup BBQ sauce
- 1 teaspoon dried rosemary
- ¼ cup of water
- 1 tablespoon avocado oil

Directions:
1. In the big bowl mix avocado oil, water, dried rosemary, and BBQ sauce.
2. Add chopped beef sirloin and carefully mix the mixture.
3. Leave it for 20 minutes to marinate.
4. After this, transfer meat and all remaining liquid in the Crock Pot.
5. Cook it on High for 5 hours.

Nutrition Info:
- Per Serving: 342 calories, 38.8g protein, 23.4g carbohydrates, 9.1g fat, 1g fiber, 114mg cholesterol, 785mg sodium, 672mg potassium.

Roast With Pepperoncini

Servings: 4 | Cooking Time: 8 Hrs.

Ingredients:
- 5 lbs. beef chuck roast
- 1 tbsp soy sauce
- 10 pepperoncini's
- 1 cup beef stock
- 2 tbsp butter, melted

Directions:
1. Add beef roast and all other ingredients to the insert of Crock Pot.
2. Put the cooker's lid on and set the cooking time to 8 hours on Low settings.
3. Shred the cooked meat with the help of 2 forks and return to the cooker.
4. Mix gently and serve warm.

Nutrition Info:
- Per Serving: Calories: 362, Total Fat: 4g, Fiber: 8g, Total Carbs: 17g, Protein: 17g

Sweet Lamb Tagine

Servings:6 | Cooking Time: 10 Hours

Ingredients:
- 12 oz lamb fillet, chopped
- 1 cup apricots, pitted, chopped
- 1 cup red wine
- 1 jalapeno pepper, sliced
- 1 teaspoon ground nutmeg
- 1 cup of water
- 1 teaspoon ground ginger

Directions:
1. Mix lamb with ground nutmeg and ground ginger.
2. Transfer the lamb meat in the Crock Pot.
3. Add water, jalapeno pepper, red wine, and apricots.
4. Close the lid and cook the tagine for 10 hours on Low.

Nutrition Info:
- Per Serving: 154 calories, 16.4g protein, 4.4g carbohydrates, 4.5g fat, 0.7g fiber, 51mg cholesterol, 47mg sodium, 307mg potassium.

Brisket Turnips Medley

Servings: 6 | Cooking Time: 8 Hrs.

Ingredients:
- 2 and ½ lbs. beef brisket
- 4 cups veggie stock
- 2 bay leaves
- 3 garlic cloves, chopped
- 4 carrots, chopped
- 1 cabbage head cut into 6 wedges
- Salt and black pepper to the taste
- 3 turnips, cut into quarters

Directions:
1. Add beef, bay leaves, stock, carrots, garlic, salt, cabbage, black pepper, and turnips to the insert of the Crock Pot.
2. Put the cooker's lid on and set the cooking time to 8 hours on Low settings.
3. Serve warm.

Nutrition Info:
- Per Serving: Calories: 321, Total Fat: 15g, Fiber: 4g, Total Carbs: 18g, Protein: 19g

Beef And Pancetta

Servings: 4 | Cooking Time: 4 Hours And 10 Minutes

Ingredients:
- 8 ounces pancetta, chopped
- 4 pounds beef, cubed
- 4 garlic cloves, minced
- 2 brown onions, chopped
- 2 tablespoons olive oil
- 4 tablespoons red vinegar
- 4 cups beef stock
- 2 tablespoons tomato paste
- 2 cinnamon sticks
- 3 lemon peel strips
- A handful parsley, chopped
- 4 thyme springs
- 2 tablespoons butter
- Salt and black pepper to the taste

Directions:
1. Heat up a pan with the oil over medium-high heat, add pancetta, onion and garlic, stir, cook for 5 minutes, add beef, stir and brown for a few minutes
2. Add vinegar, salt, pepper, stock, tomato paste, cinnamon, lemon peel, thyme and butter, stir, cook for 3 minutes more, transfer everything to your Crock Pot, cook on High for 4 hours, discard cinnamon, lemon peel and thyme, add parsley, stir, divide between plates and serve.

Nutrition Info:
- calories 250, fat 6, fiber 1, carbs 17, protein 33

Cinnamon Lamb

Servings: 2 | Cooking Time: 6 Hours

Ingredients:
- 1 pound lamb chops
- 1 teaspoon cinnamon powder
- 1 red onion, chopped
- 1 tablespoon avocado oil
- 1 tablespoon oregano, chopped
- ½ cup beef stock
- 1 tablespoon chives, chopped

Directions:
1. In your Crock Pot, mix the lamb chops with the cinnamon and the other ingredients, toss, put the lid on and cook on Low for 6 hours.
2. Divide the chops between plates and serve with a side salad.

Nutrition Info:
- calories 253, fat 14, fiber 2, carbs 6, protein 18

Tarragon Pork Chops

Servings: 2 | Cooking Time: 6 Hours

Ingredients:
- ½ pound pork chops
- ¼ tablespoons olive oil
- 2 garlic clove, minced
- ¼ teaspoon chili powder
- ½ cup beef stock
- ½ teaspoon coriander, ground

- Salt and black pepper to the taste
- ¼ teaspoon mustard powder
- 1 tablespoon tarragon, chopped

Directions:
1. Grease your Crock Pot with the oil and mix the pork chops with the garlic, stock and the other ingredients inside.
2. Toss, put the lid on, cook on Low for 6 hours, divide between plates and serve with a side salad.

Nutrition Info:
- calories 453, fat 16, fiber 8, carbs 7, protein 27

Ginger Ground Pork

Servings:3 | Cooking Time: 6 Hours

Ingredients:
- 1.5 cup ground pork
- 1 oz minced ginger
- 2 tablespoons coconut oil
- 1 tablespoon tomato paste
- ½ teaspoon chili powder

Directions:
1. Mix ground pork with minced ginger, tomato paste, and chili powder.
2. Put the ground pork in the Crock Pot.
3. Add coconut oil and close the lid.
4. Cook the meal on Low for 6 hours.

Nutrition Info:
- Per Serving: 193 calories, 7.8g protein, 7.9g carbohydrates, 15.1g fat, 1.6g fiber, 25mg cholesterol, 39mg sodium, 189mg potassium

Enchilada Pork Luncheon

Servings: 8 | Cooking Time: 4 Hrs

Ingredients:
- 1 lb. chorizo, ground
- 1 lb. pork, ground
- 3 tbsp olive oil
- 1 tomato, chopped
- 1 avocado, pitted, peeled and chopped
- Salt and black pepper to the taste
- 1 small red onion, chopped
- 2 tbsp enchilada sauce

Directions:
1. Take oil in a non-stick skillet and place it over medium-high heat,
2. Stir in pork and sauté until brown.
3. Transfer the pork along with all other ingredients to the Crock Pot.
4. Put the cooker's lid on and set the cooking time to 4 hours on Low settings.
5. Serve warm.

Nutrition Info:
- Per Serving: Calories 300, Total Fat 12g, Fiber 3g, Total Carbs 15g, Protein 17g

Spaghetti Meatballs

Servings:4 | Cooking Time: 3 Hours

Ingredients:
- 2 cups ground pork
- 1 teaspoon ground black pepper
- ½ teaspoon salt
- 1 teaspoon dried cilantro
- ½ cup tomato juice
- 1 teaspoon butter
- ¼ cup of water

Directions:
1. In the mixing bowl mix ground pork with ground black pepper.
2. Then add salt and dried cilantro.
3. Make the small balls from the mixture and press them gently.
4. Put butter in the Crock Pot.
5. Add water and meatballs.
6. Close the lid and cook the meatballs on high for 3 hours.

Nutrition Info:
- Per Serving: 141 calories, 11.2g protein, 1.6g carbohydrates, 9.8g fat, 0.3g fiber, 42mg cholesterol, 411mg sodium, 231mg potassium

Winter Pork With Green Peas

Servings:4 | Cooking Time: 7 Hours

Ingredients:
- 1-pound pork shoulder, boneless, chopped
- 1 cup green peas
- 3 cups of water
- 1 cup carrot, chopped
- 1 teaspoon chili powder
- 1 teaspoon dried thyme

Directions:
1. Sprinkle the pork shoulder with chili powder and dried thyme. Transfer the meat in the Crock Pot.
2. Add carrot, water, and green peas.
3. Close the lid and cook the meal on low for 7 hours.

Nutrition Info:
- Per Serving: 374 calories, 28.7g protein, 8.5g carbohydrates, 24.5g fat, 2.8g fiber, 102mg cholesterol, 110mg sodium, 566mg potassium

Jamaican Pork Mix

Servings:4 | Cooking Time: 4 Hours

Ingredients:
- 1 cup corn kernels, frozen
- 1 cup of water
- 1 teaspoon Jamaican spices
- 10 oz pork sirloin, chopped
- 1 tomato, chopped
- 1 teaspoon salt
- 1 teaspoon avocado oil

Directions:
1. Roast the chopped pork sirloin in the avocado oil for 1 minute per side.

2. Then mix the meat with Jamaican spices and transfer in the Crock Pot.
3. Add all remaining ingredients and close the lid.
4. Cook the meal on High for 4 hours.

Nutrition Info:
• Per Serving: 174 calories, 23.5g protein, 7.9g carbohydrates, 5.4g fat, 1.3g fiber, 65mg cholesterol, 629mg sodium, 412mg potassium

Pork Meatloaf

Servings:4 | Cooking Time: 4 Hours

Ingredients:
• 8 oz pork mince
• ¼ cup onion, diced
• 1 teaspoon ground black pepper
• 1 teaspoon chili powder
• 1 egg, beaten
• 1 teaspoon olive oil
• ½ teaspoon salt
• 1 teaspoon tomato paste
• Cooking spray

Directions:
1. Spray the bottom of the Crock Pot with cooking spray.
2. After this, mix the pork mince, onion, ground black pepper, chili powder, egg, olive oil, and salt.
3. Transfer the mixture in the Crock Pot and flatten it.
4. Then brush the surface of the meatloaf with tomato paste and cook it on High for 4 hours.

Nutrition Info:
• Per Serving: 188 calories, 1.7g protein, 36.9g carbohydrates, 4.7g fat, 1.1g fiber, 41mg cholesterol, 314mg sodium, 58mg potassium

One Pot Pork Chops

Servings:6 | Cooking Time: 10 Hours

Ingredients:
• 6 pork chops
• 2 cups broccoli florets
• ½ cup green and red bell peppers
• 1 onion, sliced
• Salt and pepper to taste

Directions:
1. Place all ingredients in the crockpot.
2. Give a stir to mix everything.
3. Close the lid and cook on low for 10 hours or on high for 8 hours.

Nutrition Info:
• Calories per serving: 496; Carbohydrates: 6g; Protein: 37.1g; Fat: 23.7g; Sugar: 0.8g; Sodium: 563mg; Fiber: 4.3g

Crockpot Cheeseburgers Casserole

Servings:4 | Cooking Time: 8 Hours

Ingredients:
• 1 white onion, chopped
• 1 ½ pounds lean ground beef
• 2 tablespoons mustard
• 1 teaspoon dried basil leaves
• 2 cups cheddar cheese

Directions:
1. Heat skillet over medium flame and sauté both white onions and ground beef for 3 minutes. Continue stirring until lightly brown.
2. Transfer to the crockpot and stir in mustard and basil leaves. Season with salt and pepper.
3. Add cheese on top.
4. Close the lid and cook on low for 8 hours and on high for 6 hours.

Nutrition Info:
• Calories per serving: 472; Carbohydrates: 3g; Protein: 32.7g; Fat: 26.2g; Sugar: 0g; Sodium: 429mg; Fiber: 2.4g

Lamb Casserole

Servings: 2 | Cooking Time: 7 Hours

Ingredients:
• 2 garlic cloves, minced
• 1 red onion, chopped
• 1 tablespoon olive oil
• 1 celery stick, chopped
• 10 ounces lamb fillet, cut into medium pieces
• Salt and black pepper to the taste
• 1 and ¼ cups lamb stock
• 2 carrots, chopped
• ½ tablespoon rosemary, chopped
• 1 leek, chopped
• 1 tablespoon mint sauce
• 1 teaspoon sugar
• 1 tablespoon tomato puree
• ½ cauliflower, florets separated
• ½ celeriac, chopped
• 2 tablespoons butter

Directions:
1. Heat up a Crock Pot with the oil over medium heat, add garlic, onion and celery, stir and cook for 5 minutes.
2. Add lamb pieces, stir, brown for 3 minutes and transfer everything to your Crock Pot.
3. Add carrot, leek, rosemary, stock, tomato puree, mint sauce, sugar, cauliflower, celeriac, butter, salt and black pepper, cover and cook on Low for 7 hours.
4. Divide lamb and all the veggies between plates and serve.

Nutrition Info:
• calories 324, fat 4, fiber 5, carbs 12, protein 20

Beef Curry

Servings:3 | Cooking Time: 8 Hours

Ingredients:
• 7 oz beef tenderloin, chopped
• 1 teaspoon curry powder
• 1 cup of coconut milk
• ¼ cup of water
• ½ cup potatoes, chopped
• 1 onion, sliced

Directions:
1. Mix coconut milk with curry powder and pour the liquid in the Crock Pot.
2. Add beef, potatoes, and sliced onion.

3. Then add water and close the lid.
4. Cook the meal on low for 8 hours.

Nutrition Info:
- Per Serving: 354 calories, 21.9g protein, 12.2g carbohydrates, 25.3g fat, 3.4g fiber, 61mg cholesterol, 55mg sodium, 612mg potassium.

Soy Pork Ribs

Servings: 4 | Cooking Time: 6 Hours

Ingredients:
- 4 cups vinegar
- 4 pounds pork ribs
- 2 tablespoons apple cider vinegar
- 2 cups water
- 3 tablespoons soy sauce
- Salt and black pepper to the taste
- A pinch of garlic powder
- A pinch of Chinese 5 spice

Directions:
1. Put your ribs in a big bowl, add white vinegar and water, toss, cover and keep in the fridge for 12 hours.
2. Drain ribs, season with salt and black pepper to the taste, garlic powder and Chinese 5 spice, rub well, transfer them to your Crock Pot and add apple cider vinegar and soy sauce as well.
3. Toss to coat well, cover Crock Pot and cook on High for 6 hours.
4. Divide ribs between plates and serve.

Nutrition Info:
- calories 300, fat 6, fiber 3, carbs 15, protein 15

Crockpot Asian Pot Roast

Servings:6 | Cooking Time: 10 Hours

Ingredients:
- 2 pounds beef chuck roast, excess fat trimmed
- 1 ½ teaspoon salt
- 3.4 teaspoon ground black pepper
- 2 tablespoons basil, chopped
- 2 large yellow onions, chopped
- 4 cloves of garlic, minced
- 2 star anise pods
- 2 cups beef stock
- 3 tablespoons sesame seed oil

Directions:
1. Place all ingredients except for the sesame oil in the Crock-Pot.
2. Close the lid and cook on high for 8 hours or on low for 10 hours.
3. Once cooked, drizzle with sesame seed oil or sesame seeds. You can also garnish it with chopped scallions if desired.

Nutrition Info:
- Calories per serving: 334; Carbohydrates: 2.3g; Protein: 32.3g; Fat: 20.1g; Sugar: 0g; Sodium: 768mg; Fiber: 0.7g

Fajita Beef

Servings:4 | Cooking Time: 4.5 Hours

Ingredients:
- 1 sweet pepper, cut into strips
- 1 red onion, sliced
- 1-pound beef sirloin, cut into strips
- 1 teaspoon fajita seasonings
- ½ cup of water
- 1 tablespoon butter

Directions:
1. Put the beef strips in the Crock Pot.
2. Add fajita seasonings, butter, and water.
3. Close the lid and cook the beef on high for 5 hours.
4. Add onion and sweet pepper.
5. Carefully mix the beef mixture and cook for 1 hour on High.

Nutrition Info:
- Per Serving: 259 calories, 35g protein, 5.4g carbohydrates, 10.1g fat, 1g fiber, 109mg cholesterol, 142mg sodium, 554mg potassium.

Chili Beef Ribs

Servings:4 | Cooking Time: 5 Hours

Ingredients:
- 10 oz beef ribs, chopped
- 1 teaspoon hot sauce
- 1 teaspoon chili powder
- 1 tablespoon sesame oil
- ½ cup of water

Directions:
1. Mix the beef ribs with chili powder.
2. Then heat the sesame oil in the skillet until hot.
3. Add beef ribs and roast them for 2-3 minutes per side or until they are light brown.
4. After this, transfer the beef ribs in the Crock Pot.
5. Add water and hot sauce.
6. Close the lid and cook them on High for 5 hours.

Nutrition Info:
- Per Serving: 164 calories, 21.6g protein, 0.4g carbohydrates, 7.9g fat, 0.2g fiber, 63mg cholesterol, 86mg sodium, 300mg potassium.

Beef And Scallions Bowl

Servings:4 | Cooking Time: 5 Hours

Ingredients:
- 1 teaspoon chili powder
- 2 oz scallions, chopped
- 1-pound beef stew meat, cubed
- 1 cup corn kernels, frozen
- 1 cup of water
- 2 tablespoons tomato paste
- 1 teaspoon minced garlic

Directions:
1. Mix water with tomato paste and pour the liquid in the Crock Pot.
2. Add chili powder, beef, corn kernels, and minced garlic.

3. Close the lid and cook the meal on high for 5 hours.
4. When the meal is cooked, transfer the mixture in the bowls and top with scallions.

Nutrition Info:
• Per Serving: 258 calories, 36.4g protein, 10.4g carbohydrates, 7.7g fat, 2g fiber, 101mg cholesterol, 99mg sodium, 697mg potassium.

Beef French Dip

Servings:4 | Cooking Time: 8 Hours

Ingredients:
• 1-pound beef chuck roast
• 1 cup onion, sliced
• ½ cup French onion soup
• 1 teaspoon garlic powder
• ½ cup of water
• 1 tablespoon coconut oil
• 2 oz provolone cheese, shredded

Directions:
1. Dice the meat and put it in the Crock Pot.
2. Add all remaining ingredients and carefully mix.
3. Close the lid and cook the dip on Low for 8 hours.

Nutrition Info:
• Per Serving: 520 calories, 32.4g protein, 6g carbohydrates, 39g fat, 0.9g fiber, 127mg cholesterol, 386mg sodium, 371mg potassium.

Balsamic Lamb Chops

Servings: 2 | Cooking Time: 6 Hours

Ingredients:
• 1 pound lamb chops
• 2 tablespoons balsamic vinegar
• 1 tablespoon chives, chopped
• 1 tablespoon olive oil
• 4 garlic cloves, minced
• ½ cup beef stock
• A pinch of salt and black pepper

Directions:
1. In your Crock Pot, mix the lamb chops with the vinegar and the other ingredients, toss, put the lid on and cook on Low for 6 hours.
2. Divide everything between plates and serve.

Nutrition Info:
• calories 292, fat 12, fiber 3, carbs 7, protein 16

French Lamb

Servings: 4 | Cooking Time: 8 Hours

Ingredients:
• 4 lamb chops
• 1 cup onion, chopped
• 2 cups canned tomatoes, chopped
• 1 cup leek, chopped
• 2 tablespoons garlic, minced
• 1 teaspoon herbs de Provence
• Salt and black pepper to the taste
• 3 cups water

Directions:
1. In your Crock Pot mix, lamb chops with onion, tomatoes, leek, garlic, herbs de Provence, salt, pepper and water, stir, cover and cook on Low for 8 hours.
2. Divide lamb and veggies between plates and serve.

Nutrition Info:
• calories 430, fat 12, fiber 8, carbs 20, protein 18

Beef In Onion Dip

Servings:4 | Cooking Time: 6 Hours

Ingredients:
• 1-pound beef sirloin
• 1 cup onion, sliced
• 1 cup of water
• 3 tablespoons butter
• 1 teaspoon salt
• 1 teaspoon white pepper
• ½ teaspoon ground clove

Directions:
1. Toss the butter in the pan and melt it.
2. Add beef sirloin and roast it for 4 minutes per side on high heat.
3. After this, transfer the beef sirloin and liquid butter in the Crock Pot.
4. Add onion, water, salt, white pepper, and ground clove.
5. Close the lid and cook the meal on High for 4 hours.
6. Then shred the beef and cook the dip for 2 hours on high more.

Nutrition Info:
• Per Serving: 301 calories, 34.9g protein, 3.2g carbohydrates, 15.8g fat, 0.9g fiber, 124mg cholesterol, 721mg sodium, 512mg potassium.

Oregano Lamb

Servings: 2 | Cooking Time: 6 Hours

Ingredients:
• 1 pound lamb stew meat, roughly cubed
• 1 teaspoon hot paprika
• 1 tablespoon oregano, chopped
• ½ teaspoon turmeric powder
• 4 scallions, chopped
• A pinch of salt and black pepper
• 1 cup beef stock

Directions:
1. In your Crock Pot, mix the lamb with the paprika, oregano and the other ingredients, toss, put the lid on and cook on Low for 6 hours.
2. Divide the mix between plates and serve with a side salad.

Nutrition Info:
• calories 200, fat 9, fiber 2, carbs 6, protein 12

Pork Liver Kebabs

Servings:6 | Cooking Time: 3.5 Hours

Ingredients:
- 15 oz pork liver, roughly chopped
- 1 teaspoon onion powder
- 1 teaspoon garlic powder
- 2 bell peppers, roughly chopped
- 1 tablespoon cornflour
- ½ teaspoon salt
- 1 cup of water
- 1 tablespoon coconut oil

Directions:
1. Sprinkle the pork liver with onion powder, garlic powder, cornflour, and salt.
2. Then string the liver int skewers (wooden sticks) and sprinkle with coconut oil.
3. Arrange the skewers in the Crock Pot.
4. Add water and close the lid.
5. Cook them on High for 3.5 hours.

Nutrition Info:
- Per Serving: 157 calories, 19g protein, 7.3g carbohydrates, 5.5g fat, 0.7g fiber, 252mg cholesterol, 231mg sodium, 194mg potassium

Egg Salad With Ground Pork

Servings:2 | Cooking Time: 4 Hours

Ingredients:
- 2 eggs, hard-boiled, peeled, chopped
- ¼ cup ground pork
- 1 teaspoon ground turmeric
- 1 teaspoon salt
- ¼ cup plain yogurt
- 1 tablespoon coconut oil
- 2 tomatoes, chopped

Directions:
1. Put the coconut oil in the Crock Pot.
2. Add ground pork, ground turmeric, salt, and yogurt.
3. Close the lid and cook the meat on High for 4 hours.
4. After this, transfer the ground pork and all remaining liquid from the Crock Pot in the salad bowl.
5. Add all remaining ingredients from the list above and mix the salad.

Nutrition Info:
- Per Serving: 198 calories, 11g protein, 8g carbohydrates, 13.9g fat, 1.7g fiber, 175mg cholesterol, 1262mg sodium, 450mg potassium

Cider Beef Mix

Servings: 2 | Cooking Time: 8 Hours

Ingredients:
- 1 pound beef stew meat, cubed
- 1 tablespoon olive oil
- Salt and black pepper to the taste
- 3 garlic cloves, minced
- ½ yellow onion, chopped
- ½ cup beef stock
- 1 tablespoon apple cider vinegar

- 1 tablespoon lime zest, grated

Directions:
1. In your Crock Pot, mix the beef with the oil, salt, pepper, garlic and the other ingredients, toss, put the lid on, and cook on Low for 8 hours.
2. Divide everything between plates and serve.

Nutrition Info:
- calories 453, fat 10, fiber 12, carbs 20, protein 36

Cilantro Beef Meatballs

Servings:6 | Cooking Time: 4 Hours

Ingredients:
- 2 tablespoons dried cilantro
- 12 oz ground beef
- 2 tablespoons semolina
- 1 teaspoon garlic powder
- 1 teaspoon chili powder
- 1 tablespoon olive oil
- ½ cup of coconut milk

Directions:
1. Put the ground beef in the Crock Pot.
2. Add semolina, garlic powder, chili powder, and dried cilantro.
3. Make the small balls and put them in the Crock Pot in one layer.
4. Add olive oil and coconut milk.
5. Close the lid and cook the meatballs on High for 4 hours.

Nutrition Info:
- Per Serving: 187 calories, 18.2g protein, 4.2g carbohydrates, 10.7g fat, 0.8g fiber, 51mg cholesterol, 45mg sodium, 303mg potassium.

Easy Pork Chop Dinner

Servings:4 | Cooking Time: 10 Hours

Ingredients:
- 2 teaspoons olive oil
- 2 cloves of garlic, chopped
- 1 onion, chopped
- 4 pork cops
- 2 cups chicken broth

Directions:
1. In a skillet, heat the oil and sauté the garlic and onions until fragrant and lightly golden. Add in the pork chops and cook for 2 minutes for 2 minutes on each side.
2. Pour the chicken broth and scrape the bottom to remove the browning.
3. Transfer to the crockpot. Season with salt and pepper to taste.
4. Close the lid and cook on low for 10 hours or on high for 7 hours.

Nutrition Info:
- Calories per serving: 481; Carbohydrates: 2.5g; Protein: 38.1g; Fat: 30.5g; Sugar: 0.3g; Sodium: 735mg; Fiber: 1.2g

Fish & Seafood Recipes

Fish & Seafood Recipes

Shrimp And Peas Soup

Servings: 4 | Cooking Time: 1 Hour

Ingredients:
- 4 scallions, chopped
- 1 tablespoon olive oil
- 1 small ginger root, grated
- 8 cups chicken stock
- ¼ cup soy sauce
- 5 ounces canned bamboo shoots, sliced
- Black pepper to the taste
- ¼ teaspoon fish sauce
- 1 pound shrimp, peeled and deveined
- ½ pound snow peas
- 1 tablespoon sesame oil
- ½ tablespoon chili oil

Directions:
1. In your Crock Pot, mix olive oil with scallions, ginger, stock, soy sauce, bamboo, black pepper, fish sauce, shrimp, peas, sesame oil and chili oil, cover and cook on High for 1 hour.
2. Stir soup, ladle into bowls and serve.

Nutrition Info:
- calories 240, fat 3, fiber 2, carbs 12, protein 14

Salmon Croquettes

Servings:6 | Cooking Time: 2 Hours

Ingredients:
- 1-pound salmon fillet, minced
- 1 tablespoon mayonnaise
- 2 tablespoons panko breadcrumbs
- ½ teaspoon ground black pepper
- 1 egg, beaten
- 1 teaspoon smoked paprika
- ½ cup of water

Directions:
1. In the bowl mix minced salmon with mayonnaise panko breadcrumbs, ground black pepper, egg, and smoked paprika.
2. Then make the small croquettes and place them in the Crock Pot.
3. Add water and close the lid.
4. Cook the meal on high for 2 hours.

Nutrition Info:
- Per Serving: 127 calories, 15.9g protein, 2.2g carbohydrates, 6.3g fat, 0.4g fiber, 61mg cholesterol, 73mg sodium, 311mg potassium.

Basil Cod And Olives

Servings: 2 | Cooking Time: 3 Hours

Ingredients:
- 1 pound cod fillets, boneless
- 1 cup black olives, pitted and halved
- ½ tablespoon tomato paste
- 1 tablespoon basil, chopped
- ¼ cup chicken stock
- 1 red onion, sliced
- 1 tablespoon lime juice
- 1 tablespoon chives, chopped
- Salt and black pepper to the taste

Directions:
1. In your Crock Pot, mix the cod with the olives, basil and the other ingredients, toss, put the lid on and cook on Low for 3 hours.
2. Divide everything between plates and serve.

Nutrition Info:
- calories 132, fat 9, fiber 2, carbs 5, protein 11

Shrimp And Sausage Boil

Servings: 4 | Cooking Time: 2 Hours And 30 Minutes

Ingredients:
- 1 and ½ pounds shrimp, head removed
- 12 ounces Andouille sausage, already cooked and chopped
- 4 ears of corn, each cut into 3 pieces
- 1 tablespoon old bay seasoning
- 16 ounces beer
- Salt and black pepper to the taste
- 1 teaspoon red pepper flakes, crushed
- 2 sweet onions, cut into wedges
- 1 pound potatoes, cut into medium chunks
- 8 garlic cloves, crushed
- French baguettes for serving

Directions:
1. In your Crock Pot mix beer with old bay seasoning, red pepper flakes, salt, black pepper, onions, garlic, potatoes, corn and sausage, cover and cook on High for 2 hours.
2. Add shrimp, cover, cook on High for 30 minutes more, divide into bowls and serve with French baguettes on the side.

Nutrition Info:
- calories 261, fat 5, fiber 6, carbs 20, protein 16

Braised Lobster

Servings:4 | Cooking Time: 3 Hours

Ingredients:
- 2-pound lobster, cleaned
- 1 cup of water
- 1 teaspoon Italian seasonings

Directions:
1. Put all ingredients in the Crock Pot.
2. Close the lid and cook the lobster in High for 3 hours.
3. Remove the lobster from the Crock Pot and cool it till room temperature

Nutrition Info:
- Per Serving: 206 calories, 43.1g protein, 0.1g carbohydrates, 2.2g fat, 0g fiber, 332mg cholesterol, 1104mg sodium, 524mg potassium.

Crockpot Tuna Spaghetti

Servings:3 | Cooking Time: 2 Hours

Ingredients:
- 2 stalks of celery, chopped
- 1/3 cup chicken broth
- 1 cup full-fat milk
- 2 tablespoons parsley flakes
- ½ pound ground tuna, boiled
- 2 zucchinis, spiralized or cut into long strips
- 1 tablespoons butter
- Salt and pepper to taste

Directions:
1. Place all ingredients in the CrockPot.
2. Give a good stir.
3. Close the lid and cook on high for 1 hours or on low for 2 hours.
4. Garnish with chopped parsley if desired.

Nutrition Info:
- Calories per serving: 320; Carbohydrates:7.3 g; Protein: 30.9g; Fat: 19.3g; Sugar: 0.2g; Sodium: 590mg; Fiber: 4.8g

Spicy Curried Shrimps

Servings:4 | Cooking Time: 2 Hours

Ingredients:
- 1 ½ pounds shrimp, shelled and deveined
- 1 tablespoon ghee or butter, melted
- 1 tablespoon curry powder
- 1 teaspoon cayenne pepper
- Salt and pepper to taste

Directions:
1. Place all ingredients in the crockpot.
2. Give a stir to incorporate everything.
3. Close the lid and allow to cook on low for 2 hours or on high for 30 minutes.

Nutrition Info:
- Calories per serving: 207; Carbohydrates:2.2 g; Protein: 35.2g; Fat: 10.5g; Sugar: 0g; Sodium: 325mg; Fiber: 1.6g

Cod Sticks In Blankets

Servings:4 | Cooking Time: 4 Hours

Ingredients:
- 4 cod fillets
- 4 oz puff pastry
- 1 teaspoon mayonnaise
- 1 teaspoon ground black pepper
- 1 teaspoon olive oil

Directions:
1. Cut the cod fillets into the sticks.
2. Then sprinkle them with mayonnaise and ground black pepper.
3. Roll up the puff pastry and cut into strips.
4. Roll every cod stick in the puff pastry and brush with olive oil.
5. Put the cod sticks in the Crock Pot in one layer and cook on high for 4 hours.

Nutrition Info:

- Per Serving: 262 calories, 22.1g protein, 13.4g carbohydrates, 13.g fat, 0.6g fiber, 55mg cholesterol, 150mg sodium, 24mg potassium

Coconut Curry Cod

Servings:2 | Cooking Time: 2.5 Hours

Ingredients:
- 2 cod fillets
- ½ teaspoon curry paste
- 1/3 cup coconut milk
- 1 teaspoon sunflower oil

Directions:
1. Mix coconut milk with curry paste, add sunflower oil, and transfer the liquid in the Crock Pot.
2. Add cod fillets.
3. Cook the meal on High for 2.5 hours.

Nutrition Info:
- Per Serving: 211 calories, 21g protein, 2.6g carbohydrates, 13.6g fat, 0.9g fiber, 55mg cholesterol, 76mg sodium, 105mg potassium

Mussels Soup

Servings: 6 | Cooking Time: 2 Hours

Ingredients:
- 2 pounds mussels
- 28 ounces canned tomatoes, crushed
- 28 ounces canned tomatoes, chopped
- 2 cup chicken stock
- 1 teaspoon red pepper flakes, crushed
- 3 garlic cloves, minced
- 1 handful parsley, chopped
- 1 yellow onion, chopped
- Salt and black pepper to the taste
- 1 tablespoon olive oil

Directions:
1. In your Crock Pot, mix mussels with canned and crushed tomatoes, stock, pepper flakes, garlic, parsley, onion, salt, pepper and oil, stir, cover and cook on High for 2 hours.
2. Divide into bowls and serve.

Nutrition Info:
- calories 250, fat 3, fiber 3, carbs 8, protein 12

Thai Salmon Cakes

Servings: 10 | Cooking Time: 6 Hrs.

Ingredients:
- 6 oz squid, minced
- 10 oz salmon fillet, minced
- 2 tbsp chili paste
- 1 tsp cayenne pepper
- 2 oz lemon leaves
- 3 tbsp green peas, mashed
- 2 tsp fish sauce
- 2 egg white
- 1 egg yolk
- 1 tsp oyster sauce
- 1 tsp salt
- ½ tsp ground coriander

- 1 tsp sugar
- 2 tbsp butter
- ¼ cup cream
- 3 tbsp almond flour

Directions:
1. Mix seafood with chili paste, cayenne pepper, lemon leaves, mashed green peas, fish sauce, whisked egg yolk and egg whites in a bowl.
2. Stir in sugar, salt, oyster sauce, sugar, almond flour, and ground coriander.
3. Mix well, then make small-sized fish cakes out of this mixture.
4. Add cream and butter to the insert of the Crock Pot.
5. Place the fish cakes in the butter and cream.
6. Put the cooker's lid on and set the cooking time to 5 hours on Low settings.
7. Serve warm with cream mixture.

Nutrition Info:
- Per Serving: Calories: 112, Total Fat: 6.7g, Fiber: 1g, Total Carbs: 2.95g, Protein: 10g

Octopus And Veggies Mix

Servings: 4 | Cooking Time: 3 Hours

Ingredients:
- 1 octopus, already prepared
- 1 cup red wine
- 1 cup white wine
- 1 cup water
- 1 cup olive oil
- 2 teaspoons pepper sauce
- 1 tablespoon hot sauce
- 1 tablespoon paprika
- 1 tablespoon tomato sauce
- Salt and black pepper to the taste
- ½ bunch parsley, chopped
- 2 garlic cloves, minced
- 1 yellow onion, chopped
- 4 potatoes, cut into quarters.

Directions:
1. Put octopus in a bowl, add white wine, red one, water, half of the oil, pepper sauce, hot sauce, paprika, tomato paste, salt, pepper and parsley, toss to coat, cover and keep in a cold place for 1 day.
2. Add the rest of the oil to your Crock Pot and arrange onions and potatoes on the bottom.
3. Add the octopus and the marinade, stir, cover, cook on High for 3 hours, divide everything between plates and serve.

Nutrition Info:
- calories 230, fat 4, fiber 1, carbs 7, protein 23

Salmon And Yam Casserole

Servings:4 | Cooking Time: 5 Hours

Ingredients:
- 1 cup yams, chopped
- 7 oz salmon fillet, sliced
- 1 zucchini, chopped
- 1 oz Monterey Jack cheese, shredded
- ½ cup of water
- 1 teaspoon sesame oil
- 1 teaspoon salt

Directions:
1. Mix yams with zucchini and put in the Crock Pot.
2. Then mix salt with salmon and sesame oil.
3. Put the fish over the vegetables and top with shredded cheese.
4. Add water and close the lid.
5. Cook the casserole on Low for 5 hours.

Nutrition Info:
- Per Serving: 149 calories, 12.5g protein, 11g carbohydrates, 6.5g fat, 1.9g fiber, 28mg cholesterol, 650mg sodium, 553mg potassium

Butter Crab Legs

Servings:4 | Cooking Time: 45 Minutes

Ingredients:
- 15 oz king crab legs
- 1 tablespoon butter
- 1 cup of water
- 1 teaspoon dried basil

Directions:
1. Put the crab legs in the Crock Pot.
2. Add basil and water and cook them on High for 45 minutes.

Nutrition Info:
- Per Serving: 133 calories, 20.4g protein, 0g carbohydrates, 4.5g fat, 0g fiber, 67mg cholesterol, 1161mg sodium, 2mg potassium

Chives Shrimp

Servings: 2 | Cooking Time: 1 Hour

Ingredients:
- 1 pound shrimp, peeled and deveined
- 1 tablespoon chives, chopped
- ½ teaspoon basil, dried
- 1 teaspoon turmeric powder
- 1 tablespoon olive oil
- ½ cup chicken stock

Directions:
1. In your Crock Pot, mix the shrimp with the basil, chives and the other ingredients, toss, put the lid on and cook on High for 1 hour.
2. Divide the shrimp between plates and serve with a side salad.

Nutrition Info:
- calories 200, fat 12, fiber 3, carbs 7, protein 9

Almond-crusted Tilapia

Servings:4 | Cooking Time: 4 Hours

Ingredients:
- 2 tablespoons olive oil
- 1 cup chopped almonds
- ¼ cup ground flaxseed
- 4 tilapia fillets
- Salt and pepper to taste

Directions:
1. Line the bottom of the crockpot with a foil.
2. Grease the foil with the olive oil.
3. In a mixing bowl, combine the almonds and flaxseed.
4. Season the tilapia with salt and pepper to taste.
5. Dredge the tilapia fillets with the almond and flaxseed mixture.
6. Place neatly in the foil-lined crockpot.
7. Close the lid and cook on high for 2 hours and on low for 4 hours.

Nutrition Info:
- Calories per serving: 233; Carbohydrates: 4.6g; Protein: 25.5g; Fat: 13.3g; Sugar: 0.4g; Sodium: 342mg; Fiber: 1.9g

Cod In Lemon Sauce

Servings:4 | Cooking Time: 2.5 Hours

Ingredients:
- 4 cod fillets
- 4 tablespoons lemon juice
- 2 tablespoons olive oil
- ½ teaspoon fennel seeds
- ¼ cup of water

Directions:
1. Put the cod fillets in the Crock Pot.
2. Add water, fennel seeds, and olive oil.
3. Cook the fish on high for 2.5 hours.
4. Then transfer the fish in the bowls and sprinkle with lemon juice.

Nutrition Info:
- Per Serving: 155 calories, 20.2g protein, 0.5g carbohydrates, 8.2g fat, 0.2g fiber, 55mg cholesterol, 74mg sodium, 23mg potassium

Butter Dipped Crab Legs

Servings: 4 | Cooking Time: 1 Hr. 30 Minutes

Ingredients:
- 4 lbs. king crab legs, broken in half
- 3 lemon wedges
- ¼ cup butter, melted
- ½ cup chicken stock

Directions:
1. Add crab legs, butter, and chicken stock to the insert of the Crock Pot.
2. Put the cooker's lid on and set the cooking time to 1.5 hours on High settings.
3. Serve warm with lemon wedges.

Nutrition Info:
- Per Serving: Calories: 100, Total Fat: 1g, Fiber: 5g, Total Carbs: 12g, Protein: 3g

Salmon And Raspberry Vinaigrette

Servings: 6 | Cooking Time: 2 Hours

Ingredients:
- 6 salmon steaks
- 2 tablespoons olive oil
- 4 leeks, sliced
- 2 garlic cloves, minced
- 2 tablespoons parsley, chopped
- 1 cup clam juice
- 2 tablespoons lemon juice
- Salt and white pepper to the taste
- 1 teaspoon sherry
- 1/3 cup dill, chopped
- For the raspberry vinegar:
- 2 pints red raspberries
- 1-pint cider vinegar

Directions:
1. In a bowl, mix red raspberries with vinegar and salmon, toss, cover and keep in the fridge for 2 hours.
2. In your Crock Pot, mix oil with parsley, leeks, garlic, clam juice, lemon juice, salt, pepper, sherry, dill and salmon, cover and cook on High for 2 hours.
3. Divide everything between plates and serve.

Nutrition Info:
- calories 251, fat 6, fiber 7, carbs 16, protein 26

Poached Cod And Pineapple Mix

Servings: 2 | Cooking Time: 4 Hours

Ingredients:
- 1 pound cod, boneless
- 6 garlic cloves, minced
- 1 small ginger pieces, chopped
- ½ tablespoon black peppercorns
- 1 cup pineapple juice
- 1 cup pineapple, chopped
- ¼ cup white vinegar
- 4 jalapeno peppers, chopped
- Salt and black pepper to the taste

Directions:
1. Put the fish in your crock, season with salt and pepper.
2. Add garlic, ginger, peppercorns, pineapple juice, pineapple chunks, vinegar and jalapenos.
3. Stir gently, cover and cook on Low for 4 hours.
4. Divide fish between plates, top with the pineapple mix and serve.

Nutrition Info:
- calories 240, fat 4, fiber 4, carbs 14, protein 10

Rosemary Sole

Servings:2 | Cooking Time: 2 Hours

Ingredients:
- 8 oz sole fillet
- 1 tablespoon dried rosemary
- 1 tablespoon avocado oil
- 1 tablespoon apple cider vinegar
- 5 tablespoons water

Directions:
1. Pour water in the Crock Pot.
2. Then rub the sole fillet with dried rosemary and sprinkle with avocado oil and apple cider vinegar.
3. Put the fish fillet in the Crock Pot and cook it on High for 2 hours.

Nutrition Info:
- Per Serving: 149 calories, 27.6g protein, 1.5g carbohydrates, 2.9g fat, 1g fiber, 77mg cholesterol, 122mg sodium, 434mg potassium.

Salmon And Strawberries Mix

Servings: 2 | Cooking Time: 2 Hours

Ingredients:
- 1 pound salmon fillets, boneless
- 1 cup strawberries, halved
- ½ cup orange juice
- Zest of 1 lemon, grated
- 4 scallions, chopped
- 1 teaspoon balsamic vinegar
- 1 tablespoon chives, chopped
- A pinch of salt and black pepper

Directions:
1. In your Crock Pot, mix the salmon with the strawberries, orange juice and the other ingredients, toss, put the lid on and cook on High for 2 hours.
2. Divide everything into bowls and serve.

Nutrition Info:
- calories 200, fat 12, fiber 4, carbs 6, protein 8

Moroccan Fish

Servings: 9 | Cooking Time: 3 Hours 20 Minutes

Ingredients:
- 1 pound cherry tomatoes, crushed slightly
- 1 teaspoon tea seed oil
- 1 teaspoon red pepper flakes, crushed
- 3 pounds salmon fillets
- 2 garlic cloves, crushed
- Salt, to taste
- 1 tablespoon fresh basil leaves, torn
- 1 teaspoon dried oregano, crushed

Directions:
1. Put the tea seed oil and salmon fillets in the Crock Pot and cover the lid.
2. Cook on LOW for about 2 hours and add cherry tomatoes, garlic, oregano, salt and red pepper flakes.
3. Cook on HIGH for about 1 hour and garnish with basil leaves to serve.

Nutrition Info:
- Calories: 243 Fat: 11.3g Carbohydrates: 2.7g

Clams In Coconut Sauce

Servings:2 | Cooking Time: 2 Hours

Ingredients:
- 1 cup coconut cream
- 1 teaspoon minced garlic
- 1 teaspoon chili flakes
- 1 teaspoon salt
- 1 teaspoon ground coriander
- 8 oz clams

Directions:
1. Pour coconut cream in the Crock Pot.
2. Add minced garlic, chili flakes, salt, and ground coriander.
3. Cook the mixture on high for 1 hour.
4. Then add clams and stir the meal well. Cook it for 1 hour on high more.

Nutrition Info:
- Per Serving: 333 calories, 3.5g protein, 19.6g carbohydrates, 28.9g fat, 3.1g fiber, 0mg cholesterol, 1592mg sodium, 425mg potassium.

Tarragon Mahi Mahi

Servings:4 | Cooking Time: 2.5 Hours

Ingredients:
- 1-pound mahi-mahi fillet
- 1 tablespoon dried tarragon
- 1 tablespoon coconut oil
- ½ cup of water

Directions:
1. Melt the coconut oil in the skillet.
2. Add mahi-mahi fillet and roast it on high heat for 2 minutes per side.
3. Put the fish fillet in the Crock Pot.
4. Add dried tarragon and water.
5. Close the lid and cook the fish on High for 2.5 hours.

Nutrition Info:
- Per Serving: 121 calories, 21.2g protein, 0.2g carbohydrates, 3.4g fat, 0g fiber, 40mg cholesterol, 97mg sodium, 14mg potassium

Tuna Spinach Casserole

Servings:5 | Cooking Time: 6 Hours

Ingredients:
- 1-pound tuna, chopped or ground finely
- 1-inch ginger grated
- 1 tablespoon lemon juice
- 2 tablespoons soy sauce
- Zest from ½ lemon
- ¼ cup butter, melted
- 4 cloves of garlic, minced
- 1 cup heavy cream
- 9 ounces spinach, rinsed and drained
- 4 eggs, beaten
- Salt and pepper to taste
- 1 cup mozzarella cheese

Directions:

1. In a mixing bowl, combine the tuna, ginger, lemon juice, soy sauce, and lemon zest. Marinate for at least 2 hours in the fridge.
2. After 2 hours, discard the juices of the tuna and transfer into the CrockPot.
3. Stir in the butter, garlic, heavy cream, and spinach. Add in the beaten eggs and season with salt and pepper to taste.
4. Sprinkle mozzarella cheese on top.
5. Close the lid and cook on high for 4 hours or on low for 6 hours.

Nutrition Info:
- Calories per serving: 573; Carbohydrates: 2.1g; Protein: 39.1g; Fat:45.3g; Sugar: 0g; Sodium: 761mg; Fiber: 1.2g

Crockpot Fish Chowder

Servings:9 | Cooking Time: 3 Hours

Ingredients:
- 2 pounds catfish fillet, sliced
- 2 tablespoons butter
- ½ cup fresh oysters
- 1 onion, chopped
- 2 cups water
- 1 red bell pepper, chopped
- 1 yellow bell pepper, chopped
- Salt and pepper to taste
- 1 cup full-fat milk

Directions:

1. Place all ingredients in the CrockPot.
2. Give a good stir.
3. Close the lid and cook on high for 2 hours or on low for 3 hours.

Nutrition Info:
- Calories per serving: 172; Carbohydrates:6.1 g; Protein: 20.5g; Fat: 9.4g; Sugar: 1.3g; Sodium: 592mg; Fiber: 3.5g

Flavored Squid

Servings: 4 | Cooking Time: 3 Hours

Ingredients:
- 17 ounces squids
- 1 and ½ tablespoons red chili powder
- Salt and black pepper to the taste
- ¼ teaspoon turmeric powder
- 2 cups water
- 5 pieces coconut, shredded
- 4 garlic cloves, minced
- ½ teaspoons cumin seeds
- 3 tablespoons olive oil
- ¼ teaspoon mustard seeds
- 1-inch ginger pieces, chopped

Directions:

1. Put squids in your Crock Pot, add chili powder, turmeric, salt, pepper and water, stir, cover and cook on High for 2 hours.
2. In your blender, mix coconut with ginger, oil, garlic and cumin and blend well.
3. Add this over the squids, cover and cook on High for 1 more hour.

4. Divide everything into bowls and serve.

Nutrition Info:
- calories 261, fat 3, fiber 8, carbs 19, protein 11

Turmeric Coconut Squid

Servings: 4 | Cooking Time: 3 Hrs.

Ingredients:
- 17 oz. squids
- 1 and ½ tbsp red chili powder
- Salt and black pepper to the taste
- ¼ tsp turmeric powder
- 2 cups of water
- 5 pieces coconut, shredded
- 4 garlic cloves, minced
- ½ tsp cumin seeds
- 3 tbsp olive oil
- ¼ tsp mustard seeds
- 1-inch ginger pieces, chopped

Directions:

1. Add squids, turmeric, chili powder, water, black pepper, and salt to the insert of the Crock Pot.
2. Put the cooker's lid on and set the cooking time to 2 hours on High settings.
3. Add ginger, garlic, cumin, and oil to a blender jug and blend well.
4. Transfer this ginger-garlic mixture to the squids in the cooker.
5. Cook again for 1 hour on High settings.
6. Serve warm.

Nutrition Info:
- Per Serving: Calories: 261, Total Fat: 3g, Fiber: 8g, Total Carbs: 19g, Protein: 11g

Italian Barramundi And Tomato Relish

Servings: 4 | Cooking Time: 2 Hours

Ingredients:
- 2 barramundi fillets, skinless
- 2 teaspoon olive oil
- 2 teaspoons Italian seasoning
- ¼ cup green olives, pitted and chopped
- ¼ cup cherry tomatoes, chopped
- ¼ cup black olives, chopped
- 1 tablespoon lemon zest
- 2 tablespoons lemon zest
- Salt and black pepper to the taste
- 2 tablespoons parsley, chopped
- 1 tablespoon olive oil

Directions:

1. Rub fish with salt, pepper, Italian seasoning and 2 teaspoons olive oil and put into your Crock Pot.
2. In a bowl, mix tomatoes with all the olives, salt, pepper, lemon zest and lemon juice, parsley and 1 tablespoon olive oil, toss, add over fish, cover and cook on High for 2 hours.
3. Divide fish between plates, top with tomato relish and serve.

Nutrition Info:
- calories 140, fat 4, fiber 2, carbs 11, protein 10

Fish Hot Dog Sticks

Servings: 4 | Cooking Time: 2 Hours

Ingredients:
- 5 oz salmon fillet, minced
- 2 oz potato, cooked, mashed
- 1 egg, beaten
- 2 tablespoons cornflour
- ½ teaspoon salt
- 1 teaspoon dried parsley
- 1 tablespoon avocado oil
- ¼ cup of water

Directions:
1. In the mixing bowl mix minced salmon with mashed potato, egg, cornflour, salt, and dried parsley.
2. Then make the medium size hot dog sticks and put them in the hot skillet.
3. Add avocado oil and roast them on high heat for 1 minute per side.
4. Transfer the hot dog sticks in the Crock Pot.
5. Add water and close the lid.
6. Cook the meal on high for 2 hours.

Nutrition Info:
- Per Serving: 92 calories, 8.9g protein, 5.6g carbohydrates, 3.9g fat, 0.7g fiber, 57mg cholesterol, 324mg sodium, 235mg potassium

Coriander Salmon Mix

Servings: 2 | Cooking Time: 3 Hours

Ingredients:
- 1 pound salmon fillets, boneless and roughly cubed
- 1 tablespoon coriander, chopped
- ½ teaspoon chili powder
- ¼ cup chicken stock
- 3 scallions, chopped
- Juice of 1 lime
- 2 teaspoons avocado oil
- A pinch of salt and black pepper

Directions:
1. In your Crock Pot, mix the salmon with the coriander, chili powder and the other ingredients, toss gently, put the lid on and cook on High for 3 hours.
2. Divide the mix between plates and serve.

Nutrition Info:
- calories 232, fat 10, fiber 4, carbs 6, protein 9

Taco Mahi Mahi

Servings: 6 | Cooking Time: 6 Hours

Ingredients:
- 2-pounds Mahi Mahi fillets
- 1 tablespoon taco seasonings
- 1 teaspoon fish sauce
- 1/3 cup chicken stock
- 1 tablespoon sunflower oil

Directions:
1. Sprinkle the fish fillets with taco seasonings and fish sauce.
2. Pour sunflower oil in the Crock Pot.

3. Add fish and chicken stock.
4. Close the lid and cook the fish on Low for 6 hours.

Nutrition Info:
- Per Serving: 163 calories, 28.7g protein, 1.4g carbohydrates, 3.8g fat, 0g fiber, 130mg cholesterol, 453mg sodium, 563mg potassium

Seabass Ragout

Servings: 4 | Cooking Time: 3.5 Hours

Ingredients:
- 7 oz shiitake mushrooms
- 1 onion, diced
- 1 tablespoon coconut oil
- 1 teaspoon ground coriander
- ½ teaspoon salt
- 1 cup of water
- 12 oz seabass fillet, chopped

Directions:
1. Heat the coconut oil in the skillet.
2. Add onion and mushrooms and roast the vegetables for 5 minutes on medium heat.
3. Then transfer the vegetables in the Crock Pot and add water.
4. Add fish fillet, salt, and ground coriander.
5. Cook the meal on High for 3.5 hours.

Nutrition Info:
- Per Serving: 241 calories, 20.4g protein, 9.4g carbohydrates, 14g fat, 2.3g fiber, 0mg cholesterol, 413mg sodium, 99mg potassium.

Coconut Pollock

Servings: 4 | Cooking Time: 5 Hours

Ingredients:
- 1-pound Pollock fillet, chopped
- 1 tablespoon coconut flakes
- 1 tablespoon coconut flour
- ½ teaspoon ground nutmeg
- ½ teaspoon salt
- 1 cup coconut cream
- 1 tablespoon sunflower oil

Directions:
1. Sprinkle the Pollock fillet with coconut flakes, coconut flour, ground nutmeg, and salt.
2. Then transfer the fillets in the Crock Pot.
3. Add coconut cream and sunflower oil.
4. Cook the fish on Low for 5 hours.

Nutrition Info:
- Per Serving: 284 calories, 24g protein, 4.7g carbohydrates, 19.6g fat, 2.1g fiber, 56mg cholesterol, 370mg sodium, 163mg potassium

Mustard Cod

Servings:4 | Cooking Time: 3 Hours

Ingredients:
- 4 cod fillets
- 4 teaspoons mustard
- 2 tablespoons sesame oil
- ¼ cup of water

Directions:
1. Mix mustard with sesame oil.
2. Then brush the cod fillets with mustard mixture and transfer in the Crock Pot.
3. Add water and cook the fish on low for 3 hours.

Nutrition Info:
- Per Serving: 166 calories, 20.8g protein, 1.2g carbohydrates, 8.8g fat, 0.5g fiber, 55mg cholesterol, 71mg sodium, 23mg potassium

Tuna Casserole

Servings:4 | Cooking Time: 7 Hours

Ingredients:
- 1 cup mushrooms, sliced
- ½ cup corn kernels, frozen
- 8 oz tuna, chopped
- 1 teaspoon Italian seasonings
- 1 cup chicken stock
- ½ cup Cheddar cheese, shredded
- 1 tablespoon sesame oil

Directions:
1. Heat the sesame oil in the skillet.
2. Add mushrooms and roast them for 5 minutes on medium heat.
3. Then transfer the mushrooms in the Crock Pot and flatten in one layer.
4. After this, mix Italian seasonings with tuna and put over the mushrooms.
5. Then top the fish with corn kernels and cheese.
6. Add chicken stock.
7. Cook the casserole on Low for 7 hours.

Nutrition Info:
- Per Serving: 219 calories, 19.9g protein, 4.7g carbohydrates, 13.4g fat, 0.7g fiber, 33mg cholesterol, 311mg sodium, 315mg potassium.

Express Shrimps And Sausage Jambalaya Stew

Servings:4 | Cooking Time: 3 Hours

Ingredients:
- 1 teaspoon canola oil
- 8 ounces andouille sausage, cut into slices
- 1 16-ounce bag frozen bell pepper and onion mix
- 1 can chicken broth
- 8 ounces shrimps, shelled and deveined

Directions:
1. In a skillet, heat the oil and sauté the sausages until the sausages have rendered their fat. Set aside.
2. Pour the vegetable mix into the crockpot.

3. Add in the sausages and pour the chicken broth.
4. Stir in the shrimps last.
5. Cook on low for 1 hour or on low for 3 hours.

Nutrition Info:
- Calories per serving: 316; Carbohydrates: 6.3; Protein: 32.1g; Fat: 25.6g; Sugar:0.2 g; Sodium: 425mg; Fiber: 3.2g

Salmon With Almond Crust

Servings:2 | Cooking Time: 2.5 Hours

Ingredients:
- 8 oz salmon fillet
- 2 tablespoons almond flakes
- 1 teaspoon butter
- 1 teaspoon ground black pepper
- 1 teaspoon salt
- 1 egg, beaten
- ¼ cup of coconut milk

Directions:
1. Sprinkle the salmon fillet with ground black pepper and salt.
2. Then dip the fish in egg and coat in the almond flakes.
3. Put butter and coconut milk in the Crock Pot.
4. Then add salmon and close the lid.
5. Cook the salmon on High for 2.5 hours.

Nutrition Info:
- Per Serving: 301 calories, 26.6g protein, 3g carbohydrates, 20.9g fat, 1.5g fiber, 137mg cholesterol, 1262mg sodium, 558mg potassium

Flavored Cod Fillets

Servings: 4 | Cooking Time: 2 Hours

Ingredients:
- 4 medium cod fillets, boneless
- ¼ teaspoon nutmeg, ground
- 1 teaspoon ginger, grated
- Salt and black pepper to the taste
- 1 teaspoon onion powder
- ¼ teaspoon sweet paprika
- 1 teaspoon cayenne pepper
- ½ teaspoon cinnamon powder

Directions:
1. In a bowl, mix cod fillets with nutmeg, ginger, salt, pepper, onion powder, paprika , cayenne black pepper and cinnamon, toss, transfer to your Crock Pot, cover and cook on Low for 2 hours.
2. Divide between plates and serve with a side salad.

Nutrition Info:
- calories 200, fat 4, fiber 2, carbs 14, protein 4

Red Thai Salmon Curry

Servings:4 | Cooking Time: 4 Hours

Ingredients:
- 2 onions, chopped
- 4 salmon fillets
- 1 can coconut milk
- 1 teaspoon coconut oil
- 1 tablespoon curry powder
- 3 curry leaves
- 1 teaspoon coriander powder
- 1 teaspoon cayenne pepper
- ½ teaspoon cumin
- 1 teaspoon cinnamon
- 2 red bell peppers, julienned

Directions:
1. Place all ingredients in the CrockPot.
2. Give a good stir.
3. Close the lid and cook on high for 3 hours or on low for 4 hours.

Nutrition Info:
- Calories per serving: 499; Carbohydrates: 5.7g; Protein: 27.6g; Fat: 38.3g; Sugar: 0.8g; Sodium: 891mg; Fiber: 3.2g

Creamy Sea Bass

Servings: 2 | Cooking Time: 1 Hour And 30 Minutes

Ingredients:
- 1 pound sea bass
- 2 scallion stalks, chopped
- 1 small ginger piece, grated
- 1 tablespoon soy sauce
- 2 cups coconut cream
- 4 bok choy stalks, chopped
- 3 jalapeno peppers, chopped
- Salt and black pepper to the taste

Directions:
1. Put the cream in your Crock Pot, add ginger, soy sauce, scallions, a pinch of salt, black pepper, jalapenos, stir, top with the fish and bok choy, cover and cook on High for 1 hour and 30 minutes.
2. Divide the fish mix between plates and serve.

Nutrition Info:
- calories 270, fat 3, fiber 3, carbs 18, protein 17

Buttery Trout

Servings: 4 | Cooking Time: 2 Hours

Ingredients:
- 4 trout fillets, boneless
- Salt and black pepper to the taste
- 3 teaspoons lemon zest, grated
- 3 tablespoons chives, chopped
- 6 tablespoons butter, melted
- 2 tablespoons olive oil
- 2 teaspoons lemon juice

Directions:
1. Put the butter in your Crock Pot, add trout fillets, season with salt, pepper, lemon zest, chives, oil and lemon juice, rub

fish a bit, cover and cook on High for 2 hours.
2. Divide fish between plates and serve with the butter sauce drizzled on top.

Nutrition Info:
- calories 320, fat 12, fiber 6, carbs 12, protein 24

Vinaigrette Dipped Salmon

Servings: 6 | Cooking Time: 2 Hrs.

Ingredients:
- 6 salmon steaks
- 2 tbsp olive oil
- 4 leeks, sliced
- 2 garlic cloves, minced
- 2 tbsp parsley, chopped
- 1 cup clam juice
- 2 tbsp lemon juice
- Salt and white pepper to the taste
- 1 tsp sherry
- 1/3 cup dill, chopped
- For the raspberry vinegar:
- 2 pints red raspberries
- 1-pint cider vinegar

Directions:
1. Mix raspberries with salmon, and vinegar in a bowl.
2. Cover the raspberry salmon and refrigerate for 2 hours.
3. Add the raspberry mixture along with the remaining ingredients to the insert of the Crock Pot.
4. Put the cooker's lid on and set the cooking time to 2 hours on High settings.
5. Serve warm.

Nutrition Info:
- Per Serving: Calories: 251, Total Fat: 6g, Fiber: 7g, Total Carbs: 16g, Protein: 26g

Cream White Fish

Servings: 6 | Cooking Time: 2 Hrs.

Ingredients:
- 17 oz. white fish, skinless, boneless and cut into chunks
- 1 yellow onion, chopped
- 13 oz. potatoes, peeled and cut into chunks
- 13 oz. milk
- Salt and black pepper to the taste
- 14 oz. chicken stock
- 14 oz. water
- 14 oz. half and half cream

Directions:
1. Add onion, fish, potatoes, water, stock, and milk to the insert of Crock Pot.
2. Put the cooker's lid on and set the cooking time to 2 hours on High settings.
3. Add half and half cream, black pepper, and salt to the fish.
4. Mix gently, then serve warm.

Nutrition Info:
- Per Serving: Calories: 203, Total Fat: 4g, Fiber: 5g, Total Carbs: 20g, Protein: 15g

Fish Soufflé

Servings: 4 | Cooking Time: 4 Hours

Ingredients:
- 3 oz white sandwich bread, chopped
- 1 cup cream
- ¼ cup Mozzarella, shredded
- 8 oz salmon, chopped
- 1 teaspoon ground black pepper
- ½ cup of water

Directions:
1. Pour water and cream in the Crock Pot,
2. Then add salmon and bread.
3. Top the mixture with Mozzarella and ground black pepper.
4. Close the lid and cook the soufflé for 4 hours on Low.

Nutrition Info:
- Per Serving: 181 calories, 13.9g protein, 13.1g carbohydrates, 8.3g fat, 0.4g fiber, 37mg cholesterol, 164mg sodium, 247mg potassium.

Mussels And Vegetable Ragout

Servings: 4 | Cooking Time: 5 Hours

Ingredients:
- 1 cup potato, chopped
- ½ onion, chopped
- 2 cups of water
- 1 bell pepper, chopped
- 1 teaspoon peppercorns
- 1 cup tomatoes, chopped
- 1 cup mussels
- 1 teaspoon salt

Directions:
1. Put all ingredients except mussels in the Crock Pot.
2. Close the lid and cook the meal on High for 3 hours.
3. Then add mussels and mix the meal.
4. Close the lid and cook the ragout on Low for 2 hours.

Nutrition Info:
- Per Serving: 71 calories, 5.8g protein, 10.3g carbohydrates, 1.1g fat, 1.8g fiber, 11mg cholesterol, 697mg sodium, 390mg potassium

Chinese Cod

Servings: 4 | Cooking Time: 2 Hours

Ingredients:
- 1 pound cod, cut into medium pieces
- Salt and black pepper to the taste
- 2 green onions, chopped
- 3 garlic cloves, minced
- 3 tablespoons soy sauce
- 1 cup fish stock
- 1 tablespoons balsamic vinegar
- 1 tablespoon ginger, grated
- ½ teaspoon chili pepper, crushed

Directions:
1. In your Crock Pot, mix fish with salt, pepper green onions, garlic, soy sauce, fish stock, vinegar, ginger and chili pepper, toss, cover and cook on High for 2 hours.

2. Divide everything between plates and serve.

Nutrition Info:
- calories 204, fat 3, fiber 6, carbs 14, protein 24

Lamb Bacon Stew

Servings: 6 | Cooking Time: 7 Hrs And 10 Minutes

Ingredients:
- 2 tbsp flour
- 2 oz. bacon, cooked and crumbled
- 1 and ½ lbs. lamb loin, chopped
- Salt and black pepper to the taste
- 1 garlic clove, minced
- 1 cup yellow onion, chopped
- 3 and ½ cups veggie stock
- 1 cup carrots, chopped
- 1 cup celery, chopped
- 2 cups sweet potatoes, chopped
- 1 tbsp thyme, chopped
- 1 bay leaf
- 2 tbsp olive oil

Directions:
1. Thoroughly mix lamb meat with salt, black pepper, and flour in a bowl.
2. Take oil in a non-stick skillet and heat over medium-high heat.
3. Stir in lamb meat and sauté for 5 minutes.
4. Transfer the sauteed meat to the Crock Pot along with the rest of the ingredients to the cooker.
5. Put the cooker's lid on and set the cooking time to 7 hours on Low settings.
6. Discard the bay leaf and serve warm.

Nutrition Info:
- Per Serving: Calories 360, Total Fat 5g, Fiber 3g, Total Carbs 16g, Protein 17g

Salmon And Berries

Servings: 2 | Cooking Time: 3 Hours

Ingredients:
- 1 pound salmon fillets, boneless and roughly cubed
- ½ cup blackberries
- Juice of 1 lime
- 1 tablespoon avocado oil
- 2 scallions, chopped
- ½ teaspoon Italian seasoning
- ½ cup fish stock
- A pinch of salt and black pepper

Directions:
1. In your Crock Pot, mix the salmon with the berries, lime juice and the other ingredients, toss, put the lid on and cook on Low for 3 hours.
2. Divide the mix between plates and serve.

Nutrition Info:
- calories 211, fat 13, fiber 2, carbs 7, protein 11

Vegetable & Vegetarian Recipes

Vegetable & Vegetarian Recipes

Crockpot Mediterranean Eggplant Salad

Servings:2 | Cooking Time: 4 Hours

Ingredients:
- 1 red onion, sliced
- 2 bell peppers, sliced
- 3 extra virgin olive oil
- 1 eggplant, quartered
- 1 cup tomatoes, crushed
- 1 tablespoon smoked paprika
- 2 teaspoons cumin
- Juice from 1 lemon, freshly squeezed
- Salt and pepper to taste

Directions:
1. Place all ingredients in the CrockPot.
2. Give a good stir.
3. Close the lid and cook on high for 3 hours or on low for 4 hours.

Nutrition Info:
- Calories per serving: 312; Carbohydrates: 30.2g; Protein: 5.6g; Fat: 22g; Sugar: 0.4g; Sodium: 519mg; Fiber: 27.1g

Bulgur Sauté

Servings:4 | Cooking Time: 4 Hours

Ingredients:
- 1 cup bell pepper, chopped
- 1 white onion, diced
- 2 tablespoons tomato paste
- 1 cup bulgur
- 3 cups vegetable stock
- 1 tablespoon olive oil
- 1 teaspoon salt
- 1 teaspoon chili flakes

Directions:
1. Put all ingredients in the Crock Pot and close the lid.
2. Cook the meal on low doe 4 hours or until the bulgur is tender.

Nutrition Info:
- Per Serving: 181 calories, 5.6g protein, 33.8g carbohydrates, 4.2g fat, 8g fiber, 0mg cholesterol, 747mg sodium, 322mg potassium.

Spinach With Halloumi Cheese Casserole

Servings:4 | Cooking Time: 2 Hours

Ingredients:
- 1 package spinach, rinsed
- ½ cup walnuts, chopped
- Salt and pepper to taste
- 1 tablespoon balsamic vinegar
- 1 ½ cups halloumi cheese, grated

Directions:
1. Place spinach and walnuts in the crockpot.
2. Season with salt and pepper. Drizzle with balsamic vinegar.
3. Top with halloumi cheese and cook on low for 2 hours or on high for 30 minutes

Nutrition Info:
- Calories per serving: 560; Carbohydrates: 7g; Protein:21 g; Fat: 47g; Sugar:2.1 g; Sodium: 231mg; Fiber:3 g

Broccoli And Cheese Casserole

Servings:4 | Cooking Time: 4 Hours

Ingredients:
- ¾ cup almond flour
- 1 head of broccoli, cut into florets
- 2 large eggs, beaten
- Salt and pepper to taste
- ½ cup mozzarella cheese

Directions:
1. Place the almond flour and broccoli in the crockpot.
2. Stir in the eggs and season with salt and pepper to taste.
3. Sprinkle with mozzarella cheese.
4. Close the lid and cook on low for 4 hours or on high for 2 hours.

Nutrition Info:
- Calories per serving: 78; Carbohydrates: 4g; Protein: 8.2g; Fat:5.8 g; Sugar: 0g; Sodium: 231mg; Fiber:2.3 g

Zucchini Mash

Servings:2 | Cooking Time: 45 Minutes

Ingredients:
- 2 cups zucchini, grated
- 1 tablespoon olive oil
- ¼ cup of water
- ½ teaspoon ground black pepper
- 2 tablespoons sour cream

Directions:
1. Put all ingredients in the Crock Pot and gently stir.
2. Cook the zucchini mash on High for 45 minutes.

Nutrition Info:
- Per Serving: 105 calories, 1.8g protein, 4.6g carbohydrates, 9.7g fat, 1.4g fiber, 5mg cholesterol, 19mg sodium, 320mg potassium.

Corn Pudding

Servings:4 | Cooking Time: 5 Hours

Ingredients:
- 3 cups corn kernels
- 2 cups heavy cream
- 3 tablespoons muffin mix
- 1 oz Parmesan, grated

Directions:
1. Mix heavy cream with muffin mix and pour the liquid in the Crock Pot.
2. Add corn kernels and Parmesan. Stir the mixture well.
3. Close the lid and cook the pudding on Low for 5 hours.

Nutrition Info:
- Per Serving: 371 calories, 21.8g protein, 31.4g carbohydrates, 26.3g fat, 3.2g fiber, 87mg cholesterol, 180mg sodium, 378mg potassium.

Teriyaki Kale

Servings:6 | Cooking Time: 30 Minutes

Ingredients:
- 5 cups kale, roughly chopped
- 1/2 cup teriyaki sauce
- 1 teaspoon sesame seeds
- 1 cup of water
- 1 teaspoon garlic powder
- 2 tablespoons coconut oil

Directions:
1. Melt the coconut oil and mix it with garlic powder, water, sesame seeds, and teriyaki sauce.
2. Pour the liquid in the Crock Pot.
3. Add kale and close the lid.
4. Cook the kale on High for 30 minutes.
5. Serve the kale with a small amount of teriyaki liquid.

Nutrition Info:
- Per Serving: 92 calories, 3.3g protein, 10g carbohydrates, 4.8g fat, 1g fiber, 0mg cholesterol, 945mg sodium, 336mg potassium.

Broccoli Egg Pie

Servings: 7 | Cooking Time: 4 Hrs 25 Minutes

Ingredients:
- 7 oz. pie crust
- ¼ cup broccoli, chopped
- 1/3 cup sweet peas
- ¼ cup heavy cream
- 2 tbsp flour
- 3 eggs
- 4 oz. Romano cheese, shredded
- 1 tsp cilantro
- 1 tsp salt
- ¼ cup spinach, chopped
- 1 tomato, chopped

Directions:
1. Cover the base of your Crock Pot with a parchment sheet.
2. Spread the pie crust in the cooker and press it with your fingertips.
3. Mix chopped broccoli, sweet peas, flour, cream, salt, and cilantro in a bowl.
4. Beat eggs and add them to the cream mixture.
5. Stir in tomatoes and spinach to this mixture.
6. Spread this broccoli filling in the crust evenly
7. Put the cooker's lid on and set the cooking time to 4 hours on High settings.
8. Drizzle cheese over the quiche and cover it again.
9. Put the cooker's lid on and set the cooking time to 25 minutes on High settings.
10. Serve warm.

Nutrition Info:
- Per Serving: Calories 287, Total Fat 18.8g, Fiber 1g, Total Carbs 17.1g, Protein 11g

Quinoa Black Bean Chili

Servings: 4 | Cooking Time: 3 Hrs

Ingredients:
- 15 oz. canned black beans, drained
- 2 and ¼ cups veggie stock
- ½ cup quinoa
- 14 oz. canned tomatoes, chopped
- ¼ cup red bell pepper, chopped
- 1 carrot, sliced
- ¼ cup green bell pepper, chopped
- 2 garlic cloves, minced
- ½ chili pepper, chopped
- ½ cup of corn
- 2 tsp chili powder
- 1 small yellow onion, chopped
- Salt and black pepper to the taste
- 1 tsp oregano, dried
- 1 tsp cumin, ground

Directions:
1. Add black beans and other ingredients to the Crock Pot.
2. Put the cooker's lid on and set the cooking time to 3 hours on High settings.
3. Serve warm.

Nutrition Info:
- Per Serving: Calories 291, Total Fat 7g, Fiber 4g, Total Carbs 28g, Protein 8g

Zucchini Basil Soup

Servings:8 | Cooking Time: 3 Hours

Ingredients:
- 9 cups zucchini, diced
- 2 cups white onions, chopped
- 4 cups vegetable broth
- 8 cloves of garlic, minced
- 1 cup basil leaves
- 4 tablespoons olive oil
- Salt and pepper to taste

Directions:
1. Place the ingredients in the CrockPot.
2. Give a good stir.
3. Close the lid and cook on high for 2 hours or on low for 3 hours.
4. Once cooked, transfer into a blender and pulse until smooth.

Nutrition Info:
- Calories per serving: 93; Carbohydrates: 5.4g; Protein: 1.3g; Fat: 11.6g; Sugar: 0g; Sodium: 322mg; Fiber: 4.2g

Pumpkin Bean Chili

Servings: 6 | Cooking Time: 5 Hrs

Ingredients:
- 1 cup pumpkin puree
- 30 oz. canned kidney beans, drained
- 30 oz. canned roasted tomatoes, chopped
- 2 cups of water
- 1 cup red lentils, dried
- 1 cup yellow onion, chopped

- 1 jalapeno pepper, chopped
- 1 tbsp chili powder
- 1 tbsp cocoa powder
- ½ tsp cinnamon powder
- 2 tsp cumin, ground
- A pinch of cloves, ground
- Salt and black pepper to the taste
- 2 tomatoes, chopped

Directions:

1. Add pumpkin puree along with other ingredients except for tomatoes, to the Crock Pot.
2. Put the cooker's lid on and set the cooking time to 5 hours on High settings.
3. Serve with tomatoes on top.
4. Enjoy.

Nutrition Info:

- Per Serving: Calories 266, Total Fat 6g, Fiber 4g, Total Carbs 12g, Protein 4g

Walnut Kale

Servings:4 | Cooking Time: 5 Hours

Ingredients:

- 5 cups kale, chopped
- 2 oz walnuts, chopped
- 1 cup of coconut milk
- 1 teaspoon vegan butter
- 1 cup of water
- 1 oz vegan Parmesan, grated

Directions:

1. Put all ingredients in the Crock Pot and gently stir.
2. Then close the lid and cook the kale on Low for 5 hours.

Nutrition Info:

- Per Serving: 298 calories, 9.6g protein, 13.7g carbohydrates, 25.1g fat, 3.5g fiber, 8mg cholesterol, 120mg sodium, 644mg potassium.

Sautéed Endives

Servings:4 | Cooking Time: 40 Minutes

Ingredients:

- 1-pound endives, roughly chopped
- ½ cup of water
- 1 tablespoon avocado oil
- 1 teaspoon garlic, diced
- 2 tablespoons coconut cream

Directions:

1. Pour water in the Crock Pot.
2. Add endives and garlic.
3. Close the lid and cook them on High for 30 minutes.
4. Then add coconut cream and avocado oil.
5. Cook the endives for 10 minutes more.

Nutrition Info:

- Per Serving: 42 calories, 1.9g protein, 4.4g carbohydrates, 2.4g fat, 3.7g fiber, 6mg cholesterol, 41mg sodium, 376mg potassium.

Hot Tofu

Servings:4 | Cooking Time: 4 Hours

Ingredients:

- 1-pound firm tofu, cubed
- 1 tablespoon hot sauce
- ½ cup vegetable stock
- 1 teaspoon miso paste

Directions:

1. Mix vegetables tock with miso paste and pour in the Crock Pot.
2. Add hot sauce and tofu.
3. Close the lid and cook the meal on Low for 4 hours.
4. Then transfer the tofu and liquid in the serving bowls.

Nutrition Info:

- Per Serving: 83 calories, 9.5g protein, 2.5g carbohydrates, 4.8g fat, 1.2g fiber, 0mg cholesterol, 168mg sodium, 176mg potassium.

Pinto Beans Balls

Servings:4 | Cooking Time: 3 Hours

Ingredients:

- ½ cup pinto beans, cooked
- 1 egg, beaten
- 1 teaspoon garam masala
- 1 onion, diced, roasted
- 2 tablespoons flour
- 1 teaspoon tomato paste
- 1 tablespoon coconut oil

Directions:

1. Mash the pinto beans with the help of the potato masher.
2. Then mix them with egg, garam masala, roasted onion, flour, and tomato paste.
3. Make the small balls from the mixture and put them in the Crock Pot.
4. Add coconut oil.
5. Cook the pinto beans balls for 3 hours on Low.

Nutrition Info:

- Per Serving: 155 calories, 7.3g protein, 21g carbohydrates, 4.9g fat, 4.5g fiber, 41mg cholesterol, 22mg sodium, 409mg potassium.

Garlic Butter

Servings:8 | Cooking Time: 20 Minutes

Ingredients:

- 1 cup vegan butter
- 1 tablespoon garlic powder
- ¼ cup fresh dill, chopped

Directions:

1. Put all ingredients in the Crock Pot and cook on High for 20 minutes.
2. Then pour the liquid in the ice cubes molds and refrigerate for 30 minutes or until butter is solid.

Nutrition Info:

- Per Serving: 211 calories, 0.7g protein, 1.6g carbohydrates, 23.1g fat, 0.3g fiber, 61mg cholesterol, 167mg sodium, 68mg potassium.

Turmeric Parsnip

Servings:2 | Cooking Time: 7 Hours

Ingredients:
- 10 oz parsnip, chopped
- 1 teaspoon ground turmeric
- 1 teaspoon chili flakes
- ½ teaspoon onion powder
- ½ teaspoon salt
- 1 cup of water
- 1 teaspoon vegan butter

Directions:
1. Put parsnip in the Crock Pot,
2. Add chili flakes and ground turmeric.
3. Then add onion powder, salt, water, and butter.
4. Close the lid and cook the meal on Low for 7 hours.

Nutrition Info:
- Per Serving: 129 calories, 1.9g protein, 26.7g carbohydrates, 2.5g fat, 7.2g fiber, 5mg cholesterol, 614mg sodium, 569mg potassium.

Tender Stuffing

Servings:4 | Cooking Time: 4 Hours

Ingredients:
- 8 oz celery stalks, chopped
- ¼ cup breadcrumbs
- 1 white onion, diced
- 1 teaspoon dried sage
- 2 tablespoons coconut oil
- ½ cup tomatoes, chopped
- 1 cup of coconut milk

Directions:
1. Put all ingredients in the Crock Pot and gently mix.
2. Then close the lid and cook the stuffing on Low for 4 hours.

Nutrition Info:
- Per Serving: 248 calories, 3.2g protein, 13.4g carbohydrates, 21.7g fat, 3.5g fiber, 0mg cholesterol, 106mg sodium, 414mg potassium.

Creamy Puree

Servings:4 | Cooking Time: 4 Hours

Ingredients:
- 2 cups potatoes, chopped
- 3 cups of water
- 1 tablespoon vegan butter
- ¼ cup cream
- 1 teaspoon salt

Directions:
1. Pour water in the Crock Pot.
2. Add potatoes and salt.
3. Cook the vegetables on high for 4 hours.
4. Then drain water, add butter, and cream.
5. Mash the potatoes until smooth.

Nutrition Info:
- Per Serving: 87 calories, 1.4g protein, 12.3g carbohydrates, 3.8g fat, 1.8g fiber, 10mg cholesterol, 617mg sodium, 314mg potassium

Curried Vegetable Stew

Servings:10 | Cooking Time: 3 Hours

Ingredients:
- 1 teaspoon olive oil
- 1 onion, diced
- 2 tablespoon curry powder
- 1 tablespoon grated ginger
- 3 cloves of garlic, minced
- 1/8 teaspoon cayenne pepper
- 1 cup tomatoes, crushed
- 1 bag baby spinach
- 1 yellow bell pepper, chopped
- 1 red bell pepper, chopped
- 2 cups vegetable broth
- 1 cup coconut milk
- Salt and pepper to taste

Directions:
1. Place all ingredients in the CrockPot.
2. Give a good stir.
3. Close the lid and cook on high for 2 hours or on low for 3 hours.

Nutrition Info:
- Calories per serving: 88; Carbohydrates: 5.1g; Protein: 2.9g; Fat: 9.3g; Sugar: 0g; Sodium: 318mg; Fiber: 3.9g

Curry Couscous

Servings:4 | Cooking Time: 20 Minutes

Ingredients:
- 1 cup of water
- 1 cup couscous
- ½ cup coconut cream
- 1 teaspoon salt

Directions:
1. Put all ingredients in the Crock Pot and close the lid.
2. Cook the couscous on High for 20 minutes.

Nutrition Info:
- Per Serving: 182 calories, 5.8g protein, 34.4g carbohydrates, 2g fat, 2.2g fiber, 6mg cholesterol, 597mg sodium, 84mg potassium.

Creamy Keto Mash

Servings:3 | Cooking Time: 4 Hours

Ingredients:
- 1 cauliflower head, cut into florets
- 1 white onion, chopped
- 2 cloves of garlic, minced
- ¼ cup vegetable stock
- ¼ cup butter
- Salt and pepper to taste
- ½ cup cream cheese

Directions:
1. Place the all ingredients except for the cream cheese in the CrockPot.
2. Close the lid and cook on high for 3 hours or on low for 4 hours.
3. Place in the food processor and pour in the cream cheese.

Pulse until slightly fine.
4. Garnish with chopped parsley if desired.

Nutrition Info:
• Calories per serving: 302; Carbohydrates: 7g; Protein: 3.7g; Fat: 28g; Sugar: 0g; Sodium: 771mg; Fiber: 3.8g

Corn Fritters

Servings:4 | Cooking Time: 3 Hours

Ingredients:
• 1 cup mashed potato
• 1/3 cup corn kernels, cooked
• 1 egg, beaten
• 2 tablespoons flour
• 1 teaspoon salt
• 1 teaspoon ground turmeric
• ½ teaspoon chili powder
• 2 tablespoons coconut oil

Directions:
1. Put the coconut oil in the Crock Pot and melt it on low for 15 minutes.
2. Meanwhile, mix mashed potato with corn kernels, egg, flour, salt, ground turmeric, and chili powder.
3. Make the medium size fritters and put them in the Crock Pot.
4. Cook them on Low for 3 hours.

Nutrition Info:
• Per Serving: 162 calories, 3.3g protein, 14.9g carbohydrates, 10.4g fat, 1.5g fiber, 41mg cholesterol, 777mg sodium, 246mg potassium.

Baked Onions

Servings:4 | Cooking Time: 2 Hours

Ingredients:
• 4 onions, peeled
• 1 tablespoon coconut oil
• 1 teaspoon salt
• 1 teaspoon brown sugar
• 1 cup coconut cream

Directions:
1. Put coconut oil in the Crock Pot.
2. Then make the small cuts in the onions with the help of the knife and put in the Crock Pot in one layer.
3. Sprinkle the vegetables with salt, and brown sugar.
4. Add coconut cream and close the lid.
5. Cook the onions on High for 2 hours.

Nutrition Info:
• Per Serving: 214 calories, 2.6g protein, 14.3g carbohydrates, 17.8g fat, 3.7g fiber, 0mg cholesterol, 595mg sodium, 320mg potassium.

Tofu Kebabs

Servings:4 | Cooking Time: 2 Hours

Ingredients:
• 2 tablespoons lemon juice
• 1 teaspoon ground turmeric
• 2 tablespoons coconut cream
• 1 teaspoon chili powder
• ¼ cup of water
• 1 teaspoon avocado oil
• 1-pound tofu, cubed

Directions:
1. Pour water in the Crock Pot.
2. After this, in the mixing bowl mix lemon juice, ground turmeric, coconut cream, chili powder, and avocado oil.
3. Coat every tofu cube in the coconut cream mixture and string on the wooden skewers. Place them in the Crock Pot.
4. Cook the tofu kebabs on Low for 2 hours.

Nutrition Info:
• Per Serving: 104 calories, 9.7g protein, 3.3g carbohydrates, 6.9g fat, 1.6g fiber, 0mg cholesterol, 24mg sodium, 227mg potassium.

Cheddar Mushrooms

Servings:4 | Cooking Time: 6 Hours

Ingredients:
• 4 cups cremini mushrooms, sliced
• 1 teaspoon dried oregano
• 1 teaspoon ground black pepper
• ½ teaspoon salt
• 1 cup Cheddar cheese, shredded
• 1 cup heavy cream
• 1 cup of water

Directions:
1. Pour water and heavy cream in the Crock Pot.
2. Add salt, ground black pepper, and dried oregano.
3. Then add sliced mushrooms, and Cheddar cheese.
4. Cook the meal on Low for 6 hours.
5. When the mushrooms are cooked, gently stir them and transfer in the serving plates.

Nutrition Info:
• Per Serving: 239 calories, 9.6g protein, 4.8g carbohydrates, 20.6g fat, 0.7g fiber, 71mg cholesterol, 484mg sodium, 386mg potassium.

Tofu And Cauliflower Bowl

Servings:3 | Cooking Time: 2.15 Hours

Ingredients:
• 5 oz firm tofu, chopped
• 1 teaspoon curry paste
• ¼ cup of coconut milk
• 1 teaspoon dried basil
• 1 tablespoon sunflower oil
• 2 cups cauliflower, chopped
• 1 cup of water

Directions:
1. Put cauliflower in the Crock Pot.

2. Add water and cook it on High for 2 hours.
3. Meanwhile, mix curry paste with coconut milk, dried basil, and sunflower oil.
4. Then add tofu and carefully mix the mixture. Leave it for 30 minutes.
5. When the cauliflower is cooked, drain water.
6. Add tofu mixture and shake the meal well. Cook it on High for 15 minutes.

Nutrition Info:
• Per Serving: 148 calories, 5.7g protein, 5.9g carbohydrates, 12.5g fat, 2.5g fiber, 0mg cholesterol, 31mg sodium, 326mg potassium.

Butter Asparagus

Servings:4 | Cooking Time: 5 Hours

Ingredients:
• 1-pound asparagus
• 2 tablespoons vegan butter
• 1 teaspoon ground black pepper
• 1 cup vegetable stock

Directions:
1. Pour the vegetable stock in the Crock Pot.
2. Chop the asparagus roughly and add in the Crock Pot.
3. Close the lid and cook the asparagus for 5 hours on Low.
4. Then drain water and transfer the asparagus in the bowl.
5. Sprinkle it with ground black pepper and butter.

Nutrition Info:
• Per Serving: 77 calories, 2.8g protein, 4.9g carbohydrates, 6.1g fat, 2.5g fiber, 15mg cholesterol, 234mg sodium, 241mg potassium.

Aromatic Marinated Mushrooms

Servings:4 | Cooking Time: 5 Hours

Ingredients:
• 1 teaspoon dried rosemary
• 1 teaspoon dried thyme
• 1 teaspoon onion powder
• 2 cups of water
• 4 cups mushrooms, roughly chopped
• 1 teaspoon salt
• 1 teaspoon sugar
• ½ cup apple cider vinegar

Directions:
1. Pour water in the Crock Pot.
2. Add all remaining ingredients and carefully mix.
3. Cook the mushrooms on Low for 5 hours.
4. After this, transfer the mushrooms with liquid in the glass cans and cool well.
5. Store the mushrooms in the fridge for up to 4 days.

Nutrition Info:
• Per Serving: 29 calories, 2.3g protein, 4.4g carbohydrates, 0.3g fat, 1g fiber, 0mg cholesterol, 591mg sodium, 256mg potassium.

Onion Chives Muffins

Servings: 7 | Cooking Time: 8 Hrs

Ingredients:
• 1 egg
• 5 tbsp butter, melted
• 1 cup flour
• ½ cup milk
• 1 tsp baking soda
• 1 cup onion, chopped
• 1 tsp cilantro
• ½ tsp sage
• 1 tsp apple cider vinegar
• 1 tbsp chives
• 1 tsp olive oil

Directions:
1. Whisk egg with melted butter, onion, milk, and all other ingredients to make a smooth dough.
2. Grease a muffin tray with olive oil and divide the batter into its cups.
3. Pour 2 cups water into the Crock Pot and set the muffin tray in it.
4. Put the cooker's lid on and set the cooking time to 8 hours on Low settings.
5. Serve.

Nutrition Info:
• Per Serving: Calories 180, Total Fat 11g, Fiber 1g, Total Carbs 16.28g, Protein 4g

Sauteed Spinach

Servings:3 | Cooking Time: 1 Hour

Ingredients:
• 3 cups spinach
• 1 tablespoon vegan butter, softened
• 2 cups of water
• 2 oz Parmesan, grated
• 1 teaspoon pine nuts, crushed

Directions:
1. Chop the spinach and put it in the Crock Pot.
2. Add water and close the lid.
3. Cook the spinach on High for 1 hour.
4. Then drain water and put the cooked spinach in the bowl.
5. Add pine nuts, Parmesan, and butter.
6. Carefully mix the spinach.

Nutrition Info:
• Per Serving: 108 calories, 7.1g protein, 1.9g carbohydrates, 8.7g fat, 0.7g fiber, 24mg cholesterol, 231mg sodium, 176mg potassium.

Green Peas Risotto

Servings: 6 | Cooking Time: 3 Hrs 30 Minutes

Ingredients:
- 7 oz. Parmigiano-Reggiano
- 2 cup chicken broth
- 1 tsp olive oil
- 1 onion, chopped
- ½ cup green peas
- 1 garlic clove, peeled and sliced
- 2 cups long-grain rice
- ¼ cup dry wine
- 1 tsp salt
- 1 tsp ground black pepper
- 1 carrot, chopped
- 1 cup beef broth

Directions:
1. Layer a nonstick skillet with olive oil and place it over medium heat.
2. Stir in carrot and onion, then sauté for 3 minutes.
3. Transfer these veggies to the Crock Pot.
4. Add rice to the remaining oil to the skillet.
5. Stir cook for 1 minute then transfers the rice to the cooker.
6. Add garlic, dry wine, green peas, black pepper, beef broth, and chicken broth.
7. Put the cooker's lid on and set the cooking time to 3 hours on Low settings.
8. Add Parmigiano-Reggiano to the risotto.
9. Put the cooker's lid on and set the cooking time to 30 minutes on Low settings.
10. Serve warm.

Nutrition Info:
- Per Serving: Calories 268, Total Fat 3g, Fiber 4g, Total Carbs 53.34g, Protein 7g

Sautéed Greens

Servings:4 | Cooking Time: 1 Hour

Ingredients:
- 1 cup spinach, chopped
- 2 cups collard greens, chopped
- 1 cup Swiss chard, chopped
- 2 cups of water
- ½ cup half and half

Directions:
1. Put spinach, collard greens, and Swiss chard in the Crock Pot.
2. Add water and close the lid.
3. Cook the greens on High for 1 hour.
4. Then drain water and transfer the greens in the bowl.
5. Bring the half and half to boil and pour over greens.
6. Carefully mix the greens.

Nutrition Info:
- Per Serving: 49 calories, 1.8g protein, 3.2g carbohydrates, 3.7g fat, 1.1g fiber, 11mg cholesterol, 45mg sodium, 117mg potassium.

Rainbow Carrots

Servings:4 | Cooking Time: 3.5 Hours

Ingredients:
- 2-pound rainbow carrots, sliced
- 1 cup vegetable stock
- 1 cup bell pepper, chopped
- 1 onion, sliced
- 1 teaspoon salt
- 1 teaspoon chili powder

Directions:
1. Put all ingredients in the Crock Pot.
2. Close the lid and cook the meal on High for 3.5 hours.
3. Then cool the cooked carrots for 5-10 minutes and transfer in the serving bowls.

Nutrition Info:
- Per Serving: 118 calories, 3.5g protein, 26.7g carbohydrates, 0.4g fat, 6.6g fiber, 0mg cholesterol, 954mg sodium, 112mg potassium.

Curry Paneer

Servings:2 | Cooking Time: 2 Hours

Ingredients:
- 6 oz paneer, cubed
- 1 teaspoon garam masala
- ½ cup coconut cream
- 1 chili pepper, chopped
- 1 teaspoon olive oil
- ½ onion, diced
- 1 teaspoon garlic paste

Directions:
1. In the mixing bowl mix diced onion, garlic paste, olive oil, chili pepper, coconut cream, and garam masala.
2. Then mix the mixture with cubed paneer and put in the Crock Pot.
3. Cook it on Low for 2 hours.

Nutrition Info:
- Per Serving: 309 calories, 7.1g protein, 22.5g carbohydrates, 22.4g fat, 3.5g fiber, 2mg cholesterol, 415mg sodium, 208mg potassium.

Garlic Sweet Potato

Servings:4 | Cooking Time: 6 Hours

Ingredients:
- 2-pounds sweet potatoes, chopped
- 1 teaspoon minced garlic
- 2 tablespoons vegan butter
- 1 teaspoon salt
- 3 cups of water

Directions:
1. Pour water in the Crock Pot. Add sweet potatoes.
2. Then add salt and close the lid.
3. Cook the sweet potato on Low for 6 hours.
4. After this, drain the water and transfer the vegetables in the big bowl.
5. Add minced garlic and butter. Carefully stir the sweet potatoes until butter is melted.

Nutrition Info:
- Per Serving: 320 calories, 3.6g protein, 63.5g carbohydrates, 6.2g fat, 9.3g fiber, 15mg cholesterol, 648mg sodium, 1857mg potassium.

Parsnip Balls

Servings:4 | Cooking Time: 3 Hours

Ingredients:
- 8 oz parsnip, peeled, grated
- 1 tablespoon coconut cream
- 1/3 cup coconut flour
- 1 tablespoon coconut oil
- 1 carrot, boiled, peeled, mashed
- 1 teaspoon salt
- 1 teaspoon chili powder

Directions:
1. In the mixing bowl mix grated parsnip, coconut cream, coconut flour, mashed carrot, salt, and chili powder.
2. With the help of the scooper make the small balls and freeze them for 10-15 minutes.
3. Then put coconut oil in the Crock Pot.
4. Add frozen parsnip balls and cook them on Low for 3 hours.

Nutrition Info:
- Per Serving: 129 calories, 2.3g protein, 18.9g carbohydrates, 5.6g fat, 7.5g fiber, 0mg cholesterol, 605mg sodium, 284mg potassium.

Quinoa Avocado Salad

Servings: 6 | Cooking Time: 7 Hrs

Ingredients:
- ½ lemon, juiced
- 1 avocado, pitted, peeled and diced
- 1 red onion, diced
- 1 cup white quinoa
- 1 cup of water
- 1 tsp canola oil
- ½ cup fresh dill
- 1 cup green peas, frozen
- 1 tsp garlic powder

Directions:
1. Add quinoa, green peas and water to the Crock Pot.
2. Put the cooker's lid on and set the cooking time to 7 hours on Low settings.
3. Transfer the cooked quinoa and peas to a salad bowl.
4. Stir in the remaining ingredients for the salad and toss well.
5. Serve fresh.

Nutrition Info:
- Per Serving: Calories 195, Total Fat 7.7g, Fiber 6g, Total Carbs 26.77g, Protein 6g

Carrot And Lentils Sauté

Servings:4 | Cooking Time: 5 Hours

Ingredients:
- 1 cup red lentils
- 1 cup carrot, diced
- 1 cup fresh parsley, chopped
- 4 cups vegetable stock
- 1 teaspoon cayenne pepper
- 1 teaspoon salt
- 1 tablespoon tomato paste

Directions:
1. Put all ingredients in the Crock Pot and gently stir.
2. Close the lid and cook the meal on low for 5 hours.

Nutrition Info:
- Per Serving: 201 calories, 13.3g protein, 35.5g carbohydrates, 2.7g fat, 16.1g fiber, 0mg cholesterol, 1336mg sodium, 679mg potassium.

Collard Greens Saute

Servings:4 | Cooking Time: 5 Hours

Ingredients:
- 1 cup potato, chopped
- 8 oz collard greens, chopped
- 1 cup tomatoes, chopped
- 1 cup of water
- 2 tablespoons coconut oil
- 1 teaspoon dried thyme
- 1 teaspoon salt

Directions:
1. Put coconut oil in the Crock Pot.
2. Then mix chopped potato with dried thyme and salt.
3. Put the potato in the Crock Pot and flatten it in one layer.
4. Add tomatoes, collard greens.
5. After this, add water and close the lid.
6. Cook the saute on Low for 5 hours.

Nutrition Info:
- Per Serving: 97 calories, 2.1g protein, 8.3g carbohydrates, 7.3g fat, 2.9g fiber, 0mg cholesterol, 596mg sodium, 188mg potassium.

Eggplant Salad

Servings:5 | Cooking Time: 3 Hours

Ingredients:
- 4 eggplants, cubed
- 1 teaspoon salt
- 1 teaspoon ground black pepper
- 1 cup of water
- 1 tablespoon sesame oil
- 1 tablespoon apple cider vinegar
- 1 teaspoon sesame seeds
- 2 cups tomatoes, chopped

Directions:
1. Mix eggplants with salt and ground black pepper and leave for 10 minutes.
2. Then transfer the eggplants in the Crock Pot. Add water and cook them for 3 hours on High.

3. Drain water and cool the eggplants to the room temperature.
4. Add sesame oil, apple cider vinegar, sesame seeds, and tomatoes.
5. Gently shake the salad.

Nutrition Info:
- Per Serving: 152 calories, 5.1g protein, 29g carbohydrates, 4g fat, 16.5g fiber, 0mg cholesterol, 479mg sodium, 1185mg potassium.

Egg Cauliflower

Servings:2 | Cooking Time: 4 Hours

Ingredients:
- 2 cups cauliflower, shredded
- 4 eggs, beaten
- 1 tablespoon vegan butter
- ½ teaspoon salt

Directions:
1. Mix eggs with salt.
2. Put the shredded cauliflower in the Crock Pot.
3. Add eggs and vegan butter. Gently mix the mixture.
4. Close the lid and cook the meal on low for 4 hours. Stir the cauliflower with the help of the fork every 1 hour.

Nutrition Info:
- Per Serving: 176 calories, 13.5g protein, 9.9g carbohydrates, 9.7g fat, 2.6g fiber, 372mg cholesterol, 746mg sodium, 421mg potassium.

Warming Butternut Squash Soup

Servings: 9 | Cooking Time: 8 Hrs

Ingredients:
- 2 lb. butternut squash, peeled and cubed
- 4 tsp minced garlic
- ½ cup onion, chopped
- 1 tsp salt
- ¼ tsp ground nutmeg
- 1 tsp ground black pepper
- 8 cups chicken stock
- 1 tbsp fresh parsley

Directions:
1. Spread the butternut squash in your Crock Pot.
2. Add stock, garlic, and onion to the squash.
3. Put the cooker's lid on and set the cooking time to 8 hours on Low settings.
4. Add salt, black pepper, and nutmeg to the squash.
5. Puree the cooked squash mixture using an immersion blender until smooth.
6. Garnish with chopped parsley.
7. Enjoy.

Nutrition Info:
- Per Serving: Calories 129, Total Fat 2.7g, Fiber 2g, Total Carbs 20.85g, Protein 7g

Vegan Pepper Bowl

Servings:4 | Cooking Time: 3.5 Hours

Ingredients:
- 2 cups bell pepper, sliced
- 1 tablespoon olive oil
- 1 tablespoon apple cider vinegar
- 4 tablespoons water
- 5 oz tofu, chopped
- ½ cup of coconut milk
- 1 teaspoon curry powder

Directions:
1. Put the sliced bell peppers in the Crock Pot.
2. Sprinkle them with olive oil, apple cider vinegar, and water.
3. Close the lid and cook the vegetables on low for 3 hours.
4. Meanwhile, mix curry powder with coconut milk. Put the tofu in the curry mixture and leave for 15 minutes.
5. Add the tofu and all remaining curry mixture in the Crock Pot. Gently mix it and cook for 30 minutes on low.

Nutrition Info:
- Per Serving: 145 calories, 4.3g protein, 7.1g carbohydrates, 12.4g fat, 2g fiber, 0mg cholesterol, 11mg sodium, 254mg potassium.

Buffalo Cremini Mushrooms

Servings:4 | Cooking Time: 6 Hours

Ingredients:
- 3 cups cremini mushrooms, trimmed
- 2 oz buffalo sauce
- ½ cup of water
- 2 tablespoons coconut oil

Directions:
1. Pour water in the Crock Pot.
2. Melt the coconut oil in the skillet.
3. Add mushrooms and roast them for 3-4 minutes per side. Transfer the roasted mushrooms in the Crock Pot.
4. Cook them on Low for 4 hours.
5. Then add buffalo sauce and carefully mix.
6. Cook the mushrooms for 2 hours on low.

Nutrition Info:
- Per Serving: 79 calories, 1.4g protein, 3.2g carbohydrates, 6.9g fat, 0.8g fiber, 0mg cholesterol, 458mg sodium, 242mg potassium.

Saag Aloo

Servings:6 | Cooking Time: 6 Hours

Ingredients:
- 1 yellow onion, chopped
- 1 cup potatoes, chopped
- 3 garlic cloves, diced
- 1 chili pepper, chopped
- 1 teaspoon ground cumin
- 1 teaspoon garam masala
- 2 cups of water
- 1 cup tomatoes, chopped
- 1 cup spinach, chopped

Directions:

1. Put onion, potatoes, and chili pepper in the Crock Pot.
2. Add tomatoes and spinach.
3. After this, add sprinkle the ingredients with garam masala, ground cumin, and garlic.
4. Add water and close the lid.
5. Cook the meal on Low for 6 hours.

Nutrition Info:
• Per Serving: 35 calories, 1.2g protein, 7.g car7bohydrates, 0.2g fat, 1.6g fiber, 0mg cholesterol, 12mg sodium, 242mg potassium.

Sweet And Tender Squash

Servings:4 | Cooking Time: 8 Hours

Ingredients:
• 2-pound butternut squash, chopped
• 1 tablespoon ground cinnamon
• ½ teaspoon ground ginger
• 1 tablespoon sugar
• ½ cup of water

Directions:
1. Mix butternut squash with ground cinnamon, ground ginger, and sugar. Leave the vegetables for 10-15 minutes.
2. Then transfer them in the Crock Pot. Add remaining butternut squash juice and water.
3. Close the lid and cook the squash on Low for 8 hours.

Nutrition Info:
• Per Serving: 118 calories, 2.4g protein, 31g carbohydrates, 0.3g fat, 5.5g fiber, 0mg cholesterol, 10mg sodium, 809mg potassium.

Garam Masala Potato Bake

Servings:2 | Cooking Time: 6 Hours

Ingredients:
• 1 cup potatoes, chopped
• 1 teaspoon garam masala
• 3 eggs, beaten
• ½ cup vegan mozzarella, shredded
• 1 tablespoon vegan butter
• 2 tablespoons coconut cream

Directions:
1. Mix potatoes with garam masala.
2. Then put them in the Crock Pot.
3. Add vegan butter and mozzarella.
4. After this, mix coconut cream with eggs and pour the liquid over the mozzarella.
5. Close the lid and cook the meal on Low for 6 hours.

Nutrition Info:
• Per Serving: 199 calories, 12.1g protein, 16.8g carbohydrates, 9.4g fat, 1.9g fiber, 252mg cholesterol, 156mg sodium, 398mg potassium.

Coconut Milk Lentils Bowl

Servings:5 | Cooking Time: 9 Hours

Ingredients:
• 2 cups brown lentils
• 3 cups of coconut milk
• 3 cups of water
• 1 teaspoon ground nutmeg
• 1 teaspoon salt

Directions:
1. Mix the brown lentils with salt and ground nutmeg and put in the Crock Pot.
2. Add coconut milk and water.
3. Close the lid and cook the lentils on Low for 9 hours.

Nutrition Info:
• Per Serving: 364 calories, 5.3g protein, 12.1g carbohydrates, 34.7g fat, 4.9g fiber, 0mg cholesterol, 491mg sodium, 382mg potassium.

Quinoa Avocado Salad

Servings: 6 | Cooking Time: 7 Hrs

Ingredients:
• ½ lemon, juiced
• 1 avocado, pitted, peeled and diced
• 1 red onion, diced
• 1 cup white quinoa
• 1 cup of water
• 1 tsp canola oil
• ½ cup fresh dill
• 1 cup green peas, frozen
• 1 tsp garlic powder

Directions:
1. Add quinoa, green peas and water to the Crock Pot.
2. Put the cooker's lid on and set the cooking time to 7 hours on Low settings.
3. Transfer the cooked quinoa and peas to a salad bowl.
4. Stir in the remaining ingredients for the salad and toss well.
5. Serve fresh.

Nutrition Info:
• Per Serving: Calories 195, Total Fat 7.7g, Fiber 6g, Total Carbs 26.77g, Protein 6g

Side Dish Recipes

Side Dish Recipes

Lemony Honey Beets

Servings: 6 | Cooking Time: 8 Hrs

Ingredients:
- 6 beets, peeled and cut into medium wedges
- 2 tbsp honey
- 2 tbsp olive oil
- 2 tbsp lemon juice
- Salt and black pepper to the taste
- 1 tbsp white vinegar
- ½ tsp lemon peel, grated

Directions:
1. Add beets, honey, oil, salt, black pepper, lemon peel, vinegar, and lemon juice to the Crock Pot.
2. Put the cooker's lid on and set the cooking time to 8 hours on Low settings.
3. Serve warm.

Nutrition Info:
- Per Serving: Calories: 80, Total Fat: 3g, Fiber: 4g, Total Carbs: 8g, Protein: 4g

Nut Berry Salad

Servings: 4 | Cooking Time: 1 Hour

Ingredients:
- 2 cups strawberries, halved
- 2 tbsp mint, chopped
- 1/3 cup raspberry vinegar
- 2 tbsp honey
- 1 tbsp canola oil
- Salt and black pepper to the taste
- 4 cups spinach, torn
- ½ cup blueberries
- ¼ cup walnuts, chopped
- 1 oz. goat cheese, crumbled

Directions:
1. Toss strawberries with walnuts, spinach, honey, oil, salt, black pepper, blueberries, vinegar, and mint in the Crock Pot.
2. Put the cooker's lid on and set the cooking time to 1 hour on High settings.
3. Serve warm with cheese on top.

Nutrition Info:
- Per Serving: Calories: 200, Total Fat: 12g, Fiber: 4g, Total Carbs: 17g, Protein: 15g

Barley Mix

Servings: 2 | Cooking Time: 6 Hours

Ingredients:
- 1 red onion, sliced
- ½ teaspoon sweet paprika
- ½ teaspoon turmeric powder
- 1 cup barley
- 1 cup veggie stock
- A pinch of salt and black pepper
- 1 garlic clove, minced

Directions:
1. In your Crock Pot, mix the barley with the onion, paprika and the other ingredients, toss, put the lid on and cook on Low for 6 hours.
2. Divide between plates and serve as a side dish.

Nutrition Info:
- calories 160, fat 3, fiber 7, carbs 13, protein 7

Asparagus Mix

Servings: 4 | Cooking Time: 6 Hours

Ingredients:
- 10 ounces cream of celery
- 12 ounces asparagus, chopped
- 2 eggs, hard-boiled, peeled and sliced
- 1 cup cheddar cheese, shredded
- 1 teaspoon olive oil

Directions:
1. Grease your Crock Pot with the oil, add cream of celery and cheese to the Crock Pot and stir.
2. Add asparagus and eggs, cover and cook on Low for 6 hours.
3. Divide between plates and serve as a side dish.

Nutrition Info:
- calories 241, fat 5, fiber 4, carbs 5, protein 12

Cheddar Potatoes Mix

Servings: 2 | Cooking Time: 3 Hours

Ingredients:
- ½ pound gold potatoes, peeled and cut into wedges
- 2 ounces heavy cream
- ½ teaspoon turmeric powder
- ½ teaspoon rosemary, dried
- ¼ cup cheddar cheese, shredded
- 1 tablespoon butter, melted
- Cooking spray
- A pinch of salt and black pepper

Directions:
1. Grease your Crock Pot with the cooking spray, add the potatoes, cream, turmeric and the other ingredients, toss, put the lid on and cook on High for 3 hours.
2. Divide between plates and serve as a side dish.

Nutrition Info:
- calories 300, fat 14, fiber 6, carbs 22, protein 6

Butter Green Beans

Servings: 2 | Cooking Time: 2 Hours

Ingredients:
- 1 pound green beans, trimmed and halved
- 2 tablespoons butter, melted
- ½ cup veggie stock
- 1 teaspoon rosemary, dried
- 1 tablespoon chives, chopped
- Salt and black pepper to the taste
- ¼ teaspoon soy sauce

Directions:
1. In your Crock Pot, combine the green beans with the melted butter, stock and the other ingredients, toss, put the lid on and cook on Low for 2 hours.
2. Divide between plates and serve as a side dish.

Nutrition Info:
- calories 236, fat 6, fiber 8, carbs 10, protein 6

Thyme Beets

Servings: 8 | Cooking Time: 6 Hours

Ingredients:
- 12 small beets, peeled and sliced
- ¼ cup water
- 4 garlic cloves, minced
- 2 tablespoons olive oil
- 1 teaspoon thyme, dried
- Salt and black pepper to the taste
- 1 tablespoon fresh thyme, chopped

Directions:
1. In your Crock Pot, mix beets with water, garlic, oil, dried thyme, salt and pepper, cover and cook on Low for 6 hours.
2. Divide beets on plates, sprinkle fresh thyme all over and serve as a side dish.

Nutrition Info:
- 66, fat 4, fiber 1, carbs 8, protein 1

Turmeric Buckwheat

Servings: 6 | Cooking Time: 4 Hrs

Ingredients:
- 4 tbsp milk powder
- 2 tbsp butter
- 1 carrot
- 4 cup buckwheat
- 4 cups chicken stock
- 1 tbsp salt
- 1 tbsp turmeric
- 1 tsp paprika

Directions:
1. Whisk milk powder with buckwheat, stock, salt, turmeric, and paprika in the Crock Pot.
2. Stir in carrot strips and mix gently.
3. Put the cooker's lid on and set the cooking time to 4 hours on High settings.
4. Stir in butter then serve warm.

Nutrition Info:
- Per Serving: Calories: 238, Total Fat: 6.6g, Fiber: 4g, Total Carbs: 37.85g, Protein: 9g

Muffin Corn Pudding

Servings: 8 | Cooking Time: 8 Hrs.

Ingredients:
- 6 oz. muffin mix
- 12 oz. corn kernels
- 1 cup heavy cream
- 1 tsp salt
- 1 tsp ground black pepper
- 3 oz. Parmesan cheese
- 1 tbsp cilantro
- 1 tsp ground cumin

Directions:
1. Whisk muffin mix with cream, salt, ground cumin, black pepper, and cilantro in a suitable bowl.
2. Stir in corn kernel then mix until smooth.
3. Spread this muffin corn mixture in the insert of Crock Pot.
4. Put the cooker's lid on and set the cooking time to 8 hours on Low settings.
5. Top with parmesan cheese and slice.
6. Serve.

Nutrition Info:
- Per Serving: Calories: 180, Total Fat: 9.6g, Fiber: 2g, Total Carbs: 18.8g, Protein: 6g

Buttery Artichokes

Servings: 5 | Cooking Time: 6 Hrs.

Ingredients:
- 13 oz. artichoke heart halved
- 1 tsp salt
- 4 cups chicken stock
- 1 tsp turmeric
- 1 garlic clove, peeled
- 4 tbsp butter
- 4 oz. Parmesan, shredded

Directions:
1. Add artichoke, stock, salt, and turmeric to the Crock Pot.
2. Put the cooker's lid on and set the cooking time to 6 hours on Low settings.
3. Drain and transfer the cooked artichoke to the serving plates.
4. Drizzle, cheese, and butter over the artichoke.
5. Serve warm.

Nutrition Info:
- Per Serving: Calories: 272, Total Fat: 12.8g, Fiber: 4g, Total Carbs: 24.21g, Protein: 17g

White Beans Mix

Servings: 4 | Cooking Time: 6 Hours

Ingredients:
- 1 celery stalk, chopped
- 2 garlic cloves, minced
- 1 carrot, chopped
- 1 cup veggie stock
- ½ cup canned tomatoes, crushed
- ½ teaspoon chili powder
- ½ tablespoon Italian seasoning
- 15 ounces canned white beans, drained
- 1 tablespoon parsley, chopped

Directions:
1. In your Crock Pot, mix the beans with the celery, garlic and the other ingredients, toss, put the lid on and cook on Low for 6 hours.
2. Divide the mix between plates and serve.

Nutrition Info:
- calories 223, fat 3, fiber 7, carbs 10, protein 7

Honey Glazed Vegetables

Servings: 12 | Cooking Time: 6 Hrs.

Ingredients:
- 4 large carrots, peeled and chopped
- 3 red onions, chopped
- 1 lb. potato, peeled and diced
- 3 sweet potatoes, peeled and diced
- ½ cup brown sugar
- 1 tbsp salt
- 1 tsp coriander
- 1 tsp cilantro
- 2 tbsp dried dill
- 1 tbsp sesame oil
- 3 oz. honey

Directions:
1. Toss onions, carrots, potato, and sweet potatoes with the rest of the ingredients in a Crock Pot.
2. Put the cooker's lid on and set the cooking time to 6 hours on Low settings.
3. Serve warm.

Nutrition Info:
- Per Serving: Calories: 148, Total Fat: 1.4g, Fiber: 3g, Total Carbs: 33g, Protein: 2g

Zucchini Mix

Servings: 2 | Cooking Time: 6 Hours

Ingredients:
- 1 pound zucchinis, sliced
- ½ teaspoon Italian seasoning
- ½ teaspoon sweet paprika
- Salt and black pepper
- ½ cup heavy cream
- ½ teaspoon garlic powder
- 1 tablespoon olive oil

Directions:
1. In your Crock Pot, mix the zucchinis with the seasoning,

paprika and the other ingredients, toss, put the lid on and cook on Low for 6 hours.
2. Divide between plates and serve as a side dish.

Nutrition Info:
- calories 170, fat 2, fiber 4, carbs 8, protein 5

Curry Broccoli Mix

Servings: 2 | Cooking Time: 3 Hours

Ingredients:
- 1 pound broccoli florets
- 1 cup tomato paste
- 1 tablespoon red curry paste
- 1 red onion, sliced
- ½ teaspoon Italian seasoning
- 1 teaspoon thyme, dried
- Salt and black pepper to the taste
- ½ tablespoon cilantro, chopped

Directions:
1. In your Crock Pot, mix the broccoli with the curry paste, tomato paste and the other ingredients, toss, put the lid on and cook on Low for 3 hours.
2. Divide the mix between plates and serve as a side dish.

Nutrition Info:
- calories 177, fat 12, fiber 2, carbs 7, protein 7

Italian Black Beans Mix

Servings: 2 | Cooking Time: 5 Hours

Ingredients:
- 2 tablespoons tomato paste
- Cooking spray
- 2 cups black beans
- ¼ cup veggie stock
- 1 red onion, sliced
- Cooking spray
- 1 teaspoon Italian seasoning
- ½ celery rib, chopped
- ½ red bell pepper, chopped
- ½ sweet red pepper, chopped
- ¼ teaspoon mustard seeds
- Salt and black pepper to the taste
- 2 ounces canned corn, drained
- 1 tablespoon cilantro, chopped

Directions:
1. Grease the Crock Pot with the cooking spray, and mix the beans with the stock, onion and the other ingredients inside.
2. Put the lid on, cook on Low for 5 hours, divide between plates and serve as a side dish.

Nutrition Info:
- calories 255, fat 6, fiber 7, carbs 38, protein 7

Veggie Mix

Servings: 2 | Cooking Time: 5 Hours

Ingredients:
- 1 eggplant, cubed
- 1 cup cherry tomatoes, halved
- 1 small zucchini, halved and sliced
- ½ red bell pepper, chopped
- ½ cup tomato sauce
- 1 carrot, peeled and cubed
- 1 sweet potato, peeled and cubed
- A pinch of red pepper flakes, crushed
- 1 tablespoon basil, chopped
- 1 tablespoon parsley, chopped
- A pinch of salt and black pepper
- ½ cup veggie stock
- 1 tablespoon capers
- 1 tablespoon red wine vinegar

Directions:
1. In your Crock Pot, mix the eggplant with the tomatoes, zucchini and the other ingredients, toss, put the lid on and cook on Low for 5 hours.
2. Divide between plates and serve as a side dish.

Nutrition Info:
- calories 100, fat 1, fiber 2, carbs 7, protein 5

Green Beans Mix

Servings: 12 | Cooking Time: 2 Hours

Ingredients:
- 16 ounces green beans
- ½ cup brown sugar
- ½ cup butter, melted
- ¾ teaspoon soy sauce
- Salt and black pepper to the taste

Directions:
1. In your Crock Pot, mix green beans with sugar, butter, soy sauce, salt and pepper, stir, cover and cook on Low for 2 hours.
2. Divide between plates and serve as a side dish.

Nutrition Info:
- calories 176, fat 4, fiber 7, carbs 14, protein 4

Scalloped Potatoes

Servings: 6 | Cooking Time: 6 Hours

Ingredients:
- Cooking spray
- 2 and ½ pounds gold potatoes, sliced
- 10 ounces canned cream of potato soup
- 1 yellow onion, roughly chopped
- 8 ounces sour cream
- 1 cup Gouda cheese, shredded
- ½ cup blue cheese, crumbled
- ½ cup parmesan, grated
- ½ cup chicken stock
- Salt and black pepper to the taste
- 1 tablespoon chives, chopped

Directions:
1. Grease your Crock Pot with cooking spray and arrange potato slices on the bottom.
2. Add cream of potato soup, onion, sour cream, Gouda cheese, blue cheese, parmesan, stock, salt and pepper, cover and cook on Low for 6 hours.
3. Add chives, divide between plates and serve as a side dish.

Nutrition Info:
- calories 306, fat 14, fiber 4, carbs 33, protein 12

Italian Veggie Mix

Servings: 8 | Cooking Time: 6 Hours

Ingredients:
- 38 ounces canned cannellini beans, drained
- 1 yellow onion, chopped
- ¼ cup basil pesto
- 19 ounces canned fava beans, drained
- 4 garlic cloves, minced
- 1 and ½ teaspoon Italian seasoning, dried and crushed
- 1 tomato, chopped
- 15 ounces already cooked polenta, cut into medium pieces
- 2 cups spinach
- 1 cup radicchio, torn

Directions:
1. In your Crock Pot, mix cannellini beans with fava beans, basil pesto, onion, garlic, Italian seasoning, polenta, tomato, spinach and radicchio, toss, cover and cook on Low for 6 hours.
2. Divide between plates and serve as a side dish.

Nutrition Info:
- calories 364, fat 12, fiber 10, carbs 45, protein 21

Garlic Risotto

Servings: 2 | Cooking Time: 2 Hours

Ingredients:
- 1 small shallot, chopped
- 1 cup wild rice
- 1 cup chicken stock
- 1 tablespoons olive oil
- 2 garlic cloves, minced
- Salt and black pepper to the taste
- 2 tablespoons cilantro, chopped

Directions:
1. In your Crock Pot, mix the rice with the stock, shallot and the other ingredients, toss, put the lid on and cook on High for 2 hours
2. Divide between plates and serve as a side dish.

Nutrition Info:
- calories 204, fat 7, fiber 3, carbs 17, protein 7

Butter Glazed Yams

Servings: 7 | Cooking Time: 4 Hrs.

Ingredients:
- 2 lb. yams, peeled and diced
- 5 tbsp butter, melted
- 5 oz. brown sugar
- 4 oz. white sugar
- ½ tsp salt
- 1 tsp vanilla extract
- 2 tbsp cornstarch

Directions:
1. Add melted butter, brown sugar, yams, white sugar, salt, and vanilla extract to the Crock Pot.
2. Put the cooker's lid on and set the cooking time to 4 hours on High settings.
3. Toss well, then stir in cornstarch, continue cooking for 10 minutes on High.
4. Mix well and serve.

Nutrition Info:
- Per Serving: Calories: 404, Total Fat: 16.4g, Fiber: 6g, Total Carbs: 63.33g, Protein: 3g

Zucchini Onion Pate

Servings: 6 | Cooking Time: 6 Hours

Ingredients:
- 3 medium zucchinis, peeled and chopped
- 2 red onions, grated
- 6 tbsp tomato paste
- ½ cup fresh dill
- 1 tsp salt
- 1 tsp butter
- 1 tbsp brown sugar
- ½ tsp ground black pepper
- 1 tsp paprika
- ¼ chili pepper

Directions:
1. Add zucchini to the food processor and blend for 3 minutes until smooth.
2. Transfer the zucchini blend to the Crock Pot.
3. Stir in onions and all other ingredients.
4. Put the cooker's lid on and set the cooking time to 6 hours on Low settings.
5. Serve warm.

Nutrition Info:
- Per Serving: Calories: 45, Total Fat: 0.8g, Fiber: 2g, Total Carbs: 9.04g, Protein: 1g

Baked Potato

Servings: 6 | Cooking Time: 8 Hours

Ingredients:
- 6 large potatoes, peeled and cubed
- 3 oz. mushrooms, chopped
- 1 onion, chopped
- 1 tsp butter
- ½ tsp salt
- ½ tsp minced garlic
- 1 tsp sour cream
- ½ tsp turmeric
- 1 tsp olive oil

Directions:
1. Grease the insert of the Crock Pot with olive oil.
2. Toss in potatoes, onion, mushrooms, and rest of the ingredients.
3. Put the cooker's lid on and set the cooking time to 8 hours on Low settings.
4. Serve warm.

Nutrition Info:
- Per Serving: Calories: 309, Total Fat: 1.9g, Fiber: 9g, Total Carbs: 66.94g, Protein: 8g

Black Beans Mix

Servings: 2 | Cooking Time: 6 Hours

Ingredients:
- ½ pound black beans, soaked overnight and drained
- A pinch of salt and black pepper
- ½ cup veggie stock
- ½ tablespoon lime juice
- 2 tablespoons cilantro, chopped
- 2 tablespoons pine nuts

Directions:
1. In your Crock Pot, mix the beans with the stock and the other ingredients, toss, put the lid on and cook on Low for 6 hours.
2. Divide everything between plates and serve.

Nutrition Info:
- calories 200, fat 3, fiber 4, carbs 7, protein 5

Mustard Brussels Sprouts

Servings: 2 | Cooking Time: 3 Hours

Ingredients:
- 1 pound Brussels sprouts, trimmed and halved
- 1 tablespoon olive oil
- 1 tablespoon mustard
- 1 tablespoon balsamic vinegar
- Salt and black pepper to the taste
- ¼ cup veggie stock
- A pinch of red pepper, crushed
- 2 tablespoons chives, chopped

Directions:
1. In your Crock Pot, mix the Brussels sprouts with the oil, mustard and the other ingredients, toss, put the lid on and cook on High for 3 hours.
2. Divide the mix between plates and serve as a side dish.

Nutrition Info:
- calories 256, fat 12, fiber 6, carbs 8, protein 15

Glazed Baby Carrots

Servings: 6 | Cooking Time: 6 Hours

Ingredients:
- ½ cup peach preserves
- ½ cup butter, melted
- 2 pounds baby carrots
- 2 tablespoon sugar
- 1 teaspoon vanilla extract
- A pinch of salt and black pepper
- A pinch of nutmeg, ground
- ½ teaspoon cinnamon powder
- 2 tablespoons water

Directions:
1. Put baby carrots in your Crock Pot, add butter, peach preserves, sugar, vanilla, salt, pepper, nutmeg, cinnamon and water, toss well, cover and cook on Low for 6 hours.
2. Divide between plates and serve as a side dish.

Nutrition Info:
- calories 283, fat 14, fiber 4, carbs 28, protein 3

Cabbage Mix

Servings: 2 | Cooking Time: 6 Hours

Ingredients:
- 1 pound red cabbage, shredded
- 1 apple, peeled, cored and roughly chopped
- A pinch of salt and black pepper to the taste
- ¼ cup chicken stock
- 1 tablespoon mustard
- ½ tablespoon olive oil

Directions:
1. In your Crock Pot, mix the cabbage with the apple and the other ingredients, toss, put the lid on and cook on Low for 6 hours.
2. Divide between plates and serve as a side dish.

Nutrition Info:
- calories 200, fat 4, fiber 2, carbs 8, protein 6

Hasselback Potatoes

Servings: 7 | Cooking Time: 8 Hours

Ingredients:
- 7 potatoes
- 2 oz. butter
- 1 tbsp olive oil
- 1 tbsp dried dill
- 1 tsp salt
- 1 tsp paprika

Directions:
1. Use a knife to make 4 slits on top of each potato.
2. Mix butter, dill, olive oil, paprika, and salt in a bowl.
3. Layer the insert of the Crock Pot with a foil sheet.
4. Place the potatoes inside and pour the butter-dill mixture on top of them.
5. Put the cooker's lid on and set the cooking time to 8 hours on Low settings.
6. Serve warm.

Nutrition Info:
- Per Serving: Calories: 363, Total Fat: 9g, Fiber:8g, Total Carbs: 65.17g, Protein: 8g

Creamy Chipotle Sweet Potatoes

Servings: 10 | Cooking Time: 4 Hours

Ingredients:
- 1 sweet onion, chopped
- 2 tablespoons olive oil
- ¼ cup parsley, chopped
- 2 shallots, chopped
- 2 teaspoons chipotle pepper, crushed
- Salt and black pepper
- 4 big sweet potatoes, shredded
- 8 ounces coconut cream
- 16 ounces bacon, cooked and chopped
- ½ teaspoon sweet paprika
- Cooking spray

Directions:
1. Heat up a pan with the oil over medium-high heat, add shallots and onion, stir, cook for 6 minutes and transfer to a bowl.
2. Add parsley, chipotle pepper, salt, pepper, sweet potatoes, coconut cream, paprika and bacon, stir, pour everything in your Crock Pot after you've greased it with some cooking spray, cover, cook on Low for 4 hours, leave aside to cool down a bit, divide between plates and serve as a side dish.

Nutrition Info:
- calories 260, fat 14, fiber 6, carbs 20, protein 15

Cabbage And Onion Mix

Servings: 2 | Cooking Time: 2 Hours

Ingredients:
- 1 and ½ cups green cabbage, shredded
- 1 cup red cabbage, shredded
- 1 tablespoon olive oil
- 1 red onion, sliced
- 2 spring onions, chopped
- ½ cup tomato paste
- ¼ cup veggie stock
- 2 tomatoes, chopped
- 2 jalapenos, chopped
- 1 tablespoon chili powder
- 1 tablespoon chives, chopped
- A pinch of salt and black pepper

Directions:
1. Grease your Crock Pot with the oil and mix the cabbage with the onion, spring onions and the other ingredients inside.
2. Toss, put the lid on and cook on High for 2 hours.
3. Divide between plates and serve as a side dish.

Nutrition Info:
- calories 211, fat 3, fiber 3, carbs 6, protein 8

Asparagus Mix

Servings: 2 | Cooking Time: 2 Hours

Ingredients:
- 1 pound asparagus, trimmed and halved
- 1 red onion, sliced
- 2 garlic cloves, minced
- 1 cup veggie stock
- 1 tablespoon lemon juice
- A pinch of salt and black pepper
- ¼ cup parsley, chopped

Directions:
1. In your Crock Pot, mix the asparagus with the onion, garlic and the other ingredients, toss, put the lid on and cook on High for 2 hours.
2. Divide between plates and serve as a side dish.

Nutrition Info:
- calories 159, fat 4, fiber 4, carbs 6, protein 2

Veggie And Garbanzo Mix

Servings: 4 | Cooking Time: 6 Hours

Ingredients:
- 15 ounces canned garbanzo beans, drained
- 3 cups cauliflower florets
- 1 cup green beans
- 1 cup carrot, sliced
- 14 ounces veggie stock
- ½ cup onion, chopped
- 2 teaspoons curry powder
- ¼ cup basil, chopped
- 14 ounces coconut milk

Directions:
1. In your Crock Pot, mix beans with cauliflower, green beans, carrot, onion, stock, curry powder, basil and milk, stir, cover and cook on Low for 6 hours.
2. Stir veggie mix again, divide between plates and serve as a side dish.

Nutrition Info:
- calories 219, fat 5, fiber 8, carbs 32, protein 7

Veggie Side Salad

Servings: 4 | Cooking Time: 2 Hours

Ingredients:
- 2 garlic cloves, minced
- ½ cup olive oil
- ¼ cup basil, chopped
- Salt and black pepper to the taste
- 1 red bell pepper, chopped
- 1 eggplant, roughly chopped
- 1 summer squash, cubed
- 1 Vidalia onion, cut into wedges
- 1 zucchini, sliced
- 1 green bell pepper, chopped

Directions:
1. In your Crock Pot, mix red bell pepper with green one, squash, zucchini, eggplant, onion, salt, pepper, basil, oil and garlic, toss gently, cover and cook on High for 2 hours.

2. Divide between plates and serve as a side dish.

Nutrition Info:
- calories 165, fat 11, fiber 3, carbs 15, protein 2

Orange Carrots Mix

Servings: 2 | Cooking Time: 6 Hours

Ingredients:
- ½ pound carrots, sliced
- A pinch of salt and black pepper
- ½ tablespoon olive oil
- ½ cup orange juice
- ½ teaspoon orange rind, grated

Directions:
1. In your Crock Pot, mix the carrots with the oil and the other ingredients, toss, put the lid on and cook on Low for 6 hours.
2. Divide between plates and serve as a side dish.

Nutrition Info:
- calories 140, fat 2, fiber 2, carbs 7, protein 6

Cauliflower Pilaf

Servings: 6 | Cooking Time: 3 Hours

Ingredients:
- 1 cup cauliflower rice
- 6 green onions, chopped
- 3 tablespoons ghee, melted
- 2 garlic cloves, minced
- ½ pound Portobello mushrooms, sliced
- 2 cups warm water
- Salt and black pepper to the taste

Directions:
1. In your Crock Pot, mix cauliflower rice with green onions, melted ghee, garlic, mushrooms, water, salt and pepper, stir well, cover and cook on Low for 3 hours.
2. Divide between plates and serve as a side dish.

Nutrition Info:
- calories 200, fat 5, fiber 3, carbs 14, protein 4

Hot Zucchini Mix

Servings: 2 | Cooking Time: 2 Hours

Ingredients:
- ¼ cup carrots, grated
- 1 pound zucchinis, roughly cubed
- 1 teaspoon hot paprika
- ½ teaspoon chili powder
- 2 spring onions, chopped
- ½ tablespoon olive oil
- ½ teaspoon curry powder
- 1 garlic clove, minced
- ½ teaspoon ginger powder
- A pinch of salt and black pepper
- 1 tablespoon cilantro, chopped

Directions:
1. In your Crock Pot, mix the carrots with the zucchinis, paprika and the other ingredients, toss, put the lid on and cook on Low for 2 hours.
2. Divide between plates and serve as a side dish.

Nutrition Info:
- calories 200, fat 5, fiber 7, carbs 28, protein 4

Zucchini Casserole

Servings: 10 | Cooking Time: 2 Hours

Ingredients:
- 7 cups zucchini, sliced
- 2 cups crackers, crushed
- 2 tablespoons melted butter
- 1/3 cup yellow onion, chopped
- 1 cup cheddar cheese, shredded
- 1 cup chicken stock
- 1/3 cup sour cream
- Salt and black pepper to the taste
- 1 tablespoon parsley, chopped
- Cooking spray

Directions:
1. Grease your Crock Pot with cooking spray and arrange zucchini and onion in the pot.
2. Add melted butter, stock, sour cream, salt and pepper and toss.
3. Add cheese mixed with crackers, cover and cook on High for 2 hours.
4. Divide zucchini casserole on plates, sprinkle parsley all over and serve as a side dish.

Nutrition Info:
- calories 180, fat 6, fiber 1, carbs 14, protein 4

Stewed Okra

Servings: 4 | Cooking Time: 3 Hours

Ingredients:
- 2 cups okra, sliced
- 2 garlic cloves, minced
- 6 ounces tomato sauce
- 1 red onion, chopped
- A pinch of cayenne peppers
- 1 teaspoon liquid smoke
- Salt and black pepper to the taste

Directions:
1. In your Crock Pot, mix okra with garlic, onion, cayenne, tomato sauce, liquid smoke, salt and pepper, cover, cook on Low for 3 hours.
2. Divide between plates and serve as a side dish.

Nutrition Info:
- calories 182, fat 3, fiber 6, carbs 8, protein 3

Okra Side Dish

Servings: 4 | Cooking Time: 3 Hours

Ingredients:
- 2 cups okra, sliced
- 1 and ½ cups red onion, roughly chopped
- 1 cup cherry tomatoes, halved
- 2 and ½ cups zucchini, sliced
- 2 cups red and yellow bell peppers, sliced
- 1 cup white mushrooms, sliced
- ½ cup olive oil
- ½ cup balsamic vinegar
- 2 tablespoons basil, chopped
- 1 tablespoon thyme, chopped

Directions:
1. In your Crock Pot, mix okra with onion, tomatoes, zucchini, bell peppers, mushrooms, basil and thyme.
2. In a bowl mix oil with vinegar, whisk well, add to the Crock Pot, cover and cook on High for 3 hours.
3. Divide between plates and serve as a side dish.

Nutrition Info:
- calories 233, fat 12, fiber 4, carbs 8, protein 4

Chorizo And Cauliflower Mix

Servings: 4 | Cooking Time: 5 Hours

Ingredients:
- 1 pound chorizo, chopped
- 12 ounces canned green chilies, chopped
- 1 yellow onion, chopped
- ½ teaspoon garlic powder
- Salt and black pepper to the taste
- 1 cauliflower head, riced
- 2 tablespoons green onions, chopped

Directions:
1. Heat up a pan over medium heat, add chorizo and onion, stir, brown for a few minutes and transfer to your Crock Pot.
2. Add chilies, garlic powder, salt, pepper, cauliflower and green onions, toss, cover and cook on Low for 5 hours.
3. Divide between plates and serve as a side dish.

Nutrition Info:
- calories 350, fat 12, fiber 4, carbs 6, protein 20

Jalapeno Meal

Servings: 6 | Cooking Time: 6 Hrs.

Ingredients:
- 12 oz. jalapeno pepper, cut in half and deseeded
- 2 tbsp olive oil
- 1 tbsp balsamic vinegar
- 1 onion, sliced
- 1 garlic clove, sliced
- 1 tsp ground coriander
- 4 tbsp water

Directions:
1. Place the jalapeno peppers in the Crock Pot.
2. Top the pepper with olive oil, balsamic vinegar, onion, garlic, coriander, and water.
3. Put the cooker's lid on and set the cooking time to 6 hours on Low settings.
4. Serve warm.

Nutrition Info:
- Per Serving: Calories: 67, Total Fat: 4.7g, Fiber: 2g, Total Carbs: 6.02g, Protein: 1g

Farro Rice Pilaf

Servings: 12 | Cooking Time: 5 Hours

Ingredients:
- 1 shallot, chopped
- 1 tsp garlic, minced
- A drizzle of olive oil
- 1 and ½ cups whole grain farro
- ¾ cup wild rice
- 6 cups chicken stock
- Salt and black pepper to the taste
- 1 tbsp parsley and sage, chopped
- ½ cup hazelnuts, toasted and chopped
- ¾ cup cherries, dried

Directions:
1. Add farro, rice, stock, and rest of the ingredients to the Crock Pot.
2. Put the cooker's lid on and set the cooking time to 5 hours on Low settings.
3. Serve warm.

Nutrition Info:
- Per Serving: Calories: 120, Total Fat: 2g, Fiber: 7g, Total Carbs: 20g, Protein: 3g

Mexican Avocado Rice

Servings: 8 | Cooking Time: 4 Hrs

Ingredients:
- 1 cup long-grain rice
- 1 and ¼ cups veggie stock
- ½ cup cilantro, chopped
- ½ avocado, pitted, peeled and chopped
- Salt and black pepper to the taste
- ¼ cup green hot sauce

Directions:
1. Add rice and stock to the Crock Pot.
2. Put the cooker's lid on and set the cooking time to 4 hours on Low settings.
3. Meanwhile, blend avocado flesh with hot sauce, cilantro, salt, and black pepper.
4. Serve the cooked rice with avocado sauce on top.

Nutrition Info:
- Per Serving: Calories: 100, Total Fat: 3g, Fiber: 6g, Total Carbs: 18g, Protein: 4g

Squash Side Salad

Servings: 8 | Cooking Time: 4 Hours

Ingredients:
- 1 tablespoon olive oil
- 1 cup carrots, chopped
- 1 yellow onion, chopped
- 1 teaspoon sugar
- 1 and ½ teaspoons curry powder
- 1 garlic clove, minced
- 1 big butternut squash, peeled and cubed
- A pinch of sea salt and black pepper
- ¼ teaspoon ginger, grated
- ½ teaspoon cinnamon powder
- 3 cups coconut milk

Directions:
1. In your Crock Pot, mix oil with carrots, onion, sugar, curry powder, garlic, squash, salt, pepper, ginger, cinnamon and coconut milk, stir well, cover and cook on Low for 4 hours.
2. Stir, divide between plates and serve as a side dish.

Nutrition Info:
- calories 200, fat 4, fiber 4, carbs 17, protein 4

Peas And Carrots

Servings: 12 | Cooking Time: 5 Hours

Ingredients:
- 1 yellow onion, chopped
- 1 pound carrots, sliced
- 16 ounces peas
- ¼ cup melted butter
- ¼ cup water
- ¼ cup honey
- 4 garlic cloves, minced
- A pinch of salt and black pepper
- 1 teaspoon marjoram, dried

Directions:
1. In your Crock Pot, mix onion with carrots, peas, butter, water, honey, garlic, salt, pepper and marjoram, cover and cook on Low for 5 hours.
2. Stir peas and carrots mix, divide between plates and serve as a side dish.

Nutrition Info:
- calories 105, fat 4, fiber 3, carbs 16, protein 4

Mashed Potatoes

Servings: 2 | Cooking Time: 6 Hours

Ingredients:
- 1 pound gold potatoes, peeled and cubed
- 2 garlic cloves, chopped
- 1 cup milk
- 1 cup water
- 2 tablespoons butter
- A pinch of salt and white pepper

Directions:
1. In your Crock Pot, mix the potatoes with the water, salt and pepper, put the lid on and cook on Low for 6 hours.
2. Mash the potatoes, add the rest of the ingredients, whisk and serve.

Nutrition Info:
- calories 135, fat 4, fiber 2, carbs 10, protein 4

Beans, Carrots And Spinach Salad

Servings: 6 | Cooking Time: 7 Hours

Ingredients:
- 1 and ½ cups northern beans
- 1 yellow onion, chopped
- 5 carrots, chopped
- 2 garlic cloves, minced
- ½ teaspoon oregano, dried
- Salt and black pepper to the taste
- 4 and ½ cups chicken stock
- 5 ounces baby spinach
- 2 teaspoons lemon peel, grated
- 1 avocado, peeled, pitted and chopped
- 3 tablespoons lemon juice
- ¾ cup feta cheese, crumbled
- 1/3 cup pistachios, chopped

Directions:
1. In your Crock Pot, mix beans with onion, carrots, garlic, oregano, salt, pepper and stock, stir, cover and cook on Low for 7 hours.
2. Drain beans and veggies, transfer them to a salad bowl, add baby spinach, lemon peel, avocado, lemon juice, pistachios and cheese, toss, divide between plates and serve as a side dish.

Nutrition Info:
- calories 300, fat 8, fiber 14, carbs 43, protein 16

Thyme Mushrooms And Corn

Servings: 2 | Cooking Time: 4 Hours

Ingredients:
- 4 garlic cloves, minced
- 1 tablespoon olive oil
- 1 pound white mushroom caps, halved
- 1 cup corn
- 1 cup canned tomatoes, crushed
- ¼ teaspoon thyme, dried
- ½ cup veggie stock
- A pinch of salt and black pepper
- 2 tablespoons parsley, chopped

Directions:
1. Grease your Crock Pot with the oil, and mix the garlic with the mushrooms, corn and the other ingredients inside.
2. Toss, put the lid on and cook on Low for 4 hours.
3. Divide between plates and serve as a side dish.

Nutrition Info:
- calories 122, fat 6, fiber 1, carbs 8, protein 5

Chicken With Sweet Potato

Servings: 6 | Cooking Time: 3 Hours

Ingredients:
- 16 oz. sweet potato, peeled and diced
- 3 cups chicken stock
- 1 tbsp salt
- 3 tbsp margarine
- 2 tbsp cream cheese

Directions:
1. Add sweet potato, chicken stock, and salt to the Crock Pot.
2. Put the cooker's lid on and set the cooking time to 5 hours on High settings.
3. Drain the slow-cooked potatoes and transfer them to a suitable bowl.
4. Mash the sweet potatoes and stir in cream cheese and margarine.
5. Serve fresh.

Nutrition Info:
- Per Serving: Calories: 472, Total Fat: 31.9g, Fiber: 6.7g, Total Carbs: 43.55g, Protein: 3g

Thai Side Salad

Servings: 8 | Cooking Time: 3 Hours

Ingredients:
- 8 ounces yellow summer squash, peeled and roughly chopped
- 12 ounces zucchini, halved and sliced
- 2 cups button mushrooms, quartered
- 1 red sweet potatoes, chopped
- 2 leeks, sliced
- 2 tablespoons veggie stock
- 2 garlic cloves, minced
- 2 tablespoon Thai red curry paste
- 1 tablespoon ginger, grated
- 1/3 cup coconut milk
- ¼ cup basil, chopped

Directions:
1. In your Crock Pot, mix zucchini with summer squash, mushrooms, red pepper, leeks, garlic, stock, curry paste, ginger, coconut milk and basil, toss, cover and cook on Low for 3 hours.
2. Stir your Thai mix one more time, divide between plates and serve as a side dish.

Nutrition Info:
- calories 69, fat 2, fiber 2, carbs 8, protein 2

Soups & Stews Recipes

Soups & Stews Recipes

Celery Stew

Servings:4 | Cooking Time: 6 Hours

Ingredients:
- 3 cups of water
- 1-pound beef stew meat, cubed
- 2 cups celery, chopped
- ½ cup cremini mushrooms, sliced
- 2 tablespoons sour cream
- 1 teaspoon smoked paprika
- 1 teaspoon cayenne pepper
- 1 tablespoon sesame oil

Directions:
1. Mix beef stew meat with cayenne pepper and put in the hot skillet.
2. Add sesame oil and roast the meat for 1 minute per side on high heat.
3. Transfer the meat in the Crock Pot.
4. Add celery, cremini mushrooms, sour cream, smoked paprika, and water.
5. Close the lid and cook the stew on high for 6 hours.

Nutrition Info:
- Per Serving: 267 calories, 35.3g protein, 2.7g carbohydrates, 12g fat, 1.2g fiber, 104g cholesterol, 124mg sodium, 660mg potassium.

Mexican Style Stew

Servings:6 | Cooking Time: 6 Hours

Ingredients:
- 1 cup corn kernels
- 1 cup green peas
- ¼ cup white rice
- 4 cups chicken stock
- 1 teaspoon taco seasoning
- 1 teaspoon dried cilantro
- 1 tablespoon butter

Directions:
1. Put butter and wild rice in the Crock Pot.
2. Then add corn kernels, green peas, chicken stock, taco seasoning, and dried cilantro.
3. Close the lid and cook the stew on Low for 6 hours.

Nutrition Info:
- Per Serving: 97 calories, 3.2g protein, 15.6g carbohydrates, 2.7g fat, 2g fiber, 5mg cholesterol, 599mg sodium, 148mg potassium.

Creamy Mediterranean Soup

Servings: 6 | Cooking Time: 4 1/4 Hours

Ingredients:
- 2 tablespoons olive oil
- 1 sweet onion, chopped
- 1 garlic clove, chopped
- 1/2 head cauliflower, cut into florets
- 1 head broccoli, cut into florets
- 1 teaspoon dried oregano
- 2 cups vegetable stock
- 2 cups water
- 2 tablespoons Italian pesto
- Salt and pepper to taste

Directions:
1. Heat the oil in a skillet and add the onion and garlic. Sauté for 2 minutes until softened.
2. Transfer in your Crock Pot and add the remaining ingredients.
3. Season with salt and pepper and cook on low settings for 4 hours.
4. When done, puree the soup with an immersion blender and serve the soup warm.

Meatball Tortellini Soup

Servings: 6 | Cooking Time: 6 1/2 Hours

Ingredients:
- 1/2 pound ground chicken
- 1/4 cup white rice
- 1 garlic clove, chopped
- 1 tablespoon chopped parsley
- 2 cups chicken stock
- 4 cups water
- 1 celery stalk, sliced
- 1 carrot, sliced
- 1 shallot, chopped
- 6 oz. spinach tortellini
- Salt and pepper to taste

Directions:
1. Mix the chicken, rice, garlic, parsley, salt and pepper in a bowl.
2. Combine the stock, water, celery, carrot, shallot, salt and pepper in your Crock Pot.
3. Form small meatballs and drop them in the liquid.
4. Add the tortellini as well and cook on low settings for 6 hours.
5. Serve the soup warm and fresh.

Roasted Chicken Stock

Servings: 10 | Cooking Time: 9 Hours

Ingredients:
- 1 whole chicken, cut into smaller pieces
- 2 carrots, cut in half
- 1 parsnip
- 1 celery root, peeled and sliced
- 2 onions, halved
- 10 cups water
- 1 bay leaf
- 1 rosemary sprig
- 1 thyme sprig
- Salt and pepper to taste

Directions:
1. Season the chicken with salt and pepper and place it in a baking tray. Roast in the preheated oven at 400F for 40 minutes.
2. Transfer the chicken in your Crock Pot and add the remaining ingredients.
3. Season with salt and pepper and cook on low settings for 8 hours.
4. Use the stock right away or store in the fridge or freezer.

Simple Chicken Noodle Soup

Servings: 8 | Cooking Time: 8 1/4 Hours

Ingredients:
- 1 1/2 pounds chicken breasts, cubed
- 2 large carrots, sliced
- 2 celery stalks, sliced
- 1 onion, chopped
- 2 cups chicken stock
- 5 cups water
- 1 thyme sprig
- 2 cups dried egg noodles
- Salt and pepper to taste

Directions:
1. Combine all the ingredients in your Crock Pot.
2. Add salt and pepper and cook on low settings for 8 hours, mixing once during cooking.
3. Serve the soup warm.

Spiced Lasagna Soup

Servings:6 | Cooking Time: 6 Hours

Ingredients:
- 2 sheets of lasagna noodles, crushed
- 1 oz Parmesan, grated
- 1 teaspoon ground turmeric
- 1 yellow onion, diced
- 2 cups ground beef
- 6 cups beef broth
- ½ cup tomatoes, chopped
- 1 tablespoon dried basil

Directions:
1. Roast the ground beef in the hot skillet for 4 minutes. Stir it constantly and transfer in the Crock Pot.
2. Add turmeric, onion, tomatoes, basil, and beef broth.
3. Stir the soup, add lasagna noodles, and close the lid.

4. Cook the soup on High for 6 hours.
5. Top the cooked soup with Parmesan.

Nutrition Info:
- Per Serving: 208 calories, 17.8g protein, 14.6g carbohydrates, 8.3g fat, 0.7g fiber, 40mg cholesterol, 840mg sodium, 390mg potassium.

Black Bean Mushroom Soup

Servings: 8 | Cooking Time: 6 1/2 Hours

Ingredients:
- 1 shallot, chopped
- 2 garlic cloves, chopped
- 1 can (15 oz.) black beans, drained
- 1/2 pound mushrooms, sliced
- 1 can fire roasted tomatoes
- 2 cups vegetable stock
- 4 cups water
- 1/2 teaspoon mustard seeds
- 1/2 teaspoon cumin seeds
- Salt and pepper to taste
- 2 tablespoons chopped parsley

Directions:
1. Combine the shallot, garlic and black beans with the mushrooms, tomatoes, stock, water and seeds in your Crock Pot.
2. Add salt and pepper to taste and cook on low settings for 6 hours.
3. When done, add the parsley and serve the soup warm.

Leek Potato Soup

Servings: 8 | Cooking Time: 6 1/2 Hours

Ingredients:
- 4 leeks, sliced
- 1 tablespoon olive oil
- 4 bacon slices, chopped
- 1 celery stalk, sliced
- 4 large potatoes, peeled and cubed
- 2 cups chicken stock
- 3 cups water
- 1 bay leaf
- Salt and pepper to taste
- 1/4 teaspoon cayenne pepper
- 1/4 teaspoon smoked paprika
- 1 thyme sprig
- 1 rosemary sprig

Directions:
1. Heat the oil in a skillet and add the bacon. Cook until crisp then stir in the leeks.
2. Sauté for 5 minutes until softened then transfer in your Crock Pot.
3. Add the remaining ingredients and cook on low settings for about 6 hours.
4. Serve the soup warm.

Tomato Beef Soup

Servings: 8 | Cooking Time: 8 1/4 Hours

Ingredients:
- 2 tablespoons olive oil
- 2 bacon slices, chopped
- 2 pounds beef roast, cubed
- 2 sweet onions, chopped
- 2 tomatoes, peeled and diced
- 2 cups tomato sauce
- 1 cup beef stock
- 3 cups water
- Salt and pepper to taste
- 1 thyme sprig
- 1 rosemary sprig

Directions:
1. Heat the oil in a skillet and add the bacon. Cook until crisp and stir in the beef roast. Cook for 5 minutes on all sides.
2. Transfer the beef and bacon in a Crock Pot.
3. Add the remaining ingredients and adjust the taste with salt and pepper.
4. Cook on low settings for 8 hours.
5. Serve the soup warm or chilled.

Tuscan White Bean Soup

Servings: 6 | Cooking Time: 6 1/2 Hours

Ingredients:
- 1 cup dried white beans
- 2 cups chicken stock
- 4 cups water
- 1 carrot, diced
- 1 celery stalk, diced
- 4 garlic cloves, chopped
- 2 tablespoons tomato paste
- 1 bay leaf
- 2 cups spinach, shredded
- Salt and pepper to taste
- 1 teaspoon dried oregano
- 1 teaspoon dried basil
- 1/2 lemon, juiced

Directions:
1. Combine the beans, stock, water, carrot, celery, garlic and tomato paste in your Crock Pot.
2. Add the bay leaf, dried herbs and lemon juice, as well as salt and pepper.
3. Cook on low settings for 4 hours then add the spinach and cook for 2 additional hours on low settings.
4. Serve the soup warm or chilled.

Sweet Potato Black Bean Chili

Servings: 6 (3/4 Cup Per Serving) | Cooking Time: 6 Hours 35 Minutes

Ingredients:
- Chili:
- 1 medium yellow onion, diced (+coconut or olive oil)
- 3 medium sweet potatoes, scrubbed and rinsed, in bite-size pieces, 4 cups
- 1 16-ounce jar salsa, chunky
- 1 15-ounce can black beans with salt
- 2 cups vegetable stock, + 2 cups of water
- Optional Spices:
- 1 tablespoon chili powder
- 2 teaspoons cumin, ground
- ½ teaspoon cinnamon, ground
- 1-2 teaspoons hot sauce
- For Toppings (optional):
- Fresh cilantro
- Chopped red onion
- Avocado
- Lime juice

Directions:
1. In a large pan, heat 1 tablespoon of oil on medium heat; add sweet onions, along with salt and pepper. Stir and cook until translucent, about 15 minutes. Add sweet potatoes and cook until potatoes begin to soften, about 20 minutes. Add all ingredients to Crock-Pot and stir; cover and cook on LOW for 6 hours. Serve hot.

Nutrition Info:
- Calories: 213, Total Fat: 6 g, Saturated Fat: 0 g, Sodium: 611 mg, Carbs: 47 g, Fiber: 9.1 g, Sugars: 4.4 g, Protein: 6.8 g

Creamy Noodle Soup

Servings: 8 | Cooking Time: 8 1/4 Hours

Ingredients:
- 2 chicken breasts, cubed
- 2 tablespoons all-purpose flour
- 2 shallots, chopped
- 1 celery stalk, sliced
- 1 can condensed chicken soup
- 2 cups water
- 2 cups chicken stock
- Salt and pepper to taste
- 1 cup green peas
- 6 oz. egg noodles

Directions:
1. Sprinkle the chicken with salt, pepper and flour and place it in your Crock Pot.
2. Add the remaining ingredients and season with salt and pepper.
3. Cover and cook on low settings for 8 hours.
4. This soup is best served warm.

Pumpkin Stew With Chicken

Servings: 2 | Cooking Time: 4 Hours

Ingredients:
- ½ cup pumpkin, chopped
- 6 oz chicken fillet, cut into strips
- 1 tablespoon curry powder
- ¼ cup coconut cream
- ½ teaspoon ground cinnamon
- 1 onion, chopped

Directions:
1. Mix pumpkin with chicken fillet strips in the mixing bowl.
2. Add curry powder, coconut cream, ground cinnamon, and onion.
3. Mix the stew ingredients and transfer them in the Crock Pot.
4. Cook the meal on high for 4 hours.

Nutrition Info:
- Per Serving: 291 calories, 16.2g protein, 25g carbohydrates, 15.8g fat, 5.7g fiber, 40mg cholesterol, 586mg sodium, 336mg potassium.

Tomato Chickpeas Stew

Servings: 4 | Cooking Time: 7 Hours

Ingredients:
- 2 tablespoons tomato paste
- 1 cup chickpeas, soaked
- 5 cups of water
- 1 yellow onion, chopped
- ½ cup fresh parsley, chopped
- 1 teaspoon ground black pepper
- 1 carrot, chopped

Directions:
1. Mix tomato paste with water and pour in the Crock Pot.
2. Add chickpeas, onion, parsley, ground black pepper, and carrot.
3. Close the lid and cook the stew on Low for 7 hours.

Nutrition Info:
- Per Serving: 210 calories, 10.7g protein, 36.7g carbohydrates, 3.2g fat, 10.4g fiber, 0mg cholesterol, 45mg sodium, 659mg potassium.

Vegetable Chickpea Soup

Servings: 6 | Cooking Time: 6 1/2 Hours

Ingredients:
- 2/3 cup dried chickpeas, rinsed
- 2 cups chicken stock
- 4 cups water
- 1 celery stalk, sliced
- 1 carrot, diced
- 1 shallot, chopped
- 2 ripe tomatoes, peeled and diced
- 1 red bell pepper, cored and diced
- 1 potato, peeled and diced
- 1 tablespoon lemon juice
- Salt and pepper to taste

Directions:

1. Combine all the ingredients in your Crock Pot.
2. Add salt and pepper to taste and cook on low settings for 6 hours.
3. Serve the soup warm and fresh.

Stroganoff Soup

Servings: 8 | Cooking Time: 8 1/4 Hours

Ingredients:
- 2 pound beef roast, cubed
- 2 tablespoons all-purpose flour
- 2 tablespoons canola oil
- 1 sweet onion, chopped
- 1 can condensed cream of mushroom soup
- 2 cups chicken stock
- 1 cup water
- 1/2 cup sour cream
- Salt and pepper to taste

Directions:
1. Season the beef with salt and pepper and sprinkle with flour.
2. Heat the oil in a skillet and stir in the beef. Cook for a few minutes on all sides then transfer the beef in your Crock Pot.
3. Add the onion, soup, stock, water and sour cream.
4. Season with salt and pepper and cook on low settings for 8 hours.
5. Serve the soup warm.

Italian Veggie Pasta Soup

Servings: 10 | Cooking Time: 8 1/2 Hours

Ingredients:
- 2 tablespoons olive oil
- 1 sweet onion, chopped
- 2 garlic cloves, chopped
- 2 red bell peppers, cored and diced
- 2 zucchinis, sliced
- 1 can white beans, drained
- 2 ripe tomatoes, peeled and diced
- 1 cup tomato sauce
- 2 cups chicken stock
- 4 cups water
- 1 bay leaf
- 1/2 teaspoon dried basil
- 1 teaspoon dried oregano
- 1/2 cup fusilli pasta
- 1/4 cup short pasta of your choice
- Salt and pepper to taste

Directions:
1. Heat the oil in a skillet or saucepan and stir in the onion, garlic, bell peppers and zucchinis.
2. Sauté for 5 minutes, stirring often, then transfer in your Crock Pot.
3. Add the remaining ingredients and season with salt and pepper.
4. Cook on low settings for 8 hours.
5. The soup can be served both warm and chilled.

Vegan Cream Of Tomato Soup

Servings: 4 | Cooking Time: 3 Hours

Ingredients:
- 4 Roma tomatoes
- ½ cup sun dried tomatoes
- 1 teaspoon sea salt
- ¼ teaspoon black pepper
- ¼ teaspoon white pepper
- ¼ cup basil, fresh, chopped
- 1 clove of garlic
- 4 cups water

Directions:
1. Add ingredients to a high-powered blender and blend until smooth, for about 5 minutes. Add the blended mix to Crock-Pot, cook on LOW for 3 hours. Serve hot.

Nutrition Info:
- Calories: 187, Total Fat: 15.9 g, Saturated Fat: 2.5 g, Sodium: 538 mg, Carbs: 11.8 g, Dietary Fiber: 4.1 g, Net Carbs: 7.7 g, Sugars: 3.4 g, Protein: 3.5 g

Lima Bean Soup

Servings: 8 | Cooking Time: 7 1/4 Hours

Ingredients:
- 2 bacon slices, chopped
- 4 cups frozen lima beans
- 2 shallots, chopped
- 2 carrots, diced
- 2 potatoes, peeled and cubed
- 1 celery stalk, sliced
- 1 can diced tomatoes
- 2 cups vegetable stock
- 3 cups water
- 1 bay leaf
- Salt and pepper to taste
- 1 tablespoon chopped cilantro

Directions:
1. Combine the bacon, lima beans, shallots, carrots, potatoes, celery and tomatoes in a Crock Pot.
2. Add the remaining ingredients, except cilantro and season with salt and pepper.
3. Cook on low settings for 7 hours.
4. When done, stir in the chopped cilantro and serve the soup warm.

Creamy Tomato Soup With Flour Dumplings

Servings: 8 | Cooking Time: 8 1/4 Hours

Ingredients:
- 2 tablespoons olive oil
- 2 shallots, chopped
- 2 garlic cloves, chopped
- 2 pounds ripe tomatoes, peeled and cubed
- 1 carrot, sliced
- 1 celery root, peeled and cubed
- 2 cups chicken stock
- 2 cups water
- 1/2 teaspoon dried oregano
- 1/2 teaspoon dried basil
- 1/2 red chili, sliced
- 1 tablespoon brown sugar
- 1 teaspoon balsamic vinegar
- Salt and pepper to taste
- 1 egg
- 1 teaspoon canola oil
- 4 teaspoons all-purpose flour

Directions:
1. Heat the olive oil in a skillet and stir in the shallots and garlic. Sauté for 2 minutes until softened then transfer in your Crock Pot.
2. Add the tomatoes, carrot, celery, stock, water, oregano and basil, as well as chili, brown sugar and balsamic vinegar.
3. Season with salt and pepper to taste and cook on low settings for 6 hours.
4. When done, puree the soup with an immersion blender.
5. In a small bowl, mix the egg, canola oil and flour. Give it a good mix and add salt to taste.
6. Drop small pieces of this dough into the tomato soup and continue cooking for 2 additional hours on low settings.
7. Serve the soup warm or chilled.

Creamy White Bean Soup

Servings: 6 | Cooking Time: 4 1/4 Hours

Ingredients:
- 1 tablespoon olive oil
- 1 sweet onion, chopped
- 2 garlic cloves, chopped
- 1/2 celery root, peeled and cubed
- 1 parsnip, diced
- 1 can (15 oz.) white beans, drained
- 2 cups chicken stock
- 3 cups water
- 1/2 teaspoon dried thyme
- Salt and pepper to taste

Directions:
1. Heat the oil in a skillet and stir in the onion, garlic, celery and parsnip. Cook for 5 minutes until softened then transfer the mix in your Crock Pot.
2. Add the rest of the ingredients and cook on low settings for 4 hours.
3. When done, puree the soup with an immersion blender and pulse until smooth and creamy.
4. Serve the soup warm and fresh.

Chicken Tortellini Clear Soup

Servings: 8 | Cooking Time: 8 1/2 Hours

Ingredients:
- 1 whole chicken, cut into smaller pieces
- 1 carrot, halved
- 1 celery stalk, halved
- 1 parsnip, halved
- 8 cups water
- 10 oz. cheese tortellini
- Salt and pepper to taste

Directions:
1. Combine the chicken, carrot, celery, parsnip and water in your Crock Pot.
2. Add salt and pepper to taste and cook on low settings for 6 hours.
3. When done, remove and discard the carrot, celery and parsnip then shred the meat off the bone and place it back in the cooker.
4. Add the tortellini and cook on high settings for 2 additional hours.
5. Serve the soup warm and fresh.

Smoked Sausage Lentil Soup

Servings: 6 | Cooking Time: 6 1/4 Hours

Ingredients:
- 2 links smoked sausages, sliced
- 1 sweet onion, chopped
- 2 carrots, diced
- 1 cup red lentils
- 1/2 cup green lentils
- 2 cups chicken stock
- 2 cups water
- 1/2 teaspoon smoked paprika
- 1 bay leaf
- 1 thyme sprig
- 1 lemon, juiced
- 1 cup fire roasted tomatoes
- Salt and pepper to taste

Directions:
1. Combine the sausages with the remaining ingredients in your Crock Pot.
2. Add salt and pepper to taste and cover with a lid.
3. Cook on low settings for 6 hours.
4. The soup can be served both warm and chilled.

Hungarian Borscht

Servings: 8 | Cooking Time: 8 1/4 Hours

Ingredients:
- 1 pound beef roast, cubed
- 2 tablespoons canola oil
- 4 medium size beets, peeled and cubed
- 1 can diced tomatoes
- 2 potatoes, peeled and cubed
- 1 sweet onion, chopped
- 2 tablespoons tomato paste
- Salt and pepper to taste
- 4 cups water

- 1 cup vegetable stock
- 1/2 teaspoon cumin seeds
- 1 teaspoon red wine vinegar
- 1 teaspoon honey
- 1/2 teaspoon dried dill
- 1 teaspoon dried parsley

Directions:
1. Heat the oil in a skillet and stir in the beef. Cook for a few minutes on all sides until golden.
2. Transfer the meat in your Crock Pot and add the beets, tomatoes, potatoes, onion and tomato paste.
3. Add salt and pepper, as well as the remaining ingredients and cook on low settings for 8 hours.
4. Serve the soup warm or chilled.

Chunky Pumpkin And Kale Soup

Servings: 6 | Cooking Time: 6 1/2 Hours

Ingredients:
- 1 sweet onion, chopped
- 1 red bell pepper, cored and diced
- 1/2 red chili, chopped
- 2 tablespoons olive oil
- 2 cups pumpkin cubes
- 2 cups vegetable stock
- 2 cups water
- 1 bunch kale, shredded
- 1/2 teaspoon cumin seeds
- Salt and pepper to taste

Directions:
1. Combine the onion, bell pepper, chili and olive oil in your Crock Pot.
2. Add the remaining ingredients and adjust the taste with salt and pepper.
3. Mix gently just to evenly distribute the ingredients then cook on low settings for 6 hours.
4. Serve the soup warm or chilled.

Italian Barley Soup

Servings: 8 | Cooking Time: 6 1/4 Hours

Ingredients:
- 2 tablespoons olive oil
- 1 shallot, chopped
- 1 garlic clove, chopped
- 1 carrot, diced
- 1 celery stalk, diced
- 2 red bell peppers, cored and diced
- 2 tomatoes, peeled and diced
- 2 cups vegetable stock
- 1 teaspoon dried oregano
- 1 teaspoon dried basil
- 2/3 cup pearl barley
- 3 cups water
- 2 cups fresh spinach, chopped
- 1 lemon, juiced
- Salt and pepper to taste

Directions:
1. Heat the oil in a skillet and stir in the shallot, garlic, carrot and celery, as well as bell peppers.

2. Cook for 5 minutes just until softened then transfer in your Crock Pot. You can skip this step, but sautéing the vegetables first improves the taste.
3. Add the remaining ingredients to the pot and season with salt and pepper.
4. Cook on low settings for 6 hours.
5. The soup is great served either warm or chilled.

Pesto Chicken Soup

Servings: 6 | Cooking Time: 6 1/4 Hours

Ingredients:
- 1 chicken breast, cubed
- 1 shallot, chopped
- 1 garlic clove, chopped
- 1 can (15 oz.) white beans, drained
- 1 parsnip, diced
- 1 celery stalk, sliced
- 2 tablespoons Italian pesto
- 1/2 cup chopped parsley
- Salt and pepper to taste

Directions:
1. Combine the chicken, shallot, garlic, beans, parsnip, celery and pesto in a Crock Pot.
2. Add the parsley and season with salt and pepper.
3. Cook on low settings for 6 hours and serve the soup warm and fresh.

Vegan Grain-free Cream Of Mushroom Soup

Servings: 2 | Cooking Time: 4 Hours

Ingredients:
- 2 cups cauliflower florets
- 1 teaspoon onion powder
- 1 2/3 cups unsweetened almond milk
- 1 ½ cups white mushrooms, diced
- ¼ teaspoon Himalayan rock salt
- ½ yellow onion, diced

Directions:
1. Place onion powder, milk, cauliflower, salt, and pepper in a pan, cover and bring to a boil over medium heat. Reduce heat to low and simmer for 8 minutes or until cauliflower is softened. Then, puree mixture in food processor. In a pan, add oil, mushrooms, and onions, heat over high heat for about 8 minutes. Add mushrooms and onion mix to cauliflower mixture in Crock-Pot. Cover and cook on LOW for 4 hours. Serve hot.

Nutrition Info:
- Calories: 95, Total Fat: 4 g, Sodium: 475 mg, Carbs: 12.3 g, Dietary Fiber: 4.4 g, Net Carbs: 7.9 g, Sugars: 4.9 g, Protein: 4.9 g

Cream Of Broccoli Soup

Servings: 6 | Cooking Time: 2 1/4 Hours

Ingredients:
- 2 shallots, chopped
- 2 garlic cloves, chopped
- 2 tablespoons olive oil
- 1 head broccoli, cut into florets
- 2 potatoes, peeled and cubed
- 1 cup chicken stock
- 2 cups water
- Salt and pepper to taste
- 1/2 teaspoon dried basil
- 1/2 teaspoon dried oregano

Directions:
1. Heat the oil in a skillet and stir in the shallots and garlic. Sauté for a few minutes until softened then transfer in your Crock Pot.
2. Add the broccoli, potatoes, chicken stock and water, as well as dried herbs, salt and pepper.
3. Cook on high settings for 2 hours then puree the soup in a blender until creamy and rich.
4. Pour the soup into bowls in order to serve.

Ground Beef Stew

Servings:5 | Cooking Time: 7 Hours

Ingredients:
- 1 cup bell pepper, diced
- 2 cups ground beef
- 1 teaspoon minced garlic
- 1 teaspoon dried rosemary
- 1 cup tomatoes, chopped
- 1 teaspoon salt
- 3 cups of water

Directions:
1. Put all ingredients in the Crock Pot and stir them.
2. Close the lid and cook the stew on Low for 7 hours.

Nutrition Info:
- Per Serving: 135 calories, 18.6g protein, 3.5g carbohydrates, 4.8g fat, 0.9g fiber, 55mg cholesterol, 524mg sodium, 419mg potassium.

Ginger And Sweet Potato Stew

Servings:3 | Cooking Time: 7 Hours

Ingredients:
- 1 cup sweet potatoes, chopped
- ½ teaspoon ground ginger
- 1 cup bell pepper, cut into the strips
- 1 apple, chopped
- 1 teaspoon ground cumin
- 2 cups beef broth

Directions:
1. Mix ingredients in the Crock Pot.
2. Close the lid and cook the stew on Low for 7 hours.

Nutrition Info:
- Per Serving: 140 calories, 4.8g protein, 28.3g carbohydrates, 1.4g fat, 4.5g fiber, 0mg cholesterol, 516mg sodium, 716mg potassium.

Roasted Bell Pepper Quinoa Soup

Servings: 6 | Cooking Time: 6 1/2 Hours

Ingredients:
- 1 shallot, chopped
- 1 garlic clove, chopped
- 4 roasted red bell peppers, chopped
- 1/2 cup tomato paste
- 2 cups vegetable stock
- 1 cup water
- 1/2 cup red quinoa, rinsed
- 1/2 teaspoon dried oregano
- 1/2 teaspoon dried basil
- 1 pinch cayenne pepper
- Salt and pepper to taste

Directions:
1. Combine the shallot, garlic, bell peppers, tomato paste, stock and water in your Crock Pot.
2. Add the quinoa, herbs and spices, as well as salt and pepper to taste and cover with a lid.
3. Cook on low settings for 6 hours.
4. Serve the soup warm or chilled.

Roasted Tomato Soup

Servings: 6 | Cooking Time: 5 Hours

Ingredients:
- 2 pounds heirloom tomatoes, halved
- 2 red onions, halved
- 4 garlic cloves
- 1 teaspoon dried oregano
- 2 tablespoons olive oil
- 2 cups vegetable stock
- 1 cup water
- 1 carrot, sliced
- 1/2 celery root, peeled and cubed
- Salt and pepper to taste

Directions:
1. Combine the tomatoes, red onions, garlic and oregano in a baking tray lined with parchment paper.
2. Season with salt and pepper and roast in the preheated oven at 400F for 30 minutes.
3. Transfer the vegetables and juices in your Crock Pot.
4. Add the remaining ingredients and cook on low settings for 4 hours.
5. When done, puree the soup with an immersion blender.
6. The soup can be served warm or chilled.

Chunky Potato Ham Soup

Servings: 8 | Cooking Time: 8 1/2 Hours

Ingredients:
- 2 cups diced ham
- 1 sweet onion, chopped
- 1 garlic clove, chopped
- 1 leek, sliced
- 1 celery stalk, sliced
- 2 carrots, sliced
- 2 pounds potatoes, peeled and cubed
- 1/2 teaspoon dried oregano
- 1/2 teaspoon dried basil
- 2 cups chicken stock
- 3 cups water
- Salt and pepper to taste

Directions:
1. Combine all the ingredients in your Crock Pot.
2. Add salt and pepper to taste and cook on low settings for 8 hours.
3. Serve the soup warm or chilled.

Okra Vegetable Soup

Servings: 8 | Cooking Time: 7 1/4 Hours

Ingredients:
- 1 pound ground beef
- 2 tablespoons canola oil
- 2 shallots, chopped
- 1 carrot, sliced
- 1 can fire roasted tomatoes, chopped
- 2 cups chopped okra
- 1/2 cup green peas
- 2 potatoes, peeled and cubed
- 1/2 cup sweet corn, drained
- Salt and pepper to taste
- 2 cups water
- 2 cups chicken stock
- 1 lemon, juiced

Directions:
1. Heat the oil in a skillet and stir in the beef. Cook for a few minutes then transfer the meat in your Crock Pot.
2. Add the shallots, carrot, tomatoes, okra, peas, potatoes, corn, water and stock, as well as lemon juice, salt and pepper.
3. Cook the soup on low settings for 7 hours.
4. Serve the soup warm and fresh.

Salmon Fennel Soup

Servings: 6 | Cooking Time: 5 1/4 Hours

Ingredients:
- 1 shallot, chopped
- 1 garlic clove, sliced
- 1 fennel bulb, sliced
- 1 carrot, diced
- 1 celery stalk, sliced
- 3 salmon fillets, cubed
- 1 lemon, juiced
- 1 bay leaf
- Salt and pepper to taste

Directions:
1. Combine the shallot, garlic, fennel, carrot, celery, fish, lemon juice and bay leaf in your Crock Pot.
2. Add salt and pepper to taste and cook on low settings for 5 hours.
3. Serve the soup warm.

Winter Veggie Soup

Servings: 8 | Cooking Time: 6 1/2 Hours

Ingredients:
- 1 sweet onion, chopped
- 2 carrots, sliced
- 1 celery stalk, sliced
- 1/2 head cabbage, shredded
- 1 parsnip, sliced
- 1 celery root, peeled and cubed
- Salt and pepper to taste
- 2 cups vegetable stock
- 3 cups water
- 1 cup diced tomatoes
- 1/4 cup white rice, rinsed
- 1 lemon, juiced

Directions:
1. Combine the onion, carrots, celery, cabbage, parsnip, celery, stock, water, tomatoes and rice in your Crock Pot.
2. Add salt and pepper to taste, as well as the rice and cook on low settings for 6 hours.
3. The soup is best served warm.

Lasagna Soup

Servings: 8 | Cooking Time: 8 1/2 Hours

Ingredients:
- 1 pound ground beef
- 2 tablespoons olive oil
- 1 large sweet onion, chopped
- 2 garlic cloves, chopped
- 1 teaspoon dried oregano
- 1 1/2 cups tomato sauce
- 1 cup diced tomatoes
- 2 cups beef stock
- 6 cups water
- 1 1/2 cups uncooked pasta shells
- Salt and pepper to taste
- Grated Cheddar for serving

Directions:
1. Heat the oil in a skillet and add the ground beef. Cook for 5 minutes then transfer in your Crock Pot.
2. Add the remaining ingredients and season with salt and pepper.
3. Cook on low settings for 8 hours.
4. When done, pour into serving bowls and top with cheese.
5. Serve the soup warm and fresh.

Mexican Chicken Stew

Servings: 6 | Cooking Time: 9 Hours 20 Minutes

Ingredients:
- 3 chicken breasts, boneless and skinless
- 1 can black beans, not drained
- 1 can corn
- 2 cans diced tomatoes and chilies
- ½ cup sour cream
- 1 cup onions, optional
- ½ cup Mexican cheese, shredded

Directions:

1. Place chicken breasts at the bottom of the Crock Pot and top with tomatoes, beans and corns.
2. Cover and cook on LOW for about 9 hours.
3. Dish out and serve hot.

Nutrition Info:
- Calories: 286 Fat: 12.7g Carbohydrates: 16.8g

Butternut Squash Chili

Servings:4 | Cooking Time: 3.5 Hours

Ingredients:
- 1 cup butternut squash, chopped
- 2 tablespoons pumpkin puree
- ½ cup red kidney beans, canned
- 1 teaspoon smoked paprika
- ½ teaspoon chili flakes
- 1 tablespoon cocoa powder
- ½ teaspoon salt
- 2 cups chicken stock

Directions:
1. Mix cocoa powder with chicken stock and stir it until smooth.
2. Then pour the liquid in the Crock Pot.
3. Add all remaining ingredients and carefully mix the chili.
4. Close the lid and cook the chili on high for 3.5 hours.

Nutrition Info:
- Per Serving: 105 calories, 6.3g protein, 20.2g carbohydrates, 0.8g fat, 5g fiber, 0mg cholesterol, 678mg sodium, 506mg potassium.

Cheddar Garlic Soup

Servings: 6 | Cooking Time: 2 1/4 Hours

Ingredients:
- 8 garlic cloves, chopped
- 2 tablespoons olive oil
- 1 teaspoon cumin seeds
- 1 teaspoon mustard seeds
- 2 tablespoons all-purpose flour
- 2 cups chicken stock
- 1/4 cup white wine
- 4 cups water
- 3 cups grated Cheddar
- Salt and pepper to taste

Directions:

1. Heat the oil in a skillet and add the garlic. Sauté on low heat for 2 minutes then add the seeds and cook for 1 minute to release flavor.
2. Add the flour and cook for 1 hour then transfer the mix in your Crock Pot.
3. Add the remaining ingredients and season with salt and pepper.
4. Cook on high settings for 2 hours.
5. The soup is best served warm.

Shrimp Chowder

Servings:4 | Cooking Time: 1 Hour

Ingredients:
- 1-pound shrimps
- ½ cup fennel bulb, chopped
- 1 bay leaf
- ½ teaspoon peppercorn
- 1 cup of coconut milk
- 3 cups of water
- 1 teaspoon ground coriander

Directions:
1. Put all ingredients in the Crock Pot.
2. Close the lid and cook the chowder on High for 1 hour.

Nutrition Info:
- Per Serving: 277 calories, 27.4g protein, 6.1g carbohydrates, 16.3g fat, 1.8g fiber, 239mg cholesterol, 297mg sodium, 401mg potassium.

Shrimp Soup

Servings: 6 | Cooking Time: 6 1/4 Hours

Ingredients:
- 2 tablespoons olive oil
- 1 large sweet onion, chopped
- 1 fennel bulb, sliced
- 4 garlic cloves, chopped
- 1 cup dry white wine
- 1/2 cup tomato sauce
- 2 cup water
- 1 teaspoon dried oregano
- 1 teaspoon dried basil
- 1 pinch chili powder
- 4 medium size tomatoes, peeled and diced
- 1 bay leaf
- 1/2 pound cod fillets, cubed
- 1/2 pound fresh shrimps, peeled and deveined
- Salt and pepper to taste
- 1 lime, juiced

Directions:
1. Heat the oil in a skillet and stir in the onion, fennel and garlic. Sauté for 5 minutes until softened.
2. Transfer the mixture in your Crock Pot and stir in the wine, tomato sauce, water, oregano, basil, chili powder, tomatoes and bay leaf.
3. Cook on high settings for 1 hour then add the cod and shrimps, as well as lime juice, salt and pepper and continue cooking on low settings for 5 additional hours.
4. Serve the soup warm or chilled.

Garlic Bean Soup

Servings:4 | Cooking Time: 8 Hours

Ingredients:
- 1 teaspoon minced garlic
- 1 cup celery stalk, chopped
- 1 cup white beans, soaked
- 5 cups of water
- 1 teaspoon salt
- 1 teaspoon ground paprika

- 1 tablespoon tomato paste

Directions:
1. Put all ingredients in the Crock Pot and carefully stir until tomato paste is dissolved.
2. Then close the lid and cook the soup on low for 8 hours.

Nutrition Info:
- Per Serving: 178 calories, 12.3g protein, 32.5g carbohydrates, 0.6g fat, 8.5g fiber, 0mg cholesterol, 623mg sodium, 1031mg potassium.

Paprika Hominy Stew

Servings:4 | Cooking Time: 4 Hours

Ingredients:
- 2 cups hominy, canned
- 1 tablespoon smoked paprika
- 1 teaspoon hot sauce
- ½ cup full-fat cream
- ½ cup ground chicken
- 1 cup of water

Directions:
1. Carefully mix all ingredients in the Crock Pot and close the lid.
2. Cook the stew on high for 4 hours.

Nutrition Info:
- Per Serving: 126 calories, 10.7g protein, 14.4g carbohydrates, 2.6g fat, 2.7g fiber, 18mg cholesterol, 380mg sodium, 140mg potassium.

Meatball Soup

Servings: 8 | Cooking Time: 6 1/2 Hours

Ingredients:
- 1 pound ground pork
- 1/4 cup white rice
- 1/2 teaspoon dried oregano
- 1/2 teaspoon dried basil
- Salt and pepper to taste
- 1 sweet onion, chopped
- 2 celery stalk, sliced
- 1 carrot, sliced
- 1 fennel bulb, sliced
- 1 cup diced tomatoes
- 2 cups chicken stock
- 4 cups water
- Salt and pepper to taste

Directions:
1. Mix the pork, rice, oregano, basil, salt and pepper in a bowl.
2. Combine the onion, celery stalk, carrot, fennel, tomatoes, stock and water in your Crock Pot.
3. Adjust the taste with salt and pepper then form small meatballs and place them in the Crock Pot.
4. Cook on low settings for 6 hours.
5. Serve the soup warm.

Kale Potato Soup

Servings: 6 | Cooking Time: 2 1/4 Hours

Ingredients:
- 1 shallot, chopped
- 1 garlic clove, chopped
- 1 celery stalk, sliced
- 2 carrots, sliced
- 1 1/2 pounds potatoes, peeled and cubed
- 1/2 cup diced tomatoes
- 1/4 pound kale, chopped
- 2 cups chicken stock
- 4 cups water
- Salt and pepper to taste
- 1/4 teaspoon chili flakes
- 2 tablespoons lemon juice

Directions:
1. Combine the shallot, garlic, celery, carrots, potatoes and tomatoes in your Crock Pot.
2. Add the kale, chili flakes, lemon juice, water and stock and season with salt and pepper.
3. Cook on high settings for 2 hours.
4. Serve the soup warm.

Kielbasa Kale Soup

Servings: 8 | Cooking Time: 6 1/4 Hours

Ingredients:
- 1 pound kielbasa sausages, sliced
- 1 sweet onion, chopped
- 1 carrot, diced
- 1 parsnip, diced
- 1 red bell pepper, cored and diced
- 1 can (15 oz.) white beans, drained
- 1 cup diced tomatoes
- 1/2 pound kale, shredded
- 2 cups chicken stock
- 2 cups water
- 1/2 teaspoon dried oregano
- 1/2 teaspoon dried basil
- Salt and pepper to taste

Directions:
1. Combine the kielbasa sausages, onion, carrot, parsnip, bell pepper, white beans, tomatoes and kale in a Crock Pot.
2. Add the remaining ingredients and season with salt and pepper.
3. Cook on low settings for 6 hours.
4. Serve the soup warm or chilled.

Hungarian Goulash Soup

Servings: 8 | Cooking Time: 8 1/2 Hours

Ingredients:
- 2 sweet onions, chopped
- 1 pound beef roast, cubed
- 2 tablespoons canola oil
- 2 carrots, diced
- 1/2 celery stalk, diced
- 2 red bell peppers, cored and diced
- 1 1/2 pounds potatoes, peeled and cubed
- 2 tablespoons tomato paste
- 1 cup diced tomatoes
- 1/2 cup beef stock
- 5 cups water
- 1/2 teaspoon cumin seeds
- 1/2 teaspoon smoked paprika
- Salt and pepper to taste

Directions:
1. Heat the oil in a skillet and stir in the beef. Cook for 5 minutes on all sides then stir in the onion. Sauté for 2 additional minutes then transfer in your Crock Pot.
2. Add the remaining ingredients and season with salt and pepper.
3. Cook on low settings for 8 hours.
4. Serve the soup warm.

Snack Recipes

Snack Recipes

Nuts Bowls

Servings: 2 | Cooking Time: 2 Hours

Ingredients:
- 2 tablespoons almonds, toasted
- 2 tablespoons pecans, halved and toasted
- 2 tablespoons hazelnuts, toasted and peeled
- 2 tablespoons sugar
- ½ cup coconut cream
- 2 tablespoons butter, melted
- A pinch of cinnamon powder
- A pinch of cayenne pepper

Directions:
1. In your Crock Pot, mix the nuts with the sugar and the other ingredients, toss, put the lid on, cook on Low for 2 hours, divide into bowls and serve as a snack.

Nutrition Info:
- calories 125, fat 3, fiber 2, carbs 5, protein 5

Potato Cups

Servings: 8 | Cooking Time: 8 Hours

Ingredients:
- 5 tbsp mashed potato
- 1 carrot, boiled, cubed
- 3 tbsp green peas
- 1 tsp paprika
- 3 tbsp sour cream
- 1 tsp minced garlic
- 7 oz. puff pastry
- 1 egg yolk, beaten
- 4 oz. Parmesan, shredded

Directions:
1. Mix mashed potato with carrot cubes in a bowl.
2. Stir in sour cream, paprika, green peas, and garlic, then mix well.
3. Spread the puff pastry and slice it into 2x2 inches squares.
4. Place the puff pastry square in the muffin cups of the muffin tray.
5. Press the puff pastry and in the muffin cups and brush it with egg yolk.
6. Divide the potatoes mixture into the muffin cups
7. Place the muffin tray in the Crock Pot.
8. Put the cooker's lid on and set the cooking time to 8 hours on Low settings.
9. Serve.

Nutrition Info:
- Per Serving: Calories: 387, Total Fat: 11.5g, Fiber: 6g, Total Carbs: 59.01g, Protein: 13g

Lentils Rolls

Servings: 4 | Cooking Time: 8 Hours

Ingredients:
- 1 cup brown lentils, cooked
- 1 green cabbage head, leaves separated
- ½ cup onion, chopped
- 1 cup brown rice, already cooked
- 2 ounces white mushrooms, chopped
- ¼ cup pine nuts, toasted
- ¼ cup raisins
- 2 garlic cloves, minced
- 2 tablespoons dill, chopped
- 1 tablespoon olive oil
- 25 ounces marinara sauce
- A pinch of salt and black pepper
- ¼ cup water

Directions:
1. In a bowl, mix lentils with onion, rice, mushrooms, pine nuts, raisins, garlic, dill, salt and pepper and whisk well.
2. Arrange cabbage leaves on a working surface, divide lentils mix and wrap them well.
3. Add marinara sauce and water to your Crock Pot and stir.
4. Add cabbage rolls, cover and cook on Low for 8 hours.
5. Arrange cabbage rolls on a platter and serve.

Nutrition Info:
- calories 281, fat 6, fiber 6, carbs 12, protein 3

Onion Dip

Servings: 6 | Cooking Time: 4 Hours

Ingredients:
- 7 cups tomatoes, chopped
- 1 yellow onion, chopped
- 1 red onion, chopped
- 3 jalapenos, chopped
- 1 red bell pepper, chopped
- 1 green bell pepper, chopped
- ¼ cup apple cider vinegar
- 1 tablespoon cilantro, chopped
- 1 tablespoon sage, chopped
- 3 tablespoons basil, chopped
- Salt to the taste

Directions:
1. In your Crock Pot, mix tomatoes with onion, jalapenos, red bell pepper, green bell pepper, vinegar, sage, cilantro and basil, stir, cover and cook on Low for 4 hours.
2. Transfer to your food processor, add salt, pulse well, divide into bowls and serve.

Nutrition Info:
- calories 162, fat 7, fiber 4, carbs 7, protein 3

Apple Chutney

Servings: 10 | Cooking Time: 9 Hours

Ingredients:
- 1 cup wine vinegar
- 4 oz. brown sugar
- 2 lbs. apples, chopped
- 4 oz. onion, chopped
- 1 jalapeno pepper
- 1 tsp ground cardamom
- ½ tsp ground cinnamon
- 1 tsp chili flakes

Directions:
1. Mix brown sugar with wine vinegar in the Crock Pot.
2. Put the cooker's lid on and set the cooking time to 1 hour on High settings.
3. Add chopped apples and all other ingredients to the cooker.
4. Put the cooker's lid on and set the cooking time to 8 hours on Low settings.
5. Mix well and mash the mixture with a fork.
6. Serve.

Nutrition Info:
- Per Serving: Calories: 101, Total Fat: 0.2g, Fiber: 3g, Total Carbs: 25.04g, Protein: 0g

Jalapeno Poppers

Servings: 4 | Cooking Time: 3 Hours

Ingredients:
- ½ pound chorizo, chopped
- 10 jalapenos, tops cut off and deseeded
- 1 small white onion, chopped
- ½ pound beef, ground
- ¼ teaspoon garlic powder
- 1 tablespoon maple syrup
- 1 tablespoon mustard
- 1/3 cup water

Directions:
1. In a bowl, mix beef with chorizo, garlic powder and onion and stir.
2. Stuff your jalapenos with the mix, place them in your Crock Pot, add the water, cover and cook on High for 3 hours.
3. Transfer jalapeno poppers to a lined baking sheet.
4. In a bowl, mix maple syrup with mustard, whisk well, brush poppers with this mix, arrange on a platter and serve.

Nutrition Info:
- calories 214, fat 2, fiber 3, carbs 8, protein 3

Eggplant Salsa

Servings: 2 | Cooking Time: 4 Hours

Ingredients:
- 1 cup cherry tomatoes, cubed
- 2 cups eggplant, cubed
- 1 tablespoon capers, drained
- 1 tablespoon black olives, pitted and sliced
- 1 tablespoon lemon juice
- 1 tablespoon olive oil
- ¼ cup mild salsa
- 2 teaspoons balsamic vinegar
- 1 tablespoon basil, chopped
- 1 tablespoon chives, chopped
- Salt and black pepper to the taste

Directions:
1. In your Crock Pot, mix the eggplant with the cherry tomatoes, capers, olives and the other ingredients, toss, put the lid on and cook on High for 4 hours.
2. Divide salsa into small bowls and serve.

Nutrition Info:
- calories 200, fat 6, fiber 5, carbs 9, protein 2

Garlic Parmesan Dip

Servings: 7 | Cooking Time: 6 Hours

Ingredients:
- 10 oz. garlic cloves, peeled
- 5 oz. Parmesan
- 1 cup cream cheese
- 1 tsp cayenne pepper
- 1 tbsp dried dill
- 1 tsp turmeric
- ½ tsp butter

Directions:
1. Add garlic cloves, cream cheese and all other ingredients to the Crock Pot.
2. Put the cooker's lid on and set the cooking time to 6 hours on Low settings.
3. Mix well and blend the dip with a hand blender.
4. Serve.

Nutrition Info:
- Per Serving: Calories: 244, Total Fat: 11.5g, Fiber: 1g, Total Carbs: 23.65g, Protein: 13g

Lentils Salsa

Servings: 2 | Cooking Time: 3 Hours

Ingredients:
- 1 cup canned lentils, drained
- 1 cup mild salsa
- 3 ounces tomato paste
- 2 tablespoons balsamic vinegar
- 1 small sweet onion, chopped
- 1 garlic clove, minced
- ½ tablespoon sugar
- A pinch of red pepper flakes
- A pinch of salt and black pepper
- 1 tablespoon chives, chopped

Directions:
1. In your Crock Pot, mix the lentils with the salsa and the other ingredients, toss, put the lid on and cook on High for 3 hours.
2. Divide into bowls and serve as a party salsa.

Nutrition Info:
- calories 260, fat 3, fiber 4, carbs 6, protein 7

Jalapeno Salsa Snack

Servings: 6 | Cooking Time: 3 Hours

Ingredients:
- 10 Roma tomatoes, chopped
- 2 jalapenos, chopped
- 1 sweet onion, chopped
- 28 oz. canned plum tomatoes
- 3 garlic cloves, minced
- 1 bunch cilantro, chopped
- Salt and black pepper to the taste

Directions:
1. Add Roma tomatoes, onion, and all other ingredients to the Crock Pot.
2. Put the cooker's lid on and set the cooking time to 3 hours on High settings.
3. Mix well and serve.

Nutrition Info:
- Per Serving: Calories: 162, Total Fat: 4g, Fiber: 6g, Total Carbs: 12g, Protein: 3g

Cauliflower Dip

Servings: 2 | Cooking Time: 5 Hours

Ingredients:
- 1 cup cauliflower florets
- ½ cup heavy cream
- 1 tablespoon tahini paste
- ½ cup white mushrooms, chopped
- 2 garlic cloves, minced
- 2 tablespoons lemon juice
- 1 tablespoon basil, chopped
- 1 teaspoon rosemary, dried
- A pinch of salt and black pepper

Directions:
1. In your Crock Pot, mix the cauliflower with the cream, tahini paste and the other ingredients, toss, put the lid on and cook on Low for 5 hours.
2. Transfer to a blender, pulse well, divide into bowls and serve as a party dip.

Nutrition Info:
- calories 301, fat 7, fiber 6, carbs 10, protein 6

Rice Snack Bowls

Servings: 2 | Cooking Time: 6 Hours

Ingredients:
- ½ cup wild rice
- 1 red onion, sliced
- ½ cup brown rice
- 2 cups veggie stock
- ½ cup baby spinach
- ½ cup cherry tomatoes, halved
- 2 tablespoons pine nuts, toasted
- 1 tablespoon raisins
- 1 tablespoon chives, chopped
- 1 tablespoon dill, chopped
- ½ tablespoon olive oil
- A pinch of salt and black pepper

Directions:
1. In your Crock Pot, mix the rice with the onion, stock and the other ingredients, toss, put the lid on and cook on Low for 6 hours.
2. Divide in to bowls and serve as a snack.

Nutrition Info:
- calories 301, fat 6, fiber 6, carbs 12, protein 3

Bulgur And Beans Salsa

Servings: 2 | Cooking Time: 8 Hours

Ingredients:
- 1 cup veggie stock
- ½ cup bulgur
- 1 small yellow onion, chopped
- 1 red bell pepper, chopped
- 1 garlic clove, minced
- 5 ounces canned kidney beans, drained
- ½ cup salsa
- 1 tablespoon chili powder
- ¼ teaspoon oregano, dried
- Salt and black pepper to the taste

Directions:
1. In your Crock Pot, mix the bulgur with the stock and the other ingredients, toss, put the lid on and cook on Low for 8 hours.
2. Divide into bowls and serve cold as an appetizer.

Nutrition Info:
- calories 351, fat 4, fiber 6, carbs 12, protein 4

White Cheese & Green Chilies Dip

Servings: 8 (4 Ounces Per Serving) | Cooking Time: 55 Minutes

Ingredients:
- 1 lb. white cheddar, cut into cubes
- 1 cup cream cheese
- 2 tablespoons butter, salted
- 1 can (11 oz.) green chilies, drained
- 1 tablespoons pepper flakes, (optional)
- 3 tablespoons milk
- 3 tablespoons water

Directions:
1. Cut chilies into quarters. Place all the ingredients (except milk and water) in Crock-Pot. Close the lid and cook on HIGH for 30 minutes. Stir the mixture until it is well combined and then add water and milk; continue to stir until it reaches desired consistency. Close lid and cook for another 20 minutes. Let cool and serve.

Nutrition Info:
- Calories: 173.76, Total Fat: 15.16 g, Saturated Fat: 7.53 g, Cholesterol: 37.71 g, Sodium: 394.08 mg, Potassium: 309.15 mg, Total Carbohydrates: 6.67 g, Fiber: 0.52 g, Sugar: 2.13 g, Protein: 2.88 g

Marsala Cheese Mushrooms

Servings: 6 | Cooking Time: 8 Hours 20 Minutes

Ingredients:
- 4 oz. marsala
- 8 oz. button mushrooms
- ½ cup fresh dill
- 2 oz. shallot, chopped
- 3 oz. chicken stock
- 5 oz. cream, whipped
- 1 oz. corn starch
- 3 garlic cloves, chopped
- 3 oz. Cheddar cheese
- 1 tsp salt
- ½ tsp paprika

Directions:
1. Add mushrooms to the base of the Crock Pot.
2. Mix Marsala wine with chicken stock and pour over the mushrooms.
3. Now add shallot, salt, and paprika to the cooker.
4. Put the cooker's lid on and set the cooking time to 8 hours on Low settings.
5. Whisk cream with dill, cornstarch, and cheese.
6. Add this cream-cheese mixture to the cooked mushrooms.
7. Put the cooker's lid on and set the cooking time to 20 minutes on High settings.
8. Serve.

Nutrition Info:
- Per Serving: Calories: 254, Total Fat: 10.3g, Fiber: 5g, Total Carbs: 35.7g, Protein: 9g

Mushroom Salsa

Servings: 4 | Cooking Time: 5 Hours

Ingredients:
- 2 cups white mushrooms, sliced
- 1 cup cherry tomatoes halved
- 1 cup spring onions, chopped
- ½ teaspoon chili powder
- ½ teaspoon rosemary, dried
- ½ teaspoon oregano, dried
- ½ cup black olives, pitted and sliced
- 3 garlic cloves, minced
- 1 cup mild salsa
- Salt and black pepper to the taste

Directions:
1. In your Crock Pot, mix the mushrooms with the cherry tomatoes and the other ingredients, toss, put the lid on and cook on Low for 5 hours.
2. Divide into bowls and serve as a snack.

Nutrition Info:
- calories 205, fat 4, fiber 7, carbs 9, protein 3

Apple And Carrot Dip

Servings: 2 | Cooking Time: 6 Hours

Ingredients:
- 2 cups apples, peeled, cored and chopped
- 1 cup carrots, peeled and grated
- ¼ teaspoon cloves, ground
- ¼ teaspoon ginger powder
- 1 tablespoon lemon juice
- ½ tablespoon lemon zest, grated
- ½ cup coconut cream
- ¼ teaspoon nutmeg, ground

Directions:
1. In your Crock Pot, mix the apples with the carrots, cloves and the other ingredients, toss, put the lid on and cook on Low for 6 hours.
2. Bend using an immersion blender, divide into bowls and serve.

Nutrition Info:
- calories 212, fat 4, fiber 6, carbs 12, protein 3

Crispy Sweet Potatoes With Paprika

Servings: 4 (3.2 Ounces Per Serving) | Cooking Time: 4 Hours And 45 Minutes

Ingredients:
- 2 medium sweet potatoes
- 2 tablespoons olive oil
- 1 teaspoon Cayenne pepper, optional
- 1 tablespoon nutritional yeast, optional
- Sea salt

Directions:
1. Wash and peel the sweet potatoes. Slice them into wedges. In a bowl, mix the potatoes with the other ingredients. Grease the bottom of Crock-Pot and place the sweet potato wedges in it. Cover and cook on LOW for 4- 4 ½ hours. Serve hot.

Nutrition Info:
- Calories: 120.72, Total Fat: 7.02 g, Saturated Fat: 0.98 g, Cholesterol: 0 mg, Sodium: 37.07 mg, Potassium: 260.14 mg, Total Carbohydrates: 9.06 g, Fiber: 2.57 g, Sugar: 2.9 g

Mushroom Dip

Servings: 6 | Cooking Time: 4 Hours

Ingredients:
- 2 cups green bell peppers, chopped
- 1 cup yellow onion, chopped
- 3 garlic cloves, minced
- 1 pound mushrooms, chopped
- 28 ounces tomato sauce
- ½ cup goat cheese, crumbled
- Salt and black pepper to the taste

Directions:
1. In your Crock Pot, mix bell peppers with onion, garlic, mushrooms, tomato sauce, cheese, salt and pepper, stir, cover and cook on Low for 4 hours.
2. Divide into bowls and serve.

Nutrition Info:
- calories 255, fat 4, fiber 7, carbs 9, protein 3

Chickpea Hummus

Servings: 10 | Cooking Time: 8 Hrs

Ingredients:
- 1 cup chickpeas, dried
- 2 tbsp olive oil
- 3 cup of water
- A pinch of salt and black pepper
- 1 garlic clove, minced
- 1 tbsp lemon juice

Directions:
1. Add chickpeas, salt, water, and black pepper to the Crock Pot.
2. Put the cooker's lid on and set the cooking time to 8 hours on Low settings.
3. Drain and transfer the chickpeas to a blender jug.
4. Add salt, black pepper, lemon juice, garlic, and olive oil.
5. Blend the chickpeas dip until smooth.
6. Serve.

Nutrition Info:
- Per Serving: Calories: 211, Total Fat: 6g, Fiber: 7g, Total Carbs: 8g, Protein: 4g

Tacos

Servings: 2 | Cooking Time: 4 Hours

Ingredients:
- 13 ounces canned pinto beans, drained
- ¼ cup chili sauce
- 2 ounces chipotle pepper in adobo sauce, chopped
- ½ tablespoon cocoa powder
- ¼ teaspoon cinnamon powder
- 4 taco shells

Directions:
1. In your Crock Pot, mix the beans with the chili sauce and the other ingredients except the taco shells, toss, put the lid on and cook on Low for 4 hours.
2. Divide the mix into the taco shells and serve them as an appetizer.

Nutrition Info:
- calories 352, fat 3, fiber 6, carbs 12, protein 10

Salsa Beans Dip

Servings: 2 | Cooking Time: 1 Hour

Ingredients:
- ¼ cup salsa
- 1 cup canned red kidney beans, drained and rinsed
- ½ cup mozzarella, shredded
- 1 tablespoon green onions, chopped

Directions:
1. In your Crock Pot, mix the salsa with the beans and the other ingredients, toss, put the lid on cook on High for 1 hour.
2. Divide into bowls and serve as a party dip

Nutrition Info:
- calories 302, fat 5, fiber 10, carbs 16, protein 6

Sausage Cream Dip

Servings: 8 | Cooking Time: 5 Hours

Ingredients:
- 8 oz. sausage, cooked, chopped
- 4 tbsp sour cream
- 2 tbsp Tabasco sauce
- ½ cup cream cheese
- 3 tbsp chives
- 5 oz. salsa
- 4 oz. Monterey Cheese

Directions:
1. Mix chopped sausages with sour cream in the Crock Pot.
2. Stir in Tabasco sauce, cream cheese, salsa, chives, and Monterey cheese.
3. Put the cooker's lid on and set the cooking time to 5 hours on Low settings.
4. Continue mixing the dip after every 30 minutes of cooking.
5. Serve.

Nutrition Info:
- Per Serving: Calories: 184, Total Fat: 14.4g, Fiber: 1g, Total Carbs: 5.11g, Protein: 10g

Beets Salad

Servings: 2 | Cooking Time: 6 Hours

Ingredients:
- 2 cups beets, cubed
- ¼ cup carrots, grated
- 2 ounces tempeh, rinsed and cubed
- 1 cup cherry tomatoes, halved
- ¼ cup veggie stock
- 3 ounces canned black beans, drained
- Salt and black pepper to the taste
- ½ teaspoon nutmeg, ground
- ½ teaspoon sweet paprika
- ½ cup parsley, chopped

Directions:
1. In your Crock Pot, mix the beets with the carrots, tempeh and the other ingredients, toss, put the lid on and cook on Low for 6 hours.
2. Divide into bowls and serve cold as an appetizer.

Nutrition Info:
- calories 300, fat 6, fiber 6, carbs 16, protein 6

Fava Bean Onion Dip

Servings: 6 | Cooking Time: 5 Hours

Ingredients:
- 1 lb. fava bean, rinsed
- 1 cup yellow onion, chopped
- 4 and ½ cups of water
- 1 bay leaf
- ¼ cup olive oil
- 1 garlic clove, minced
- 2 tbsp lemon juice
- Salt to the taste

Directions:
1. Add 4 cups water, bay leaf, salt, and fava beans to the

Crock Pot.

2. Put the cooker's lid on and set the cooking time to 3 hours on low settings.

3. Drain the Crock Pot beans and discard the bay leaf.

4. Return the cooked beans to the cooker and add onion, garlic, and ½ cup water.

5. Put the cooker's lid on and set the cooking time to 2 hours on Low settings.

6. Blend the slow-cooked beans with lemon juice and olive oil.

7. Serve.

Nutrition Info:
- Per Serving: Calories: 300, Total Fat: 3g, Fiber: 1g, Total Carbs: 20g, Protein: 6g

Crock-pot Citrus Cake

Servings: 10 (4.3 Ounces Per Serving) | Cooking Time: 6 Hours

Ingredients:
- ½ teaspoon orange rind, grated
- ½ cup almond flour
- 1 ½ tablespoons lemon rind, grated
- 1 tablespoon grapefruit juice (freshly squeezed)
- 1 ½ cup almond milk
- 1 cup sweetener
- 1 cup butter, softened
- 4 egg whites
- 3 egg yolks
- 3 tablespoons lime juice (freshly squeezed)

Directions:
1. In a bowl, beat sweetener and butter. Mix in flour and stir until well blended. Add the lime, lemon, and orange rinds and all citrus juices. Whisk egg yolks and milk in another bowl; pour into bowl with flour mixture and stir well. In a separate bowl, beat egg whites until they form stiff peaks, then fold into the batter; stir. Spoon the mixture into a lightly greased heat-proof bowl/dish and cover with foil. Pour a cup of water into Crock-Pot and place the batter dish into it. Cover and cook on LOW for 5-6 hours.

Nutrition Info:
- Calories: 269.63, Total Fat: 20.5 g, Saturated Fat: 12.6 g, Cholesterol: 105.77 mg, Potassium: 102.9 mg, Total Carbohydrates: 18.23 g, Fiber: 0.08 g, Sugar: 16.01 g, Protein: 4.08 g

Cashew Dip

Servings: 10 | Cooking Time: 3 Hours

Ingredients:
- 1 cup water
- 1 cup cashews
- 10 ounces hummus
- ¼ teaspoon garlic powder
- ¼ teaspoon onion powder
- A pinch of salt and black pepper
- ¼ teaspoon mustard powder
- 1 teaspoon apple cider vinegar

Directions:

1. In your Crock Pot, mix water with cashews, salt and pepper, stir, cover and cook on High for 3 hours.

2. Transfer to your blender, add hummus, garlic powder, onion powder, mustard powder and vinegar, pulse well, divide into bowls and serve.

Nutrition Info:
- calories 192, fat 7, fiber 7, carbs 12, protein 4

Chicken Meatballs

Servings: 2 | Cooking Time: 7 Hours

Ingredients:
- A pinch of red pepper flakes, crushed
- ½ pound chicken breast, skinless, boneless, ground
- 1 egg, whisked
- ½ cup salsa Verde
- 1 teaspoon oregano, dried
- ½ teaspoon chili powder
- ½ teaspoon rosemary, dried
- 1 tablespoon parsley, chopped
- A pinch of salt and black pepper

Directions:
1. In a bowl, mix the chicken with the egg and the other ingredients except the salsa, stir well and shape medium meatballs out of this mix.

2. Put the meatballs in the Crock Pot, add the salsa Verde, toss gently, put the lid on and cook on Low for 7 hours.

3. Arrange the meatballs on a platter and serve.

Nutrition Info:
- calories 201, fat 4, fiber 5, carbs 8, protein 2

Beer And Cheese Dip

Servings: 10 | Cooking Time: 1 Hour

Ingredients:
- 12 ounces cream cheese
- 6 ounces beer
- 4 cups cheddar cheese, shredded
- 1 tablespoon chives, chopped

Directions:
1. In your Crock Pot, mix cream cheese with beer and cheddar, stir, cover and cook on Low for 1 hour.

2. Stir your dip, add chives, divide into bowls and serve.

Nutrition Info:
- calories 212, fat 4, fiber 7, carbs 16, protein 5

Cajun Almonds And Shrimp Bowls

Servings: 2 | Cooking Time: 2 Hours

Ingredients:
- 1 cup almonds
- 1 pound shrimp, peeled and deveined
- ½ cup kalamata olives, pitted and halved
- ½ cup black olives, pitted and halved
- ½ cup mild salsa
- ½ tablespoon Cajun seasoning

Directions:
1. In your Crock Pot, mix the shrimp with the almonds, olives and the other ingredients, toss, put the lid on and cook on High

for 2 hours.
2. Divide between small plates and serve as an appetizer.

Nutrition Info:
- calories 100, fat 2, fiber 3, carbs 7, protein 3

Almond Bowls

Servings: 2 | Cooking Time: 4 Hours

Ingredients:
- 1 tablespoon cinnamon powder
- 1 cup sugar
- 2 cups almonds
- ½ cup water
- ½ teaspoons vanilla extract

Directions:
1. In your Crock Pot, mix the almonds with the cinnamon and the other ingredients, toss, put the lid on and cook on Low for 4 hours.
2. Divide into bowls and serve as a snack.

Nutrition Info:
- calories 260, fat 3, fiber 4, carbs 12, protein 8

Macadamia Nuts Snack

Servings: 2 | Cooking Time: 2 Hours

Ingredients:
- ½ pound macadamia nuts
- 1 tablespoon avocado oil
- ¼ cup water
- ½ tablespoon chili powder
- ½ teaspoon oregano, dried
- ½ teaspoon onion powder

Directions:
1. In your Crock Pot, mix the macadamia nuts with the oil and the other ingredients, toss, put the lid on, cook on Low for 2 hours, divide into bowls and serve as a snack.

Nutrition Info:
- calories 108, fat 3, fiber 2, carbs 9, protein 2

Lentils Hummus

Servings: 2 | Cooking Time: 4 Hours

Ingredients:
- 1 cup chicken stock
- 1 cup canned lentils, drained
- 2 tablespoons tahini paste
- ¼ teaspoon onion powder
- ¼ cup heavy cream
- A pinch of salt and black pepper
- ¼ teaspoon turmeric powder
- 1 teaspoon lemon juice

Directions:
1. In your Crock Pot, mix the lentils with the stock, onion powder, salt and pepper, toss, put the lid on and cook on High for 4 hours.
2. Drain the lentils, transfer to your blender, add the rest of the ingredients, pulse well, divide into bowls and serve.

Nutrition Info:
- calories 192, fat 7, fiber 7, carbs 12, protein 4

Apple Jelly Sausage Snack

Servings: 15 | Cooking Time: 2 Hours

Ingredients:
- 2 pounds sausages, sliced
- 18 ounces apple jelly
- 9 ounces Dijon mustard

Directions:
1. Place sausage slices in your Crock Pot, add apple jelly and mustard, toss to coat well, cover and cook on Low for 2 hours.
2. Divide into bowls and serve as a snack.

Nutrition Info:
- calories 200, fat 3, fiber 1, carbs 9, protein 10

Eggplant Salsa

Servings: 4 | Cooking Time: 7 Hours

Ingredients:
- 1 and ½ cups tomatoes, chopped
- 3 cups eggplant, cubed
- 2 teaspoons capers
- 6 ounces green olives, pitted and sliced
- 4 garlic cloves, minced
- 2 teaspoons balsamic vinegar
- 1 tablespoon basil, chopped
- Salt and black pepper to the taste

Directions:
1. In your Crock Pot, mix tomatoes with eggplant cubes, capers, green olives, garlic, vinegar, basil, salt and pepper, toss, cover and cook on Low for 7 hours.
2. Divide salsa into bowls and serve.

Nutrition Info:
- calories 200, fat 6, fiber 5, carbs 9, protein 2

Lemon Shrimp Dip

Servings: 2 | Cooking Time: 2 Hours

Ingredients:
- 3 ounces cream cheese, soft
- ½ cup heavy cream
- 1 pound shrimp, peeled, deveined and chopped
- ½ tablespoon balsamic vinegar
- 2 tablespoons mayonnaise
- ½ tablespoon lemon juice
- A pinch of salt and black pepper
- 2 ounces mozzarella, shredded
- 1 tablespoon parsley, chopped

Directions:
1. In your Crock Pot, mix the cream cheese with the shrimp, heavy cream and the other ingredients, whisk, put the lid on and cook on Low for 2 hours.
2. Divide into bowls and serve as a dip.

Nutrition Info:
- calories 342, fat 4, fiber 3, carbs 7, protein 10

Broccoli Dip

Servings: 2 | Cooking Time: 2 Hours

Ingredients:
- 1 green chili pepper, minced
- 2 tablespoons heavy cream
- 1 cup broccoli florets
- 1 tablespoon mayonnaise
- 2 tablespoons cream cheese, cubed
- A pinch of salt and black pepper
- 1 tablespoon chives, chopped

Directions:
1. In your Crock Pot, mix the broccoli with the chili pepper, mayo and the other ingredients, toss, put the lid on and cook on Low for 2 hours.
2. Blend using an immersion blender, divide into bowls and serve as a party dip.

Nutrition Info:
- calories 202, fat 3, fiber 3, carbs 7, protein 6

Candied Pecans

Servings: 4 | Cooking Time: 3 Hours

Ingredients:
- 1 cup white sugar
- 1 and ½ tablespoons cinnamon powder
- ½ cup brown sugar
- 1 egg white, whisked
- 4 cups pecans
- 2 teaspoons vanilla extract
- ¼ cup water

Directions:
1. In a bowl, mix white sugar with cinnamon, brown sugar and vanilla and stir.
2. Dip pecans in egg white, then in sugar mix and put them in your Crock Pot, also add the water, cover and cook on Low for 3 hours.
3. Divide into bowls and serve as a snack.

Nutrition Info:
- calories 152, fat 4, fiber 7, carbs 16, protein 6

Tamales

Servings: 24 | Cooking Time: 8 Hours And 30 Minutes

Ingredients:
- 8 ounces dried corn husks, soaked for 1 day and drained
- 4 cups water
- 3 pounds pork shoulder, boneless and chopped
- 1 yellow onion, chopped
- 2 garlic cloves, crushed
- 1 tablespoon chipotle chili powder
- 2 tablespoons chili powder
- Salt and black pepper to the taste
- 1 teaspoon cumin, ground
- 4 cups masa harina
- ¼ cup corn oil
- ¼ cup shortening
- 1 teaspoon baking powder

Directions:

1. In your Crock Pot, mix 2 cups water with salt, pepper, onion, garlic, chipotle powder, chili powder, cumin and pork, stir, cover the Crock Pot and cook on Low for 7 hours.
2. Transfer meat to a cutting board, shred it with 2 forks, add to a bowl, mix with 1 tablespoon of cooking liquid, more salt and pepper, stir and leave aside.
3. In another bowl, mix masa harina with salt, pepper, baking powder, shortening and oil and stir using a mixer.
4. Add cooking liquid from the instant Crock Pot and blend again well.
5. Unfold corn husks, place them on a work surface, add ¼ cup masa mix near the top of the husk, press into a square and leaves 2 inches at the bottom.
6. Add 1 tablespoon pork mix in the center of the masa, wrap the husk around the dough, place all of them in your Crock Pot, add the rest of the water, cover and cook on High for 1 hour and 30 minutes.
7. Arrange tamales on a platter and serve.

Nutrition Info:
- calories 162, fat 4, fiber 3, carbs 10, protein 5

Beef Tomato Meatballs

Servings: 8 | Cooking Time: 8 Hrs

Ingredients:
- 1 and ½ lbs. beef, ground
- 1 egg, whisked
- 16 oz. canned tomatoes, crushed
- 14 oz. canned tomato puree
- ¼ cup parsley, chopped
- 2 garlic cloves, minced
- 1 yellow onion, chopped
- Salt and black pepper to the taste

Directions:
1. Mix beef with parsley, egg, garlic, onion, and black pepper in a bowl.
2. Make 16 small meatballs out of this beef mixture.
3. Add tomato puree, tomatoes, and meatballs to the Crock Pot.
4. Put the cooker's lid on and set the cooking time to 8 hours on Low settings.
5. Serve warm.

Nutrition Info:
- Per Serving: Calories: 160, Total Fat: 5g, Fiber: 3g, Total Carbs: 10g, Protein: 7g

Peppers Salsa

Servings: 2 | Cooking Time: 5 Hours And 5 Minutes

Ingredients:
- 1 yellow onion, chopped
- 2 spring onions, chopped
- 2 teaspoons olive oil
- 1 teaspoon turmeric powder
- 1 red bell pepper, roughly cubed
- 1 green bell pepper, roughly cubed
- 1 orange bell pepper, roughly cubed
- 1 cup cherry tomatoes, halved
- 1 tablespoon chili powder
- 3 garlic cloves, minced

- ½ cup mild salsa
- 1 teaspoon oregano, dried
- A pinch of salt and black pepper

Directions:

1. Heat up a pan with the oil over medium-high heat, add the spring onions, onion and garlic, sauté for 5 minutes and transfer to the Crock Pot.
2. Add the rest of the ingredients, toss, put the lid on and cook on Low for 5 hours.
3. Divide the mix into bowls and serve as a snack.

Nutrition Info:

- calories 221, fat 5, fiber 4, carbs 9, protein 3

Peanut Snack

Servings: 4 | Cooking Time: 1 Hour And 30 Minutes

Ingredients:

- 1 cup peanuts
- 1 cup chocolate peanut butter
- 12 ounces dark chocolate chips
- 12 ounces white chocolate chips

Directions:

1. In your Crock Pot, mix peanuts with peanut butter, dark and white chocolate chips, cover and cook on Low for 1 hour and 30 minutes.
2. Divide this mix into small muffin cups, leave aside to cool down and serve as a snack.

Nutrition Info:

- calories 200, fat 4, fiber 6, carbs 10, protein 5

Almond Spread

Servings: 2 | Cooking Time: 8 Hours

Ingredients:

- ¼ cup almonds
- 1 cup heavy cream
- ½ teaspoon nutritional yeast flakes
- A pinch of salt and black pepper

Directions:

1. In your Crock Pot, mix the almonds with the cream and the other ingredients, toss, put the lid on and cook on Low for 8 hours.
2. Transfer to a blender, pulse well, divide into bowls and serve.

Nutrition Info:

- calories 270, fat 4, fiber 4, carbs 8, protein 10

Beef And Chipotle Dip

Servings: 10 | Cooking Time: 2 Hours

Ingredients:

- 8 ounces cream cheese, soft
- 2 tablespoons yellow onion, chopped
- 2 tablespoons mayonnaise
- 2 ounces hot pepper Monterey Jack cheese, shredded
- ¼ teaspoon garlic powder
- 2 chipotle chilies in adobo sauce, chopped
- 2 ounces dried beef, chopped
- ¼ cup pecans, chopped

Directions:

1. In your Crock Pot, mix cream cheese with onion, mayo, Monterey Jack cheese, garlic powder, chilies and dried beef, stir, cover and cook on Low for 2 hours.
2. Add pecans, stir, divide into bowls and serve.

Nutrition Info:

- calories 130, fat 11, fiber 1, carbs 3, protein 4

Dill Butter Muffins

Servings: 6 | Cooking Time: 9 Hours

Ingredients:

- 2 egg
- 5 tbsp butter
- 1 cup fresh dill
- 1 tsp baking soda
- 1 tbsp lemon juice
- 1 tsp cilantro
- 1 cup milk
- 2 cups flour
- 1 tsp salt
- ¼ tsp cooking spray

Directions:

1. Whisk eggs with butter, baking soda, lemon juice, flour, salt, milk, dill, and cilantro in a bowl.
2. Divide this dill batter into a greased muffin tray.
3. Place the muffin tray in the Crock Pot.
4. Put the cooker's lid on and set the cooking time to 9 hours on Low settings.
5. Serve.

Nutrition Info:

- Per Serving: Calories: 306, Total Fat: 14.6g, Fiber: 1g, Total Carbs: 34.37g, Protein: 9g

Chickpeas Spread

Servings: 2 | Cooking Time: 8 Hours

Ingredients:

- ½ cup chickpeas, dried
- 1 tablespoons olive oil
- 1 tablespoon lemon juice
- 1 cup veggie stock
- 1 tablespoon tahini
- A pinch of salt and black pepper
- 1 garlic clove, minced
- ½ tablespoon chives, chopped

Directions:

1. In your Crock Pot, combine the chickpeas with the stock, salt, pepper and the garlic, stir, put the lid on and cook on Low for 8 hours.
2. Drain chickpeas, transfer them to a blender, add the rest of the ingredients, pulse well, divide into bowls and serve as a party spread.

Nutrition Info:

- calories 211, fat 6, fiber 7, carbs 8, protein 4

Veggie Spread

Servings: 4 | Cooking Time: 7 Hours

Ingredients:
- 1 cup carrots, sliced
- 1 and ½ cups cauliflower florets
- 1/3 cup cashews
- ½ cup turnips, chopped
- 2 and ½ cups water
- 1 cup almond milk
- 1 teaspoon garlic powder
- Salt and black pepper to the taste
- ¼ teaspoon smoked paprika
- ¼ teaspoon mustard powder
- A pinch of salt

Directions:
1. In your Crock Pot, mix carrots with cauliflower, cashews, turnips and water, stir, cover and cook on Low for 7 hours.
2. Drain, transfer to a blender, add almond milk, garlic powder, paprika, mustard powder, salt and pepper, blend well, divide into bowls and serve as a snack.

Nutrition Info:
- calories 291, fat 7, fiber 4, carbs 14, protein 3

Tex Mex Dip

Servings: 6 | Cooking Time: 1 Hour

Ingredients:
- 15 ounces canned chili con carne
- 1 cup Mexican cheese, shredded
- 1 yellow onion, chopped
- 8 ounces cream cheese, cubed
- ½ cup beer
- A pinch of salt
- 12 ounces macaroni, cooked
- 1 tablespoons cilantro, chopped

Directions:
1. In your Crock Pot, mix chili con carne with cheese, onion, cream cheese, beer and salt, stir, cover and cook on High for 1 hour.
2. Add macaroni and cilantro, stir, divide into bowls and serve.

Nutrition Info:
- calories 200, fat 4, fiber 6, carbs 17, protein 5

Zucchini Sticks

Servings: 13 | Cooking Time: 2 Hours

Ingredients:
- 9 oz. green zucchini, cut into thick sticks
- 4 oz. Parmesan, grated
- 1 egg
- 1 tsp salt
- 1 tsp ground white pepper
- 1 tsp olive oil
- 2 tbsp milk

Directions:
1. Grease of the base of your Crock Pot with olive oil.
2. Whisk egg with milk, white pepper, and salt in a bowl.
3. Dip the prepared zucchini sticks in the egg mixture then place them in the Crock Pot.
4. Put the cooker's lid on and set the cooking time to 2 hours on High settings.
5. Spread the cheese over the zucchini sticks evenly.
6. Put the cooker's lid on and set the cooking time to 2 hours on High settings.
7. Serve.

Nutrition Info:
- Per Serving: Calories: 51, Total Fat: 1.7g, Fiber: 0g, Total Carbs: 4.62g, Protein: 5g

Eggplant Salsa

Servings: 2 | Cooking Time: 7 Hours

Ingredients:
- 2 cups eggplant, chopped
- 1 teaspoon capers, drained
- 1 cup black olives, pitted and halved
- ½ cup mild salsa
- 2 garlic cloves, minced
- ½ tablespoon basil, chopped
- 1 teaspoon balsamic vinegar
- A pinch of salt and black pepper

Directions:
1. In your Crock Pot, mix the eggplant with the capers and the other ingredients, toss, put the lid on and cook on Low for 7 hours.
2. Divide into bowls and serve as an appetizer.

Nutrition Info:
- calories 170, fat 3, fiber 5, carbs 10, protein 5

Dessert Recipes

Dessert Recipes

Clove Pastry Wheels

Servings:4 | Cooking Time: 3 Hours

Ingredients:
- 1 teaspoon ground clove
- 4 oz puff pastry
- 1 tablespoon brown sugar
- 1 tablespoon butter, softened

Directions:
1. Roll up the puff pastry into a square.
2. Then grease the puff pastry with butter and sprinkle with ground clove.
3. Roll it in the shape of a log and cut it into pieces (wheels).
4. Put the baking paper at the bottom of the Crock Pot.
5. Then put puff pastry wheels inside in one layer and close the lid.
6. Cook the meal on High for 3 hours.

Nutrition Info:
- Per Serving: 192 calories, 2.1g protein, 15.3g carbohydrates, 13.8g fat, 0.6g fiber, 8mg cholesterol, 93mg sodium, 27mg potassium.

Apple Dump Cake

Servings: 8 | Cooking Time: 4 1/2 Hours

Ingredients:
- 6 Granny Smith apples, peeled, cored and sliced
- 1/4 cup light brown sugar
- 1 teaspoon cinnamon
- 1 box yellow cake mix
- 1/2 cup butter, melted

Directions:
1. Mix the apples, brown sugar and cinnamon in a Crock Pot.
2. Top with the cake mix and drizzle with butter.
3. Cover the pot and cook on low settings for 4 hours.
4. Allow the cake to cool in the pot before serving.

Cardamom Apple Jam

Servings:4 | Cooking Time: 2.5 Hours

Ingredients:
- 1 cup apples, chopped
- 1 teaspoon ground cardamom
- 2 tablespoons brown sugar
- 1 teaspoon agar

Directions:
1. Mix apples with brown sugar and transfer in the Crock Pot.
2. Leave the apples until they get the juice.
3. Then add ground cardamom and agar. Mix the mixture.
4. Close the lid and cook the jam on High for 2.5 hours.
5. Then blend the mixture until smooth and cool to room temperature.

Nutrition Info:
- Per Serving: 48 calories, 0.2g protein, 12.5g carbohydrates, 0.1g fat, 1.5g fiber, 0mg cholesterol, 2mg sodium, 72mg potassium.

Carrot Cake

Servings: 12 | Cooking Time: 2 3/4 Hours

Ingredients:
- 3/4 cup white sugar
- 1/4 cup dark brown sugar
- 2 eggs
- 1/2 cup canola oil
- 1 teaspoon vanilla extract
- 1 1/2 cups all-purpose flour
- 1 teaspoon baking powder
- 1/2 teaspoon baking soda
- 1/2 teaspoon ground ginger
- 1 teaspoon cinnamon powder
- 1/4 teaspoon cardamom powder
- 1/2 teaspoon salt
- 1 cup grated carrots
- 1 cup crushed pineapple, drained
- 1/2 cup pecans, chopped

Directions:
1. Mix the two types of sugar, eggs, canola oil and vanilla in a bowl until creamy.
2. Fold in the flour, baking powder, baking soda, ginger, cinnamon, cardamom powder and salt then add the carrots, crushed pineapple and pecans.
3. Pour the batter in your Crock Pot and cook for 2 1/4 hours on high settings.
4. Allow the cake to cool in the pot before slicing and serving.

Boozy Bread Pudding

Servings: 10 | Cooking Time: 6 1/2 Hours

Ingredients:
- 8 cups bread cubes
- 1/4 cup dark chocolate chips
- 1/2 cup golden raisins
- 1/2 cup dried apricots, chopped
- 1/2 cup dried cranberries
- 1/2 cup brandy
- 4 eggs
- 2 cups whole milk
- 1/2 cup fresh orange juice
- 1/2 cup light brown sugar

Directions:
1. Combine the bread cubes and chocolate chips in your Crock Pot.
2. Mix the raisins, apricots, cranberries and brandy in a bowl and allow to soak up for 30 minutes at least, preferably overnight.
3. In a bowl, mix the eggs, milk, orange juice and brown sugar.
4. Spoon the dried fruits and brandy over the bread cubes and top with the egg and milk mixture.
5. Cover the pot and bake for 6 hours on low settings.
6. The pudding is best served slightly warm.

Servings: 8 | Cooking Time: 6 1/2 Hours

Ingredients:
- 10 oz. brioche bread, cubed
- 4 eggs, beaten
- 2 cups whole milk
- 1/4 cup brandy
- 1/2 cup light brown sugar
- 1 teaspoon vanilla extract

Directions:
1. Place the brioche in a Crock Pot.
2. Mix the eggs, milk, brandy, sugar and vanilla in a bowl then pour this mixture over the brioche.
3. Cover the pot and cook on low settings for 6 hours.
4. Serve the pudding slightly warm.

Lemon Cream

Servings: 4 | Cooking Time: 1 Hour

Ingredients:
- 1 cup heavy cream
- 1 teaspoon lemon zest, grated
- ¼ cup lemon juice
- 8 ounces mascarpone cheese

Directions:
1. In your Crock Pot, mix heavy cream with mascarpone, lemon zest and lemon juice, stir, cover and cook on Low for 1 hour.
2. Divide into dessert glasses and keep in the fridge until you serve.

Nutrition Info:
- calories 165, fat 7, fiber 0, carbs 7, protein 4

Vanilla Pears

Servings: 2 | Cooking Time: 2 Hours

Ingredients:
- 2 tablespoons avocado oil
- 1 teaspoon vanilla extract
- 2 pears, cored and halved
- ½ tablespoon lime juice
- 1 tablespoon sugar

Directions:
1. In your Crock Pot combine the pears with the sugar, oil and the other ingredients, toss, put the lid on and cook on High for 2 hours.
2. Divide between plates and serve.

Nutrition Info:
- calories 200, fat 4, fiber 6, carbs 16, protein 3

Soft Sable Cookies

Servings:2 | Cooking Time: 2 Hours

Ingredients:
- 1 teaspoon sesame seeds
- 2 tablespoons butter, softened
- 1 egg yolk, whisked
- ½ teaspoon baking powder
- 2 teaspoons brown sugar
- 1/3 cup flour
- ½ teaspoon olive oil

Directions:
1. Mix butter with baking powder, brown sugar, and flour.
2. Knead a soft dough and cut into 2 pieces.
3. Then roll the balls from the dough and press them gently.
4. Brush every ball with the help of the egg yolk and sprinkle with sesame seeds.
5. Brush the Crock Pot bowl with olive oil and put the cookies inside.
6. Cook them on High for 2 hours. Then cool the cookies well.

Nutrition Info:
- Per Serving: 236 calories, 3.9g protein, 20.1g carbohydrates, 15.9g fat, 0.8g fiber, 135mg cholesterol, 88mg sodium, 172mg potassium.

White Chocolate Apricot Bread Pudding

Servings: 8 | Cooking Time: 5 1/2 Hours

Ingredients:
- 8 cups one day old bread cubes
- 1 cup dried apricots, diced
- 1 cup white chocolate chips
- 2 cups milk
- 1 cup heavy cream
- 4 eggs
- 1 teaspoon vanilla extract
- 1 teaspoon orange zest
- 1/2 cup white sugar

Directions:
1. Mix the bread, apricots and chocolate chips in your Crock Pot.
2. Combine the milk, cream, eggs, vanilla, orange zest and sugar in a bowl.
3. Pour this mixture over the bread pudding then cover the pot with a lid and cook on low settings for 5 hours.
4. The pudding is best served slightly warm.

Creamy Lemon Mix

Servings: 4 | Cooking Time: 1 Hr.

Ingredients:
- 2 cups heavy cream
- Sugar to the taste
- 2 lemons, peeled and roughly chopped

Directions:
1. Whisk the cream with lemons and sugar to the insert of Crock Pot.
2. Put the cooker's lid on and set the cooking time to 1 hour on Low settings.
3. Serve when chilled.

Nutrition Info:
- Per Serving: Calories: 177, Total Fat: 0g, Fiber: 0g, Total Carbs: 6g, Protein: 1g

Avocado Peppermint Pudding

Servings: 3 | Cooking Time: 1 Hr.

Ingredients:
- ½ cup vegetable oil
- ½ tbsp sugar
- 1 tbsp cocoa powder
- For the pudding:
- 1 tsp peppermint oil
- 14 oz. coconut milk
- 1 avocado, pitted, peeled and chopped
- 1 tbsp sugar

Directions:
1. Start by mixing vegetable oil, ½ tbsp sugar, and cocoa powder in a bowl.
2. Spread this mixture in a container and refrigerate for 1 hour.
3. Blend this mixture with coconut milk, avocado, 1 tbsp sugar, peppermint oil in a blender.
4. Transfer this mixture to the insert of the Crock Pot.
5. Put the cooker's lid on and set the cooking time to 1 hour on Low settings.
6. Stir in chocolate chips then divide the pudding the serving bowls.
7. Refrigerate for 1 hour then enjoy.

Nutrition Info:
- Per Serving: Calories: 140, Total Fat: 3g, Fiber: 2g, Total Carbs: 3g, Protein: 4g

Oatmeal Soufflé

Servings:3 | Cooking Time: 2.5 Hours

Ingredients:
- 6 oz oatmeal
- 1 egg yolk
- 3 tablespoons sugar
- 1 cup milk
- 1 tablespoon butter

Directions:
1. Whisk egg yolk with sugar until you get a lemon color mixture.
2. Then add milk and pour the liquid in the Crock Pot.
3. Add butter and oatmeal.
4. Cook the soufflé on High for 2.5 hours.

Nutrition Info:
- Per Serving: 352 calories, 11.1g protein, 54.6g carbohydrates, 10.7g fat, 5.7g fiber, 87mg cholesterol, 72mg sodium, 259mg potassium.

Mint Lava Cake

Servings:6 | Cooking Time: 1 Hour

Ingredients:
- 1 cup fudge cake mix
- 1 teaspoon dried mint
- 4 tablespoons sunflower oil
- 2 eggs, beaten

Directions:
1. Mix cake mix with dried mint, sunflower oil, and eggs.

2. When the mixture is smooth, pour it in the ramekins and place in the Crock Pot.
3. Cook the lava cakes on High for 1 hour.

Nutrition Info:
- Per Serving: 291 calories, 4.4g protein, 32g carbohydrates, 17.6g fat, 1.1g fiber, 55mg cholesterol, 381mg sodium, 165mg potassium.

Strawberries Marmalade

Servings: 10 | Cooking Time: 4 Hours

Ingredients:
- 32 ounces strawberries, chopped
- 2 pounds sugar
- Zest of 1 lemon, grated
- 4 ounces raisins
- 3 ounces water

Directions:
1. In your Crock Pot, mix strawberries with coconut sugar, lemon zest, raisins and water, stir, cover and cook on High for 4 hours.
2. Divide into small jars and serve cold.

Nutrition Info:
- calories 140, fat 3, fiber 2, carbs 2, protein 1

Apricot Spoon Cake

Servings:10 | Cooking Time: 2.5 Hours

Ingredients:
- 2 cups cake mix
- 1 cup milk
- 1 cup apricots, canned, pitted, chopped, with juice
- 2 eggs, beaten
- 1 tablespoon sunflower oil

Directions:
1. Mix milk with cake mix and egg.
2. Then sunflower oil and blend the mixture until smooth.
3. Then place the baking paper in the Crock Pot.
4. Pour the cake mix batter in the Crock Pot, flatten it gently, and close the lid.
5. Cook the cake on High for 2.5 hours.
6. Then transfer the cooked cake in the plate and top with apricots and apricot juice.
7. Leave the cake until it is warm and cut into servings.

Nutrition Info:
- Per Serving: 268 calories, 4.5g protein, 43.8g carbohydrates, 8.6g fat, 0.8g fiber, 35mg cholesterol, 372mg sodium, 127mg potassium.

One Large Vanilla Pancake

Servings: 6 | Cooking Time: 2 1/4 Hours

Ingredients:
- 3/4 cup all-purpose flour
- 2 tablespoons white sugar
- 3/4 teaspoon baking powder
- 1/4 teaspoon baking soda
- 1/4 teaspoon salt
- 2 tablespoons butter, melted
- 1 teaspoon vanilla extract

- 2 eggs
- 1 cup buttermilk
- Maple syrup for serving

Directions:
1. Mix all the ingredients in a bowl and give it a quick mix just until combined.
2. Grease your Crock Pot with butter then pour the batter in the pot.
3. Cook for 2 hours on high settings.
4. Serve the pancake with maple syrup if you want.

Spiced Plum Butter

Servings: 8 | Cooking Time: 8 1/2 Hours

Ingredients:
- 6 pounds ripe plums, pitted
- 3 cups white sugar
- 2 star anise
- 2 cinnamon stick
- 4 cardamom pods, crushed
- 2 whole cloves

Directions:
1. Combine all the ingredients in your Crock Pot.
2. Cover the pot and cook on low settings for 8 hours.
3. Remove and discard the spices then pour the hot butter into glass jars and seal them with a lid.

Turtle Cake

Servings: 12 | Cooking Time: 4 1/2 Hours

Ingredients:
- 6 oz. dark chocolate, melted
- 1/2 cup butter, melted
- 3/4 cup white sugar
- 2 eggs
- 3/4 cup all-purpose flour
- 1 teaspoon baking powder
- 1/4 teaspoon salt
- 1 cup crushed graham crackers
- 1/2 cup mini marshmallows
- 1/2 cup mixed nuts, chopped
- 1/2 cup white chocolate chips
- 1/2 cup pretzels, chopped

Directions:
1. Mix the melted chocolate and butter in a bowl.
2. Stir in the sugar and eggs and give it a good mix then add the flour, baking powder and salt.
3. Pour the batter in a greased Crock Pot and top with the remaining ingredients.
4. Cover and cook for 4 hours on low settings.
5. When chilled, cut into small squares and serve.

Peppermint Chocolate Clusters

Servings: 20 | Cooking Time: 4 1/4 Hours

Ingredients:
- 2 cups pretzels, chopped
- 1 1/2 cups dark chocolate chips
- 1/2 cup milk chocolate chips
- 1 teaspoon peppermint extract
- 1 cup pecans, chopped

Directions:
1. Combine all the ingredients in your Crock Pot.
2. Cover the pot and cook on low settings for 4 hours.
3. When done, drop small clusters of mixture on a baking tray lined with baking paper.
4. Allow to cool and set before serving.

Peaches And Wine Sauce

Servings: 2 | Cooking Time: 2 Hours

Ingredients:
- 3 tablespoons brown sugar
- 1 pound peaches, pitted and cut into wedges
- ½ cup red wine
- ½ teaspoon vanilla extract
- 1 teaspoon lemon zest, grated

Directions:
1. In your Crock Pot, mix the peaches with the sugar and the other ingredients, toss, put the lid on and cook on High for 2 hours.
2. Divide into bowls and serve.

Nutrition Info:
- calories 200, fat 4, fiber 6, carbs 9, protein 4

White Chocolate Apple Cake

Servings: 8 | Cooking Time: 6 1/2 Hours

Ingredients:
- 5 eggs, separated
- 3/4 cup white sugar
- 1/2 cup butter, melted
- 1/2 cup whole milk
- 1 cup all-purpose flour
- 1 teaspoon baking powder
- 1/4 teaspoon salt
- 1/2 cup white chocolate chips
- 4 tart apples, peeled, cored and sliced
- 1/2 teaspoon cinnamon powder

Directions:
1. Mix the egg yolks with half of the sugar until double in volume. Stir in the butter and milk then fold in the flour, baking powder and salt.
2. Whip the egg whites until stiff then add the remaining sugar and whip for a few minutes until glossy and stiff. Fold this meringue into the egg yolks and flour mixture then add the chocolate chips.
3. Spoon the batter in your Crock Pot and top with apple slices.
4. Sprinkle with cinnamon and cook on low settings for 6 hours.
5. Allow to cool before slicing and serving.

Strawberry Cake

Servings: 2 | Cooking Time: 1 Hour

Ingredients:
- ¼ cup coconut flour
- ¼ teaspoon baking soda
- 1 tablespoon sugar
- ¼ cup strawberries, chopped
- ½ cup coconut milk
- 1 teaspoon butter, melted
- ½ teaspoon lemon zest, grated
- ¼ teaspoon vanilla extract
- Cooking spray

Directions:
1. In a bowl, mix the coconut flour with the baking soda, sugar and the other ingredients except the cooking spray and stir well.
2. Grease your Crock Pot with the cooking spray, line it with parchment paper, pour the cake batter inside, put the lid on and cook on High for 1 hour.
3. Leave the cake to cool down, slice and serve.

Nutrition Info:
- calories 200, fat 4, fiber 4, carbs 10, protein 4

Sweet Zucchini Pie

Servings:6 | Cooking Time: 4 Hours

Ingredients:
- 2 cups zucchini, chopped
- ½ cup of sugar
- 2 cups all-purpose flour
- 1 teaspoon baking powder
- 4 eggs, beaten
- 1 tablespoon butter, melted
- 1 cup milk
- 1 teaspoon vanilla extract

Directions:
1. Mix sugar with flour, baking powder, eggs, butter, milk, and vanilla extract.
2. Stir the mixture until smooth.
3. Then line the Crock Pot with baking paper and pour the smooth dough inside.
4. Top the dough with zucchini and close the lid.
5. Cook the pie on High for 4 hours.

Nutrition Info:
- Per Serving: 302 calories, 9.8g protein, 52.4g carbohydrates, 6.2g fat, 1.6g fiber, 118mg cholesterol, 79mg sodium, 291mg potassium.

Banana Muffins

Servings:2 | Cooking Time: 2.5 Hours

Ingredients:
- 2 eggs, beaten
- 2 bananas, chopped
- 4 tablespoons flour
- ½ teaspoon vanilla extract
- ½ teaspoon baking powder

Directions:
1. Mash the chopped bananas and mix them with eggs.
2. Then add vanilla extract and baking powder.
3. Add flour and stir the mixture until smooth.
4. Pour the banana mixture in the muffin molds (fill ½ part of every muffin mold) and transfer in the Crock Pot.
5. Cook the muffins on High for 2.5 hours.

Nutrition Info:
- Per Serving: 229 calories, 84g protein, 39.9g carbohydrates, 4.9g fat, 3.5g fiber, 164mg cholesterol, 64mg sodium, 626mg potassium.

Spiced Rice Pudding

Servings: 6 | Cooking Time: 4 1/4 Hours

Ingredients:
- 1 cup Arborio rice
- 1/2 cup white sugar
- 3 cups whole milk
- 1 cinnamon stick
- 1 star anise
- 2 whole cloves
- 1/2-inch piece of ginger, sliced
- 1/2 teaspoon rose water

Directions:
1. Combine all the ingredients in your Crock Pot.
2. Cover the pot and cook on low settings for 4 hours.
3. The pudding can be served both warm and chilled.

Granola Apples

Servings:6 | Cooking Time: 2.5 Hours

Ingredients:
- 6 apples, cored
- 6 teaspoons granola
- 3 teaspoons maple syrup
- ½ cup of water

Directions:
1. Mix maple syrup with granola.
2. Fill the apples with granola mixture and transfer in the Crock Pot.
3. Add water and close the lid.
4. Cook the apples on High for 2.5 hours.

Nutrition Info:
- Per Serving: 131 calories, 1.4g protein, 35.7g carbohydrates, 1.6g fat, 5.9g fiber, 0mg cholesterol, 4mg sodium, 273mg potassium.

Berry Cream

Servings: 2 | Cooking Time: 2 Hours

Ingredients:
- 2 tablespoons cashews, chopped
- 1 cup heavy cream
- ½ cup blueberries
- ½ cup maple syrup
- ½ tablespoon coconut oil, melted

Directions:
1. In your Crock Pot, mix the cream with the berries and the other ingredients, whisk, put the lid on and cook on Low for 2 hours.

2. Divide the mix into bowls and serve cold.

Nutrition Info:
- calories 200, fat 3, fiber 5, carbs 12, protein 3

Blondie Pie

Servings:6 | Cooking Time: 2.5 Hours

Ingredients:
- 1 teaspoon vanilla extract
- 1 cup cream
- 1 cup flour
- 1 egg, beaten
- ¼ cup of sugar
- 1 teaspoon baking powder
- 2 oz chocolate chips
- 1 tablespoon coconut oil, softened

Directions:
1. Mix vanilla extract, cream, flour, and egg.
2. Then add sugar, baking powder, and coconut oil.
3. When the mixture is smooth, add chocolate chips and mix them with the help of the spatula.
4. Then pour the mixture in the Crock Pot and close the lid.
5. Cook the pie on High for 2.5 hours.

Nutrition Info:
- Per Serving: 216 calories, 4.1g protein, 31.6g carbohydrates, 8.2g fat, 0.9g fiber, 37mg cholesterol, 32mg sodium, 167mg potassium.

Blueberry Tapioca Pudding

Servings:4 | Cooking Time: 3 Hours

Ingredients:
- 4 teaspoons blueberry jam
- 4 tablespoons tapioca
- 2 cups of milk

Directions:
1. Mix tapioca with milk and pour it in the Crock Pot.
2. Close the lid and cook the liquid on low for 3 hours.
3. Then put the blueberry jam in 4 ramekins.
4. Cool the cooked tapioca pudding until warm and pour over the jam.

Nutrition Info:
- Per Serving: 112 calories, 4.1g protein, 18.8g carbohydrates, 2.5g fat, 0.1g fiber, 10mg cholesterol, 58mg sodium, 71mg potassium.

Bread And Berries Pudding

Servings: 2 | Cooking Time: 3 Hours

Ingredients:
- 2 cups white bread, cubed
- 1 cup blackberries
- 2 tablespoons butter, melted
- 2 tablespoons white sugar
- 1 cup almond milk
- ¼ cup heavy cream
- 2 eggs, whisked
- 1 tablespoon lemon zest, grated
- ¼ teaspoon vanilla extract

Directions:
1. In your Crock Pot, mix the bread with the berries, butter and the other ingredients, toss gently, put the lid on and cook on Low for 3 hours.
2. Divide pudding between dessert plates and serve.

Nutrition Info:
- calories 354, fat 12, fiber 4, carbs 29, protein 11

Strawberry And Orange Mix

Servings: 2 | Cooking Time: 1 Hour

Ingredients:
- 2 tablespoons sugar
- 1 cup orange segments
- 1 cup strawberries, halved
- A pinch of ginger powder
- ½ teaspoon vanilla extract
- ½ cup orange juice
- 1 tablespoon chia seeds

Directions:
1. In your Crock Pot, mix the oranges with the berries, ginger powder and the other ingredients, toss, put the lid on and cook on High for 1 hour.
2. Divide into bowls and serve cold.

Nutrition Info:
- calories 100, fat 2, fiber 2, carbs 10, protein 2

Ginger Pears Mix

Servings: 2 | Cooking Time: 2 Hours

Ingredients:
- 2 pears, peeled and cored
- 1 cup apple juice
- ½ tablespoon brown sugar
- 1 tablespoon ginger, grated

Directions:
1. In your Crock Pot, mix the pears with the apple juice and the other ingredients, toss, put the lid on and cook on Low for 2 hour.
2. Divide the mix into bowls and serve warm.

Nutrition Info:
- calories 250, fat 1, fiber 2, carbs 12, protein 4

Blueberries Jam

Servings: 2 | Cooking Time: 4 Hours

Ingredients:
- 2 cups blueberries
- ½ cup water
- ¼ pound sugar
- Zest of 1 lime

Directions:
1. In your Crock Pot, combine the berries with the water and the other ingredients, toss, put the lid on and cook on High for 4 hours.
2. Divide into small jars and serve cold.

Nutrition Info:
- calories 250, fat 3, fiber 2, carbs 6, protein 1

Chocolate Mango Mix

Servings: 2 | Cooking Time: 1 Hour

Ingredients:
- 1 cup crème fraiche
- ¼ cup dark chocolate, cut into chunks
- 1 cup mango, peeled and chopped
- 2 tablespoons sugar
- ½ teaspoon almond extract

Directions:
1. In your Crock Pot, mix the crème fraiche with the chocolate and the other ingredients, toss, put the lid on and cook on Low for 1 hour.
2. Blend using an immersion blender, divide into bowls and serve.

Nutrition Info:
- calories 200, fat 12, fiber 4, carbs 7, protein 3

Tomato Jam

Servings: 2 | Cooking Time: 3 Hours

Ingredients:
- ½ pound tomatoes, chopped
- 1 green apple, grated
- 2 tablespoons red wine vinegar
- 4 tablespoons sugar

Directions:
1. In your Crock Pot, mix the tomatoes with the apple and the other ingredients, whisk, put the lid on and cook on Low for 3 hours.
2. Whisk the jam well, blend a bit using an immersion blender, divide into bowls and serve cold.

Nutrition Info:
- calories 70, fat 1, fiber 1, carbs 18, protein 1

Strawberry Pie

Servings: 12 | Cooking Time: 2 Hours

Ingredients:
- For the crust:
- 1 cup coconut, shredded
- 1 cup sunflower seeds
- ¼ cup butter
- Cooking spray
- For the filling:
- 1 teaspoon gelatin
- 8 ounces cream cheese
- 4 ounces strawberries
- 2 tablespoons water
- ½ tablespoon lemon juice
- ¼ teaspoon stevia
- ½ cup heavy cream
- 8 ounces strawberries, chopped for serving
- 16 ounces heavy cream for serving

Directions:
1. In your food processor, mix sunflower seeds with coconut and butter and stir well.
2. Put this into your Crock Pot greased with cooking spray.
3. Heat up a pan with the water over medium heat, add gela-tin, stir until it dissolves, take off heat and leave aside to cool down.
4. Add this to your food processor, mix with 4 ounces strawberries, cream cheese, lemon juice and stevia and blend well.
5. Add ½ cup heavy cream, stir well and spread this over crust.
6. Top with 8 ounces strawberries, cover and cook on High for 2 hours.
7. Spread heavy cream all over, leave the cake to cool down and keep it in the fridge until you serve it.

Nutrition Info:
- calories 234, fat 23, fiber 2, carbs 6, protein 7

Orange Curd

Servings:6 | Cooking Time: 7 Hours

Ingredients:
- 2 cups orange juice
- 1 tablespoon orange zest, grated
- 4 egg yolks
- 1 cup of sugar
- 1 tablespoon cornflour
- 1 teaspoon vanilla extract

Directions:
1. Whisk the egg yolks with sugar until you get a lemon color mixture.
2. Then add orange juice, vanilla extract, cornflour, and orange zest. Whisk the mixture until smooth.
3. Pour the liquid in the Crock Pot and close the lid.
4. Cook the curd on low for 7 hours. Stir the curd every 1 hour.

Nutrition Info:
- Per Serving: 206 calories, 2.5g protein, 43.6g carbohydrates, 3.2g fat, 0.4g fiber, 140mg cholesterol, 6mg sodium, 185mg potassium.

Mango Tapioca Pudding

Servings: 6 | Cooking Time: 6 1/4 Hours

Ingredients:
- 1 cup tapioca pearls
- 2 cups coconut milk
- 1 cup water
- 1 ripe mango, peeled and cubed
- 1/2 cup shredded coconut
- 1/4 cup white sugar
- 1 cinnamon stick

Directions:
1. Combine all the ingredients in your Crock Pot.
2. Cover the pot and cook on low settings for 6 hours.
3. Allow the pudding to cool completely before serving.

Orange And Apricot Jam

Servings:4 | Cooking Time: 3 Hours

Ingredients:
- 2 oranges, peeled, chopped
- 1 cup apricots, chopped
- 1 tablespoon orange zest, grated
- 4 tablespoons sugar

Directions:
1. Put all ingredients in the bowl and blend them until smooth with the help of the immersion blender.
2. Then pour the mixture in the Crock Pot and cook it on High for 3 hours.
3. Transfer the hot jam in the glass cans and close with a lid.
4. Cool the jam well.

Nutrition Info:
- Per Serving: 108 calories, 1.4g protein, 27.4g carbohydrates, 0.4g fat, 3.1g fiber, 0mg cholesterol, 1mg sodium, 270mg potassium.

Sweet Mascarpone Cream

Servings: 12 | Cooking Time: 1 Hour

Ingredients:
- 8 ounces mascarpone cheese
- ¾ teaspoon vanilla extract
- 1 tablespoon sugar
- 1 cup whipping cream
- ½ pint blueberries
- ½ pint strawberries

Directions:
1. In your Crock Pot, mix whipping cream with sugar, vanilla and mascarpone and blend well.
2. Add blueberries and strawberries, cover cook on High for 1 hour, stir your cream, divide it into glasses and serve cold.

Nutrition Info:
- calories 143, fat 12, fiber 1, carbs 6, protein 2

Cashew Cake

Servings: 6 | Cooking Time: 2 Hours

Ingredients:
- For the crust:
- ½ cup dates, pitted
- 1 tablespoon water
- ½ teaspoon vanilla
- ½ cup almonds
- For the cake:
- 2 and ½ cups cashews, soaked for 8 hours
- 1 cup blueberries
- ¾ cup maple syrup
- 1 tablespoon vegetable oil

Directions:
1. In your blender, mix dates with water, vanilla and almonds, pulse well, transfer dough to a working surface, flatten and arrange on the bottom of your Crock Pot.
2. In your blender, mix maple syrup with the oil, cashews and blueberries, blend well, spread over crust, cover and cook on High for 2 hours.

3. Leave the cake to cool down, slice and serve.

Nutrition Info:
- calories 200, fat 3, fiber 5, carbs 12, protein 3

Cranberry Walnut Bread

Servings: 10 | Cooking Time: 4 1/4 Hours

Ingredients:
- 1 cup all-purpose flour
- 1 cup ground walnuts
- 1 1/2 teaspoons baking powder
- 1/4 teaspoon salt
- 2 ripe bananas, mashed
- 2 eggs
- 1/2 cup buttermilk
- 1 cup frozen cranberries

Directions:
1. Mix the flour, walnuts, baking powder and salt in a bowl.
2. Add the bananas, eggs and buttermilk and mix well then fold in the cranberries.
3. Pour the bread in your Crock Pot and bake for 4 hours on low settings.
4. Allow the bread to cool in the pot before slicing and serving.

Gluten Free Coconut Cake

Servings: 8 | Cooking Time: 2 1/4 Hours

Ingredients:
- 2 cups gluten free oat flour
- 1 cup coconut sugar
- 1/4 cup cocoa powder
- 1 teaspoon baking powder
- 1/2 teaspoon salt
- 1 cup coconut milk
- 2 eggs
- 1/4 cup butter, melted
- 1 teaspoon vanilla extract

Directions:
1. Mix the oat flour, coconut sugar, cocoa powder, baking powder and salt in a bowl.
2. Add the remaining ingredients and give it a quick mix.
3. Pour the batter in your greased Crock Pot and bake for 2 hours on high settings.
4. Allow the cake to cool completely before slicing and serving.

Saucy Peach And Apple Dessert

Servings: 4 | Cooking Time: 4 1/4 Hours

Ingredients:
- 2 Granny Smith apples, peeled, cored and sliced
- 2 ripe peaches, pitted and sliced
- 1 cinnamon stick
- 1 cup fresh orange juice
- 1 teaspoon orange zest
- 3 tablespoons honey
- 1 teaspoon cornstarch
- Ice cream or whipped cream for serving

Directions:
1. Combine all the ingredients in your Crock Pot.
2. Cover the pot and cook for 4 hours on low settings.
3. Allow the dessert to cool in the pot before serving.
4. Ice cream or whipped cream can be a great match for this dessert.

Mango Muffins

Servings:2 | Cooking Time: 3 Hours

Ingredients:
- 3 tablespoons mango puree
- 1 tablespoon butter, softened
- 1 teaspoon vanilla extract
- 3 tablespoons flour
- ¼ teaspoon baking powder

Directions:
1. Mix mango puree with butter, vanilla extract, flour, and baking powder.
2. Stir the mixture until you get a smooth batter.
3. Then fill the muffin molds with batter (fill ½ part of every muffin mold) and transfer them in the Crock Pot.
4. Close the lid and cook the muffins on High for 3 hours.

Nutrition Info:
- Per Serving: 110 calories, 1.4g protein, 11.8g carbohydrates, 5.9g fat, 0.6g fiber, 15mg cholesterol, 42mg sodium, 107mg potassium.

Crème Brule

Servings:4 | Cooking Time: 8 Hours

Ingredients:
- 6 egg yolks
- 1 ½ cup heavy cream
- ½ cup of sugar
- 1 teaspoon flour

Directions:
1. Blend the egg yolks with sugar until you get a smooth lemon color mixture.
2. Add heavy cream and flour. Mix the liquid until smooth.
3. Pour the liquid in the ramekins and place in the Crock Pot.
4. Cover the ramekins with foil and close the lid of the Crock Pot.
5. Cook the dessert on Low for 8 hours.

Nutrition Info:
- Per Serving: 332 calories, 5g protein, 27.7g carbohydrates, 23.4g fat, 0g fiber, 376mg cholesterol, 29mg sodium, 62mg potassium.

Fudge Raspberry Cake

Servings: 8 | Cooking Time: 4 1/4 Hours

Ingredients:
- 1 cup all-purpose flour
- 1/4 cup cocoa powder
- 1 1/2 teaspoons baking powder
- 1/4 teaspoon salt
- 1 cup whole milk
- 1/2 cup canola oil
- 2 eggs
- 1/4 cup seedless raspberry jam
- 1 teaspoon vanilla extract

Directions:
1. Mix the flour, cocoa powder, baking powder and salt in a bowl. Add the remaining ingredients and give it a quick mix.
2. Pour the batter in a greased Crock Pot and cook for 4 hours on low settings.
3. Allow the cake to cool before slicing and serving.

Milky Custard

Servings:6 | Cooking Time: 7 Hours

Ingredients:
- 3 cups of milk
- 3 tablespoons corn starch
- 1 teaspoon ground cardamom
- 1 cup of sugar

Directions:
1. Mix sugar with ground cardamom and corn starch.
2. Add milk and whisk the mixture until smooth.
3. After this, pour the liquid in the Crock Pot and cook it on Low for 7 hours. Stir the mixture every 1 hour.
4. Then cool the cooked custard well and transfer in the ramekins.

Nutrition Info:
- Per Serving: 205 calories, 4g protein, 44.1g carbohydrates, 2.5g fat, 0.1g fiber, 10mg cholesterol, 58mg sodium, 74mg potassium.

Sweet Lemon Mix

Servings: 4 | Cooking Time: 1 Hour

Ingredients:
- 2 cups heavy cream
- Sugar to the taste
- 2 lemons, peeled and roughly chopped

Directions:
1. In your Crock Pot, mix cream with sugar and lemons, stir, cover and cook on Low for 1 hour.
2. Divide into glasses and serve very cold.

Nutrition Info:
- calories 177, fat 0, fiber 0, carbs 6, protein 1

C

D

Made in the USA
Middletown, DE
11 October 2023

40595800R00077